Mastery Study Guide

Macroeconomics

Principles and Applications, Updated

Second Edition

Robert E. Hall
Stanford University

Marc Lieberman
New York University

Prepared by

Geoffrey A. Jehle
Vassar College

THOMSON
SOUTH-WESTERN

Australia · Canada · Mexico · Singapore · Spain · United Kingdom · United States

THOMSON
SOUTH-WESTERN

Mastery Study Guide to accompany Macroeconomics: Principles and Applications, Updated 2e

Robert E. Hall and Marc Lieberman

Prepared by Geoffrey A. Jehle

Editor-in-Chief:
Jack W. Calhoun

Vice President, Team Director:
Michael P. Roche

Publisher of Economics
Michael B. Mercier

Acquisitions Editor:
Michael W. Worls

Senior Developmental Editor:
Susanna C. Smart

Developmental Editor:
Bob Sandman

Executive Marketing Manager:
Lisa L. Lysne

Senior Marketing Manager:
Janet Hennies

Production Editor:
Daniel C. Plofchan

Manufacturing Coordinator:
Sandee Milewski

Media Developmental Editor:
Peggy Buskey

Media Production Editor:
Pam Wallace

Design Project Manager:
Rik Moore

Internal Designer:
Hespenheide Design

Cover Designer:
Paul Neff Design

Photography Managers:
Carey Benbow, Deanna Ettinger

Photo Researchers:
Susan Van Etten, Terri Miller

Printer:
QuebecorWorld
Versailles, KY

Production House:
Pre-Press Company, Inc.

Printed in the United States of America
2 3 4 5 05 04 03

For more information contact South-Western, 5191 Natorp Boulevard, Mason, Ohio 45040.
Or you can visit our Internet site at:
http://www.swcollege.com

Text ISBN: 0-324-15190-X

PREFACE TO UPDATED SECOND EDITION

TO THE STUDENT

There's a secret to learning economics. Those who discover it learn economics more quickly, understand it more deeply, and do better on exams than those who don't. The secret is this: Economics must be learned actively, not passively.

Passive learning relies on "taking things in." Merely listening to your professor, reading the book, flipping through your notes, and feeling like you "get it" because it all makes sense when someone else says it—these are the hallmarks of passive learning. While passive learning can work in some subjects, generations of students have discovered it does not work very well in economics.

Active learning, by contrast, works very well in economics. Active learning means periodically closing your book, closing your notes, and reproducing the material on your own. It means knowing how to *use* the vocabulary of economics—not just recognizing terms when you hear them. It means drawing graphs on your own, explaining what happens as we move along a curve, and what makes a curve shift—not just making sense of a graph when someone else draws it for you. It means solving problems from the ground up—not just following along as someone else solves them for you.

This updated Mastery Study Guide will help you to study economics actively. Other than this preface, you will find nothing here for you to just read, review, or "take in." As soon as you turn the page, you will be asked to *do* things—again and again and again.

Each chapter of this study guide corresponds to the same numbered chapter in Hall and Lieberman's *Macroeconomics: Principles and Applications, Updated 2nd edition.* Every chapter includes the following sections:

- ***Speaking Economics*** asks you to fill in key vocabulary terms when you are given their definitions;

- ***Chapter Highlights*** asks you to identify missing parts of important conclusions from the text;

- ***Important Concepts*** asks you to provide lists and brief explanations about central ideas in the text;

- ***Skills and Tools*** gives you practice solving quantitative problems and using graphs—plotting them, interpreting them, and drawing conclusions from them;

- ***Practice Tests*** offer multiple choice and true/false questions to help you decide when you've mastered a chapter of the text, and when you need to go back and review.

For this update, we have not only adjusted all of these features for changes in the text, we have also added a new feature, designed to help you gauge your mastery of *all* the material, not just that of any single chapter:

- ***Sample Final Exam in Macroeconomics*** offers multiple choice exam questions, carefully coordinated with the text, along with answers and full explanations.

TO THE INSTRUCTOR

Nothing is more frustrating than inconsistency between a textbook and its associated study guide. I know this firsthand. Over the years, I've suffered—as have my students—with study guides and texts that seem to come from different planets.

In writing this updated Mastery Study Guide, I've worked closely with the textbook's authors, Bob Hall and Marc Lieberman, to ensure complete consistency in approach, language, and content. Indeed, the authors themselves contributed many of the questions and problems in this guide. From the beginning our goal has been to make the transition from text to study guide—and back again—as seamless as possible.

ACKNOWLEDGEMENTS

Bob Hall and Marc Lieberman have written a gem of a text, and it was a pleasure to prepare this Mastery Study Guide with them. Their devotion to their subject, and to their reader, is inspiring.

Geoffrey A. Jehle
Poughkeepsie, New York

CONTENTS

ANSWERS TO QUESTIONS

CHAPTER 1

WHAT IS ECONOMICS?

SPEAKING ECONOMICS

Fill in each blank with the appropriate word or phrase from the list provided in the word bank. (For a challenge, fill in as many blanks as you can *without* using the word bank.)

________________________ 1. The study of choice under conditions of scarcity.

________________________ 2. A situation in which the amount of something available is insufficient to satisfy the desire for it.

________________________ 3. The land, labor, and capital that are used to produce goods and services.

________________________ 4. The time human beings spend producing goods and services.

________________________ 5. Long-lasting tools used in producing goods and services.

________________________ 6. The skills and training of the labor force.

________________________ 7. The physical space on which production occurs, and the natural resources that come with it.

________________________ 8. The study of the behavior of individual households, firms, and governments, the choices they make, and their interaction in specific markets.

________________________ 9. The study of the economy as a whole.

________________________ 10. The study of what *is*; of how the economy works.

________________________ 11. The study of what *should be*, it is used to make value judgments, identify problems, and prescribe solutions.

________________________ 12. An abstract representation of reality.

________________________ 13. Any assumption that makes a model simpler without affecting any of its important conclusions.

________________________ 14. Any assumption that affects the conclusions of a model in an important way.

Word Bank

capital
critical assumption
economics
human capital
labor
land
macroeconomics
microeconomics
model
normative economics
positive economics
resources
scarcity
simplifying assumption

CHAPTER HIGHLIGHTS

Fill in the blanks with the appropriate words or phrases. If you have difficulty, review the chapter and then try again.

1. Economics is the study of choice under conditions of ___________________.

2. Society's problem is a scarcity of ___________________.

3. Economists generally classify resources into three categories: ___________________, ___________________, and ___________________.

4. ___________________ economics takes a close-up view of the economy, and is concerned with the behavior of *individual* actors on the economic scene.

5. ___________________ economics deals with the overall economy, and focuses on variables like total output, total employment, and the general level of interest rates.

6. ___________________ economics deals with what *is*—with *how* the economy works.

7. ___________________ economics concerns itself with what *should be*. It is used to make judgments about the economy, identify problems, and prescribe solutions.

8. To understand the economy, economists make extensive use of *models*, which are ___________________ representations of reality.

9. A simplifying assumption is a way of making a model simpler, without changing any of its important ___________________.

10. A ___________________ assumption is an assumption that affects the conclusions of a model in important ways.

IMPORTANT CONCEPTS

Write a brief answer below each of the following items.

1. State whether each of the following questions is primarily microeconomic or macroeconomic, and whether it is primarily positive or normative. Don't worry about the answers to the questions—just classify them. (For example, the first question is a microeconomic, positive question.)

   a. If the price of compact discs rises, what will happen to the equilibrium price of cassette tapes?

   ____________________ ____________________

   b. If we raise the social security tax on wages and salaries, what will happen to total employment in the United States?

   ____________________ ____________________

   c. How much have pollution-control devices raised the price of automobiles?

   ____________________ ____________________

   d. Should the federal government use our tax dollars to support the arts?

   ____________________ ____________________

   e. What policies would help improve the average standard of living in less-developed countries?

   ____________________ ____________________

   f. Should less-developed countries like Ethiopia or Ghana use government funds to subsidize basic necessities like bread or milk?

   ____________________ ____________________

   g. Which is worse for society: a one percentage-point rise in the unemployment rate, or a one percentage-point rise in the inflation rate?

   ____________________ ____________________

2. Each of the following is an example of one of the three categories of resources. In the blanks, identify the categories.

   a. A surgeon's time in performing an operation ____________________

   b. The surgeon's scalpel ____________________

   c. The surgeon's skills and training ____________________

   d. The iron ore used to make steel ____________________

   e. The workers who make steel out of iron ore ____________________

   f. The factory in which iron ore is made into steel ____________________

g. The services performed by a waiter at a restaurant ____________________

h. A restaurant's pots, pans and dishes ____________________

Indicate whether the following statements are true or false, and then explain briefly.

3. "The more details we include in a model, the better the model will work."

4. Economists make two types of assumptions in their economics models: positive assumptions and normative assumptions.

SKILLS AND TOOLS

Note to the Student: Some of the basic principles of graphs and graphing are reviewed in the Appendix to Chapter 1 in your text. If it has been a while since you used graphs you might want to take a look at that section of the text before you do these exercises. Those already comfortable with graphs can proceed with the exercises.

For each of the following items, write the correct answer in the blank or circle the correct answer.

1. This table reports estimates of the United States' population (in millions) each year during the 1980s. The data are population in millions by year.

Year	US Population
1980	228
1981	230
1982	233
1983	235
1984	237
1985	239
1986	242
1987	244
1988	246
1989	248

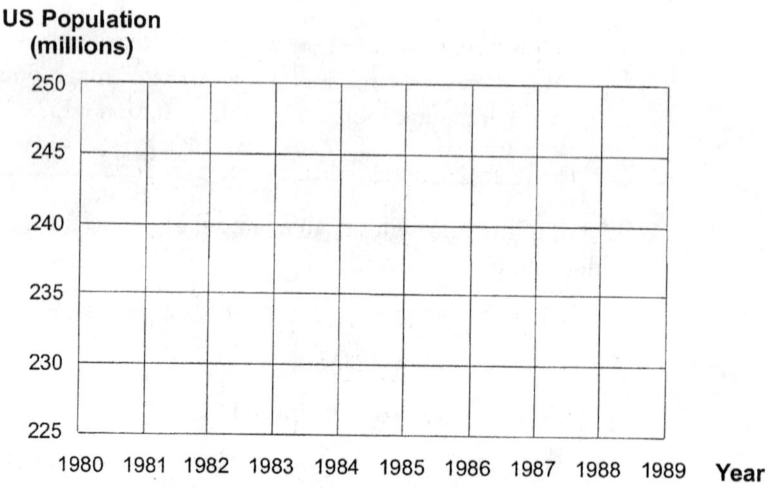

a. On the axes provided, carefully plot the data from the table.

b. Looking at your graph in (1), which of the following best describes how population changed in the 1980s? ____________________

i. Population generally decreased over the decade.
ii. Population stayed roughly constant over the decade.
iii. Population increased and decreased erratically over the decade.
iv. Population increased at a roughly constant rate over the decade.

c. On your graph for (1) use a ruler and draw in a single straight line which seems to best fit the data you plotted.

d. Slope measures the rate of change in the y-axis variable for a one unit change in the x-axis variable. Bearing this in mind, what is the rate at which population changed over the decade of the 1980s? ____________________

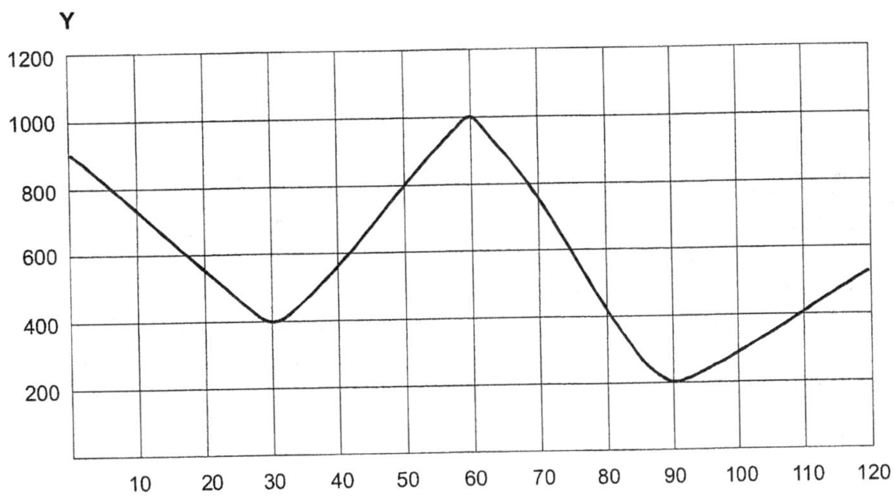

2. Study the graph in the preceding figure.

a. In the figure, Y increases when X increases from ____________________ to ____________________, and then again when X increases from ____________________ to ____________________. In these two regions, the slope of the relationship between X and Y is (positive/negative/zero).

b. In the same figure, Y decreases when X increases from ____________________ to ____________________, and then again when X increases from ____________________ to ____________________. In these two regions, the slope of the relationship between X and Y is (positive/negative/zero).

c. Y reaches its maximum value of ____________________ when X has the value ____________________. Y reaches its minimum value of ____________________ when X has the value ____________________.

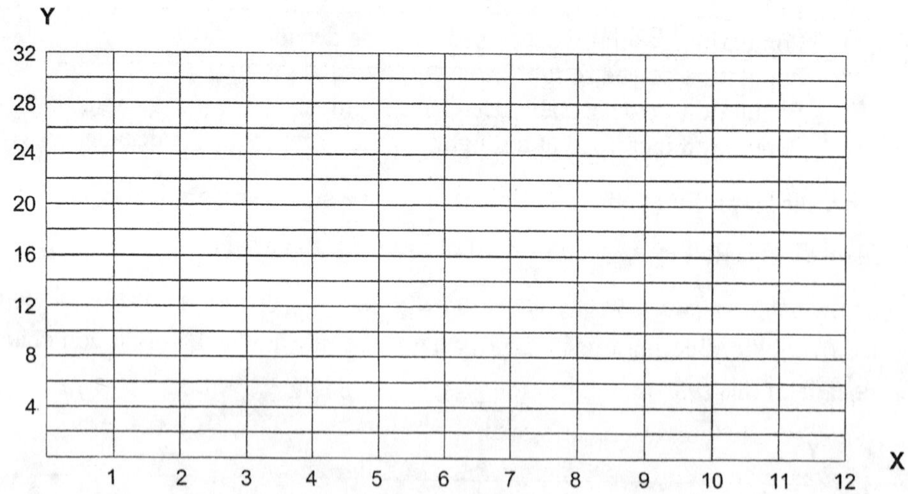

3. Graph each of the following equations on the grid provided. Then describe your graph by filling in the blanks.

   a. Y = 2X + 10

   This graph has a vertical intercept of ____________________ and a constant slope of ____________________. As X increases, Y always (increases/decreases) at a (constant/changing) rate.

   b. Y = 2X + 5

   This graph has a vertical intercept of ____________________ and a constant slope of ____________________. As X increases, Y always (increases/decreases) at a (constant/changing) rate.

   c. Y = X + 10

   This graph has a vertical intercept of ____________________ and a constant slope of ____________________. As X increases, Y always (increases/decreases) at a (constant/changing) rate.

   d. Y = 30 – 5X

   This graph has a vertical intercept of ____________________ and a constant slope of ____________________. As X increases, Y always (increases/decreases) at a (constant/changing) rate.

   e. Y = 30 – 3X

   This graph has a vertical intercept of ____________________ and a constant slope of ____________________. As X increases, Y always (increases/decreases) at a (constant/changing) rate.

10-MINUTE PRACTICE TEST

Set a timer, giving yourself just ten minutes to answer all of the following questions. To see what you *really* know and remember, take the test at least a day *after* you've read the chapter in the text and completed the exercises in this study guide.

Multiple Choice: Circle the letter in front of the single best answer.

1. Economics can be defined as the study of
   a. business firms and how they can increase their profit.
   b. financial markets, like the stock market and the bond market.
   c. choice under conditions of scarcity.
   d. how households allocate their income to different uses.
   e. how businesses and government agencies allocate their revenue to different uses.

2. *Micro*economics studies the economic behavior of
   a. very small nations.
   b. very small people.
   c. individual businesses only.
   d. individual households only.
   e. individual decision-makers, including households and businesses.

3. Which of the following is a *resource,* from society's point of view?
   a. Meat
   b. Clothing
   c. The income tax
   d. An office building
   e. Electricity

4. Regardless of its truth or falsehood, the statement "A tax cut will cause faster growth in total output than an increase in government spending" is an example of
   a. positive microeconomics.
   b. positive macroeconomics.
   c. normative microeconomics.
   d. normative macroeconomics.
   e. none of the above.

5. Which of the following is the best example of a *model*?
   a. A dollar bill
   b. A coffee cup
   c. A drawing of a house
   d. A stop sign
   e. A laptop computer

6. The best way to study economics is
   a. *passively*, reading the book over and over again until you can follow the logical flow.
   b. *actively*, making sure you can reproduce the material on your own.
   c. with a phone in one hand and a remote control in the other.
   d. bent at the waist, making a 90-degree angle with your upper torso.
   e. with Country-and-Western music in the background.

True/False: For each of the following statements, circle T if the statement is true or F if the statement is false.

T F 1. All assumptions in an economic model are *simplifying* assumptions.

T F 2. Economists classify resources into three categories: labor, physical capital and human capital.

T F 3. Normative economics deals with how the economy normally functions in ordinary times.

T F 4. In economics, we assume that individuals face scarcities of time and spending power.

T F 5. *Macro*economics studies the economies of large, industrialized nations, such as the United States or Japan.

CHAPTER 2

SCARCITY, CHOICE, AND ECONOMIC SYSTEMS

SPEAKING ECONOMICS

Fill in each blank with the appropriate word or phrase from the list provided in the word bank. (For a challenge, fill in as many blanks as you can *without* using the word bank.)

____________________ 1. What is given up when making a choice or taking an action.

____________________ 2. A curve showing all combinations of two goods that can be produced with the resources and technology currently available.

____________________ 3. The more of something we produce, the more we must sacrifice to produce one more unit.

____________________ 4. A situation in which we could produce more of one good without sacrificing production of any other good.

____________________ 5. A method of production in which each person concentrates on a limited number of activities.

____________________ 6. The act of trading with others to obtain what we desire.

____________________ 7. The ability to produce a good or service using *fewer resources* than other producers use.

____________________ 8. The ability to produce a good or service at a *lower opportunity cost* than other producers.

____________________ 9. The determination of which goods and services are produced, how they are produced, and who gets them.

____________________ 10. An economy in which resources are allocated according to long-lived practices from the past.

____________________ 11. Two names for an economic system in which resources are allocated according to explicit instructions from a central authority.

____________________ 12. An economic system in which resources are allocated through individual decision making.

____________________ 13. A group of buyers and sellers with the potential to trade with one another.

____________________ 14. The amount of money that must be paid to a seller to obtain a good or service.

____________________ 15. Communal ownership of most resources.

____________________ 16. State ownership of most resources.

____________________ 17. Private ownership of most resources.

____________________ 18. A system of resource allocation and resource ownership.

Word Bank

absolute advantage
capitalism
centrally planned economy
command economy
communism
comparative advantage
economic system
exchange
law of increasing opportunity cost
market
market economy
opportunity cost
price
production possibilities frontier (PPF)
resource allocation
socialism
specialization
productive inefficiency
traditional economy

CHAPTER HIGHLIGHTS

Fill in the blanks with the appropriate words or phrases. If you have difficulty, review the chapter and then try again.

1. The ____________________ of any choice is all that we give up when we make that choice.

2. All production carries an ____________________: to produce more of one thing, society must shift ____________________ away from producing something else.

3. The law of ____________________ opportunity cost tells us that the more of something we produce, the ____________________ is the opportunity cost of producing still more.

4. A firm, industry or an entire economy is productively ____________________ if it could produce more of some good without pulling resources from the production of any other good.

5. ____________________ and ____________________ enable us to enjoy greater production and higher living standards than would otherwise be possible. As a result, all economies exhibit high degrees of ____________________ and ____________________.

6. A person has a (an) ____________________ in producing some good if he or she can produce it using fewer resources than another person can.

7. A person has a (an) ____________________ in producing some good if he or she can produce it with a smaller opportunity cost than some other person can.

8. Total production of every good or service will be greatest when individuals specialize according to their ____________________.

9. In a ____________________ economy, resources are allocated by explicit instructions from some higher authority.

10. In a ____________________ economy, resources are allocated through individual decision making.

IMPORTANT CONCEPTS

Write a brief answer below each of the following questions.

1. Indicate whether the following statement is true or false, and then explain briefly: To determine the opportunity cost of a year of college, we would add the direct money cost and the income foregone. Thus, for someone who could have earned $30,000 as a full-time fisherman during the year, or $45,000 as a full-time truck driver that year, or $20,000 as a full-time tour guide that year, the opportunity cost would be the direct money cost plus a total income foregone of $30,000 + $45,000 + $20,000 = $95,000."

2. What economic law gives the production possibilities frontier its characteristic concave (upside-down bowl) shape?

3. Name two types of economic situations in which a "free lunch" for society might be possible.

   a.

   b.

4. List three separate reasons why specialization and exchange can lead to increased production.

   a.

   b.

   c.

5. College professors can usually locate books and articles in their college library faster than students. Yet most college professors hire students to find these materials. Is this consistent with the idea of comparative advantage? Briefly, why or why not?

6. List the three methods of resource allocation.

   a.

   b.

   c.

7. List the three methods of resource ownership.

   a.

   b.

   c.

8. List the four major types of economic systems. For each system, identify the method of resource allocation and how resources are owned.

   a.

   b.

   c.

   d.

SKILLS AND TOOLS

For each of the following items, follow the instructions, write the correct answer in the blank, or circle the correct answer.

1. By using its existing resources efficiently, an island society can produce the following alternative combinations of mangoes and oranges each day.

	Daily Production of:	
	Mangoes	**Oranges**
A	0	50
B	5	49
C	10	46
D	15	40
E	20	30
F	25	0

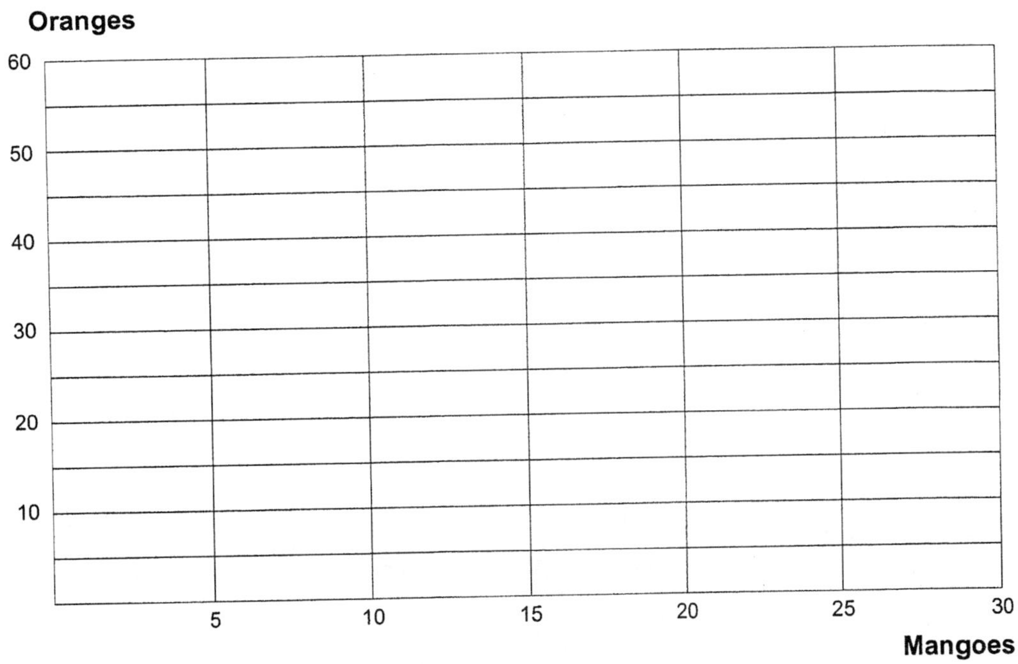

a. Plot this society's production possibility frontier (PPF) on the axes provided. Label the points A–F on your graph.

b. Assume the islanders are currently producing at point A, devoting all their resources to orange production. In moving to point B, this society gives up ____________________ orange(s). The resources released from producing oranges are then able to produce ____________________ mangoes. The opportunity cost to society of these first ____________________ mangoes is ____________________ orange(s).

Starting at point B, this society can move to point C and produce an additional ____________________ mangoes only if it foregoes an additional ____________________ oranges. The opportunity cost of the additional mangoes obtained in moving from B to C is an additional ____________________ oranges foregone.

In moving from C to D, the opportunity cost of ____________________ additional mangoes is ____________________ more oranges. In moving from D to E, the opportunity cost of ____________________ more mangoes is ____________________ more oranges. In moving from E to F, the opportunity cost of ____________________ more mangoes is ____________________ more oranges.

Moving along the PPF from A to F, the opportunity cost of mangoes is (increasing/decreasing/constant) as more and more mangoes are produced.

c. Now assume the islanders are currently producing at point F, devoting all their resources to mango production. In moving to point E, this society gives up ____________________ mangoes. The resources released from producing these mangoes are then able to produce ____________________ oranges. The opportunity cost to society of these first ____________________ oranges is ____________________ mangoes.

Starting at point E, this society can move to point D and produce an additional ____________________ oranges only if it foregoes an additional ____________________ mangoes. The opportunity cost of the additional oranges obtained in moving from E to D is an additional ____________________ mangoes foregone.

In moving from D to C, the opportunity cost of ____________________ additional oranges is ____________________ more mangoes. In moving from C to B, the opportunity cost of ____________________ more oranges is ____________________ more mangoes.

Moving along the PPF from F to A, the opportunity cost of oranges is (increasing/decreasing/constant) as more and more oranges are produced.

2. On the PPF above, plot the point representing total production of 10 mangoes and 30 oranges. Label this point G. Plot the point representing production of 15 mangoes and 50 oranges. Label this point H.

   a. At point G, the islanders (are/are not) using all their resources efficiently. Starting from point G, the opportunity cost of an additional 5 mangoes would be ____________________ oranges. The opportunity cost of an additional 5 oranges would be ____________________ mangoes. At point G, does this society achieve technical efficiency (yes/no)?

b. The point H represents a combination of mango and orange production that this society (can/cannot) achieve with existing resources. To achieve point H, the technology of production will have to (improve/decline/remain the same) or society will have to (acquire more/use less) resources.

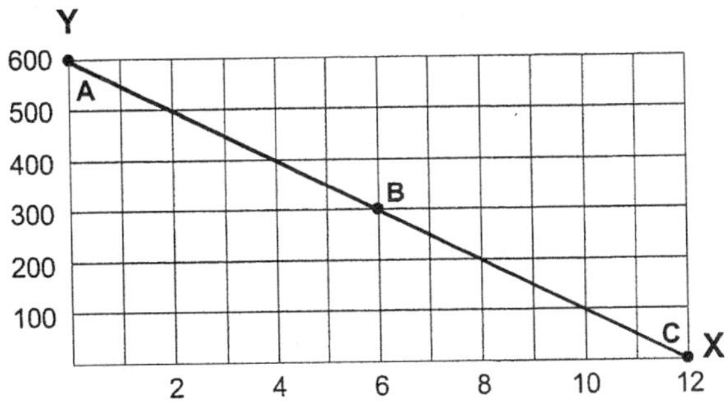

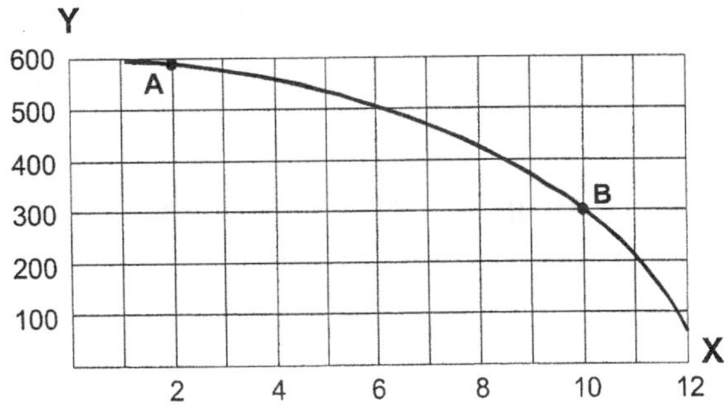

3. In the panel on the left above, the absolute value of the PPF's slope is (constant/increasing/decreasing) as we move from A to B. Starting at A, the opportunity cost of the first unit of good X will be ____________________ units of (X/Y). Starting at B, the opportunity cost of one more unit of X will be ____________________ units of (X/Y). If we begin at point C, the opportunity cost of one more unit of X will be ____________________ units of (X/Y). With this PPF, as we move from A to B to C, the opportunity cost of additional units of X is (constant/increasing/decreasing).

4. In the panel on the right above, as we move from point A to point B, the absolute value of the PPF's slope (remains constant/increases/decreases). At point A, the opportunity cost of an additional unit of X is (the same as/greater than/less than) the opportunity cost of an additional unit of X at point B. At the same time, at point A the opportunity cost of an additional unit of Y is (the same as/greater than/less than) the opportunity cost of an additional unit of Y at point B.

5. Each entry in the following table gives the number of hours it takes a typical worker in the given country to produce one unit of the indicated good. Thus, it takes a worker in Norway two hours to produce one sweater, and four hours to catch a fish, and so forth.

	Sweaters	**Fish**
Norway	2 hours	4 hours
Sweden	6 hours	2 hours

a. From these data, we can see that Norway has an absolute advantage in producing (sweaters/fish/both goods/neither good). At the same time, Sweden has an absolute advantage in producing (sweaters/fish/both goods/neither good).

b. From these same data, we can see that the opportunity cost of producing a fish in Norway is ____________________ sweater(s). The opportunity cost of producing a fish in Sweden is ____________________ sweater(s). From this we can conclude that Sweden has a comparative advantage in producing (sweaters/fish/both goods/neither good), while Norway has a comparative advantage in producing (sweaters/fish/both goods/neither good).

15-MINUTE PRACTICE TEST

Set a timer, giving yourself just 15 minutes to answer all of the following questions. To see what you *really* know and remember, take the test at least a day *after* you've read the chapter in the text and completed the exercises in this study guide.

Multiple Choice: Circle the letter in front of the single best answer.

1. The opportunity cost of any choice is
   a. the money given up for that choice.
   b. the time given up for that choice.
   c. what is actually sacrificed to make that choice.
   d. how much you would pay to make that choice.
   e. how much you would pay to avoid that choice.

2. For society, opportunity cost arises because of a scarcity of
   a. technology.
   b. land.
   c. money.
   d. resources.
   e. markets.

3. As we move rightward along a production possibilities frontier, we also move
   a. downward, and the frontier becomes steeper.
   b. downward, and the frontier becomes flatter.
   c. upward, and the frontier becomes steeper.
   d. upward, and the frontier becomes flatter.
   e. neither upward nor downward, and the slope of the frontier remains unchanged.

4. A point inside a production possibilities frontier might represent
   a. productive efficiency.
   b. a recession.
   c. a situation of very high opportunity cost.
   d. full employment of resources.
   e. none of the above.

5. The production possibilities frontier is concave shaped (like an upside-down bowl) because of
   a. the scarcity of resources.
   b. the law of increasing opportunity cost.
   c. productive inefficiency.
   d. absolute advantage.
   e. none of the above.

6. Which of the following is consistent with specialization according to comparative advantage?
   a. Famous attorney Alan Dershowitz prepares and addresses his own bills and takes them to the post office each day.
   b. John Travolta walks his own dog.
   c. The President of the United States drafts his own speeches.
   d. All of the above.
   e. None of the above.

7. One reason why specialization and exchange lead to greater production is
   a. comparative advantage.
   b. the development of expertise.
   c. the time saving from not having to switch tasks.
   d. all of the above.
   e. none of the above.

8. Which of the following is a method of resource allocation?
   a. Capitalism
   b. Socialism
   c. Command
   d. All of the above
   e. None of the above

9. Resource allocation involves an answer to which of the following questions?
   a. How are the economy's goods and services produced?
   b. What determines the rate of unemployment?
   c. How can business firms increase their profit?
   d. All of the above.
   e. None of the above.

10. Under *market capitalism*, resources are
    a. owned by society as a whole.
    b. owned by the market itself.
    c. owned by no one.
    d. allocated in an entirely random way.
    e. none of the above.

True/False: For each of the following statements, circle T if the statement is true or F if the statement is False.

T F 1. The correct measure of the cost of a choice is the time used up by that choice.

T F 2. The law of increasing opportunity cost tells us that the opportunity costs of our choices tend to rise over time.

T F 3. If we can produce more of one good without producing less of any other goods, the economy is productively inefficient.

T F 4. An individual has a comparative advantage in producing a good if he or she can produce it at a lower opportunity cost than some other individual.

T F 5. The United States is an example of a pure market economy, in which all resource allocation is accomplished through the market.

T F 6. An economic system is comprised of two components: a system of resource allocation and a system of resource ownership.

T F 7. A recession can be illustrated by a movement downward and rightward along a country's production possibilities frontier.

T F 8. The economic system of the former Soviet Union was market socialism.

CHAPTER 3

SUPPLY AND DEMAND

SPEAKING ECONOMICS

Fill in the blank with the appropriate word or phrase from the list provided in the word bank. (For a challenge, fill in as many blanks as you can *without* using the word bank.)

________________________ 1. The process of combining distinct things into a single whole.

________________________ 2. A market in which a single buyer or seller has the power to influence the price of the product.

________________________ 3. A market in which *no* buyer or seller has the power to influence the price of the product.

________________________ 4. The total amount of a good an individual would choose to purchase at a given price.

________________________ 5. The total amount of a good that buyers in a market would choose to purchase at a given price.

________________________ 6. "As the price of a good increases, the quantity demanded decreases."

________________________ 7. A list showing the quantities of a good that consumers would choose to purchase at different prices, with all other variables held constant.

________________________ 8. A line showing the quantity of a good or service demanded at various prices, with all other variables held constant.

________________________ 9. A movement along a demand curve in response to a change in price.

________________________ 10. A shift of a demand curve in response to a change in some variable other than price.

________________________ 11. The amount that a person or firm earns over a particular period.

________________________ 12. The total value of everything a person or firm owns at a point in time, minus the total value of everything owed.

____________________ 13. A good that people demand more of as their incomes rise.

____________________ 14. A good that people demand less of as their incomes rise.

____________________ 15. A good that can be used in place of some other good and that fulfills more or less the same purpose.

____________________ 16. A good that is used together with some other good.

____________________ 17. The set of methods a firm can use to turn inputs into outputs.

____________________ 18. The amount of a good or service an individual firm would choose to produce and sell at a given price.

____________________ 19. The total amount of a good or service that sellers in a market would choose to produce and sell at a given price.

____________________ 20. "As the price of a good increases, the quantity supplied increases."

____________________ 21. A list showing the quantities of a good or service that firms would choose to produce and sell at different prices, with all other variables held constant.

____________________ 22. A line showing the quantity of a good or service supplied at various prices, with all other variables held constant.

____________________ 23. A movement along a supply curve in response to a change in price.

____________________ 24. A shift of a supply curve in response to some variable other than price.

____________________ 25. Another good that a firm could produce using some of the same inputs as the good in question.

____________________ 26. A situation that, once achieved, will not change unless some external factor, previously held constant, changes.

____________________ 27. At a given price, the excess of quantity demanded over quantity supplied.

____________________ 28. At a given price, the excess of quantity supplied over quantity demanded.

Word Bank

aggregation
alternate good
change in demand
change in quantity demanded
change in quantity supplied
change in supply
complement
(market) demand curve
demand schedule
equilibrium
excess demand
excess supply
firm's quantity supplied
imperfectly competitive market
income
individual's quantity demanded
inferior good
law of demand
law of supply
normal good
perfectly competitive market
market quantity demanded
market quantity supplied
substitute
supply curve
supply schedule
technology
wealth

CHAPTER HIGHLIGHTS

Fill in the blanks with the appropriate words or phrases. If you have difficulty, review the chapter and then try again.

1. A ____________________ is a group of buyers and sellers with the potential to trade.
2. In defining a market, we must choose the geographic area in which ____________________ and ____________________ are located. The geographic area we choose depends on the specific question we are trying to answer.
3. In ____________________ markets, individual buyers and sellers have some influence over the price of the product.
4. In ____________________ markets, each buyer and seller treats the ____________________ as given.
5. Supply and demand explain how prices are determined in ____________________ markets.
6. The individual's quantity ____________________ of any good is the amount that an individual would choose to buy at a particular ____________________.

7. The ____________________ of any good is the total amount that all buyers in a market would choose to purchase at a given ____________________.

8. The ____________________ of demand states that when the price of a good rises, and everything else remains the same, the quantity of the good demanded will ____________________.

9. The ____________________ shows the relationship between the price of a good and the quantity demanded, holding constant all other variables that affect demand. Each point on the curve shows the quantity that buyers would choose to buy at a specific ____________________.

10. The law of demand tells us that demand curves slope ____________________.

11. A change in a good's price causes us to *move along* the demand curve. We call this a change in ____________________.

12. A change in any determinant of demand—except for the good's price—causes the demand curve to ____________________. We call this a ____________________.

13. The demand for most goods (normal goods) is positively related to ____________________ or ____________________. A rise in either ____________________ or ____________________ will increase demand for these goods, and shift the demand curve to the ____________________.

14. When the price of a substitute rises, the demand for a good will ____________________, shifting the demand curve to the ____________________.

15. A rise in the price of a complement will ____________________ the demand for a good, shifting the demand curve to the ____________________.

16. A firm's ____________________ is the set of methods it can use to turn ____________________ into ____________________.

17. A competitive firm faces three constraints: (1) it's production technology, (2) the ____________________ of its inputs, and (3) the ____________________ of its output.

18. A firm's quantity ____________________ of any good is the amount it would choose to produce and sell at a particular ____________________.

19. The ____________________ of any good is the total amount that sellers in a market would choose to produce and sell at a given price.

20. The *law of supply* states that when the price of a good rises, and everything else remains the same, the quantity of the good supplied will ____________________.

21. The *supply curve* shows the relationship between the ____________________ of a good and the quantity supplied, holding constant the values of all other variables that affect supply. Each point on the curve shows the quantity that sellers would choose to sell at a specific ____________________.

22. The *law of supply* tells us that supply curves slope ____________________.

23. A change in a good's price causes us to *move along* the supply curve. We call this a change in ____________________.

24. A change in any influence on supply—except for the good's price—causes the supply curve to ____________________. We call this a ____________________.

25. A rise in the price of an input will cause supply to ____________________, shifting the supply curve to the ____________________.

26. When an alternate good becomes more profitable to produce—because its price ____________________ or the cost of producing it ____________________—the supply curve for the good in questions will shift to the ____________________.

27. Cost-saving technological advances cause supply to ____________________, shifting the supply curve to the ____________________.

28. An increase in sellers' productive capacity shifts the supply curve to the ____________________.

29. A rise in the expected price of a good will ____________________ the supply of the good, shifting the supply curve to the ____________________.

30. A(n) ____________________ is a situation that, once achieved, will not change unless something we have been holding constant changes.

31. To find the ____________________ price and quantity in a competitive market, draw the supply and demand curves. The ____________________ is the point where the two curves intersect.

32. Any change that shifts the supply curve to the ____________________ will increase the equilibrium price and decrease the equilibrium quantity.

33. Any change that shifts the demand curve to the ____________________ will cause both the equilibrium price and quantity to increase.

The next four problems concern the four key steps that economists use again and again to answer questions about the economy.

34. Key Step #1—Characterize the ____________________: Decide which ____________________ best suits the problem being analyzed, and identify the decision makers (buyers and sellers) who interact in that ____________________.

35. Key Step #2—Identify ____________________ and ____________________: Identify the ____________________ that the decision makers are trying to achieve, and the ____________________ they face in achieving those ____________________.

36. Key Step #3—Find the ____________________: Describe the conditions necessary for ____________________ in the market, and a method for determining that ____________________.

37. Key Step #4—What Happens when Things Change: Explore how events or government policies change the market ____________________.

IMPORTANT CONCEPTS

Write a brief answer for each of the following items.

1. List as many distinct variables as you can that *shift* the demand curve for a good. For each variable, indicate the direction of change that causes the demand curve to shift to the *left*. Assume that the good is *normal*.

2. List as many distinct variables as you can that *shift* the supply curve for a good. For each variable, indicate the direction of change that causes the supply curve to shift to the *right*.

3. What is the key difference between a perfectly competitive market and an imperfectly competitive market?

Indicate whether each of the next two statements is true or false, and then explain briefly.

4. "Income and wealth mean basically the same thing in economics."

5. "The phrase 'change in demand' can refer either to a shift in the demand curve or a movement along the demand curve."

SKILLS AND TOOLS

For each of the following items, follow the instructions, write the correct answer in the blank, or circle the correct answer.

1. In the following demand schedule, P is the market price and Q^D is the quantity of limousine rides demanded per week by buyers in Patterson, New Jersey.

DEMAND

P	Q^D
$100	0
80	4
60	8
40	12
20	16
0	20

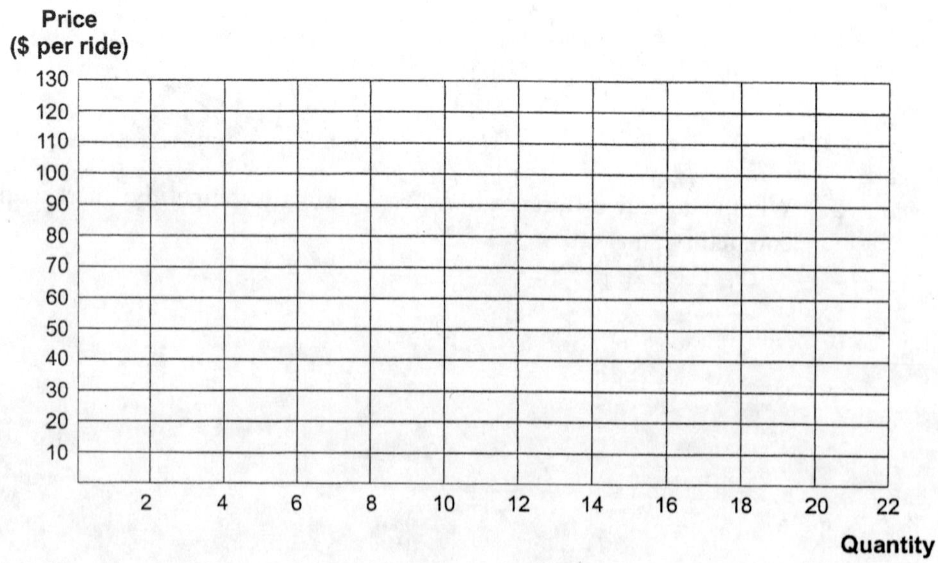

a. Plot the market demand curve for limousine rides. Label this curve D.

b. From this demand curve, we can see that when the market price is $50, the quantity of limousine rides demanded will be ____________________. If the market price rises to $90, however, the quantity demanded will (rise/fall) to ____________________ units per week. However, if the market price falls as low as $10, the quantity demanded will (rise/fall) to ____________________ units per week.

2. In the following supply schedule, P is the market price of limousine rides and Q is the quantity of rides supplied per week by sellers in Patterson, New Jersey.

SUPPLY

P	Q^S
$ 20	0
40	4
60	8
80	12
100	16
120	20

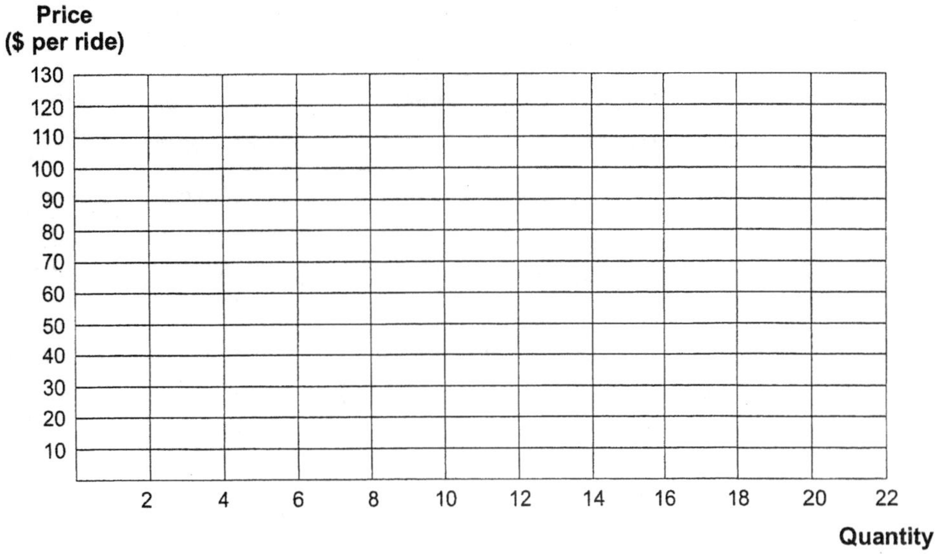

a. Plot the market supply curve for limousine rides in the space provided. Label this curve S.

b. From this supply curve, we can see that when the market price is $50, the quantity of rides supplied will be ____________________. If the market price rises to $90, however, the quantity supplied will (rise/fall) to ____________________ units per week. However, if the market price falls as low as $30, the quantity supplied will (rise/fall) to ____________________ units per week.

3. In the space below, re-plot the demand curve and the supply curve for limousine rides using the data from the previous two questions.

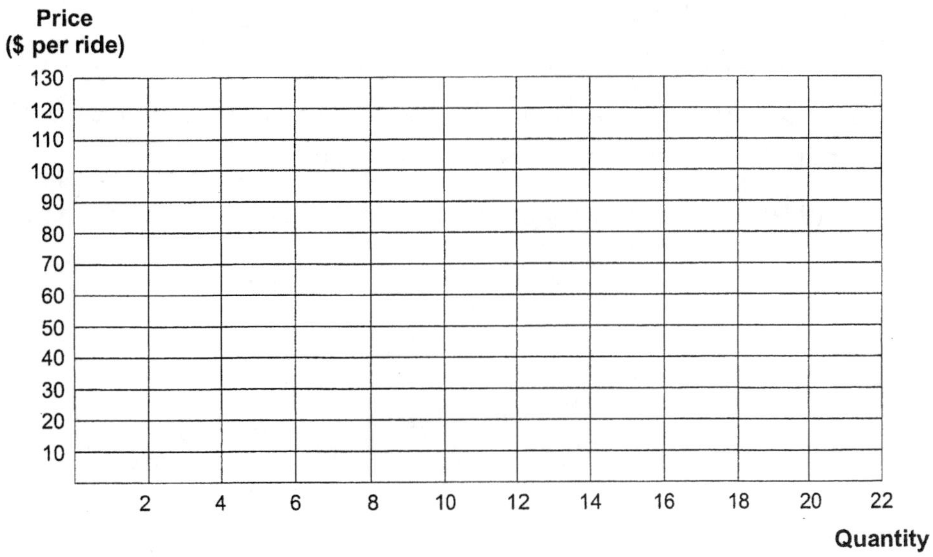

a. By examining demand and supply together, we can see that the equilibrium price in the market for limousine rides will be ____________________. The number of rides bought and sold per week will be ____________________.

b. At a price of $80 per week, there would be an excess (demand/supply) of ____________________ units per week in this market. Market price would tend to (rise/fall) as (buyers/sellers) compete with one another to (buy/sell) more limousine rides.

c. At a price of $40 per week, there would be an excess (demand/supply) of ____________________ units per week. Market price would tend to (rise/fall) as (buyers/sellers) compete with one another to (buy/sell) more limousine rides.

4. Under current conditions, the monthly demand curve and monthly supply curve for 13-inch color TVs in Golden, Colorado, are plotted below.

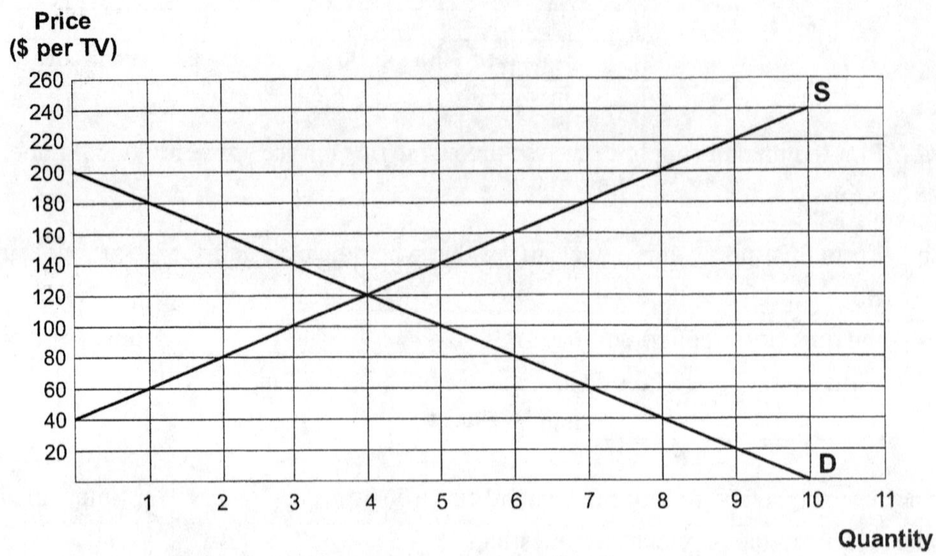

a. What is the equilibrium price of TVs? ____________________.

b. Suppose the price of recliner chairs, a complement to TVs, falls. This will tend to (increase/decrease) the quantity of TVs demanded every month, and so shift market demand for TVs (rightward/leftward).

The table below shows data on market demand for TVs *after* the price of recliners has fallen.

P	Q^D
$200	2
160	4
120	6
80	8
40	10

c. Plot the new demand curve for TVs on the graph above.

d. What is the new equilibrium price for TVs? ____________________.

e. Suppose the price of copper wire, an important component in the production of TVs, rises. This will tend to (increase/decrease) the quantity of TVs supplied every month, and so shift market supply of TVs (leftward/rightward).

Data on market supply of TVs after the price of copper wire has fallen are recorded in the table below.

P	Q^S
$120	2
160	4
200	6
240	8
280	10

f. Plot the new supply curve for TVs on the graph on the previous page.

g. What is the new equilibrium price for TVs after this latest change?

____________________.

5. Monthly data from Tuscaloosa on market demand and market supply of leather handbags have been graphed below.

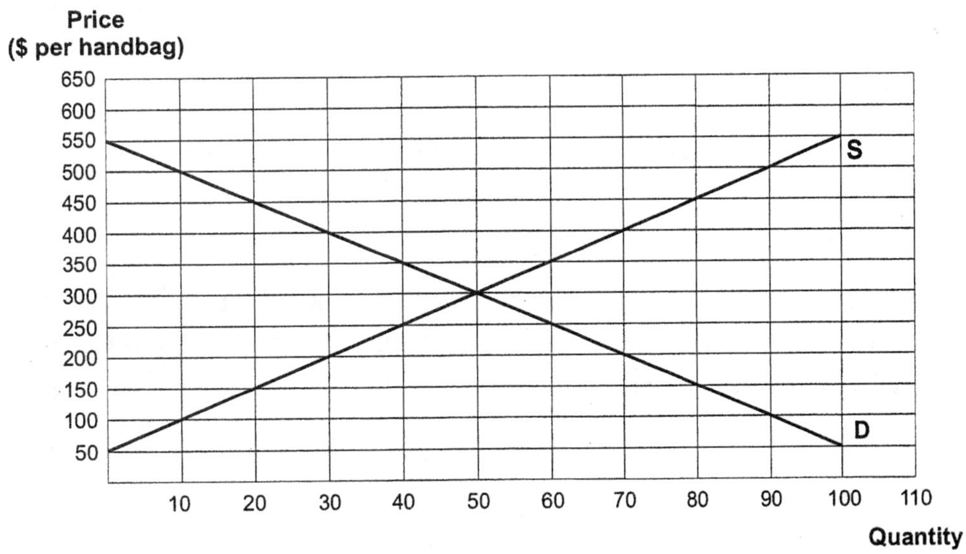

a. Complete the combined demand and supply schedules for leather handbags.

P	Q^D	Q^S
$450	_____	_____
400	_____	_____
350	_____	_____
300	_____	_____
250	_____	_____
200	_____	_____
150	_____	_____

b. If the market price were $400, quantity (demanded/supplied) would exceed quantity (demanded/supplied) and there would be an (excess demand/excess supply) equal to ____________________ units per period. This would cause the market price to (rise/fall) toward its equilibrium level of ____________________.

c. If the market price were $150, quantity (demanded/supplied) would exceed quantity (demanded/supplied) and there would be (excess demand/excess supply) equal to ____________________ units per period. This would cause the market price to (rise/fall) toward its equilibrium level of ____________________.

6. So far, we have studied market demand and market supply either as tables or as graphs. Sometimes, however, it is more convenient to express those same relationships in the form of equations. For example, suppose we know that, every week, the quantity of deep sea fishing trips buyers will demand (Q^D) is related to market price according to the equation

$$Q^D = 20 - P/15,$$

while the quantity of fishing trips supplied (Q^S) is related to market price according to the equation

$$Q^S = P/12 - 2.5.$$

Using these equations, complete the combined demand and supply schedules below. (To fill out the table, just plug market price into the demand or supply equation given above and solve for the corresponding quantity demanded or supplied.)

P	Q^D	Q^S
270	____	____
210	____	____
90	____	____
30	____	____

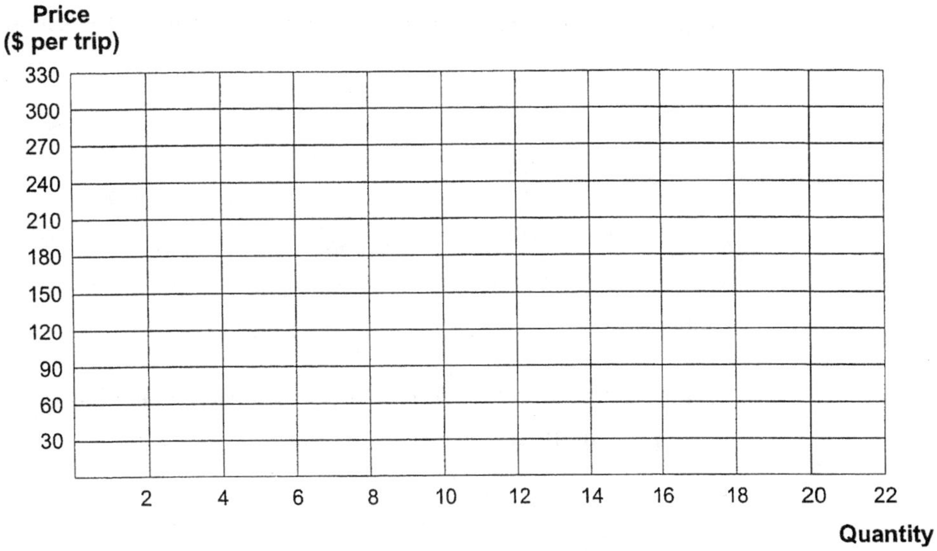

Now look at the table you just completed. Notice that at very low market prices, quantity demanded exceeds quantity supplied, while at higher prices quantity supplied exceeds quantity demanded. Just by looking at the data in these demand and supply schedules, we are therefore unable to determine the equilibrium price in this market.

But we *can* find the equilibrium with our equations. Suppose we let P_e stand for the unknown value of the equilibrium price in this market. While we do not know P_e, we know it is special: it is the only price at which quantity demanded will equal quantity supplied. To find P_e, we therefore simply set the equation for quantity demanded equal to the equation for quantity supplied. Setting $Q^D = Q^S$ in this way, we obtain

$$20 - P_e/15 = P_e/12 - 2.5.$$

To solve for P_e, we add 2.5 to each side, then add $P_e/15$ to each side, and get

$$22.5 = P_e/12 + P_e/15.$$

Next, putting the two terms on the righthand side over the common denominator $12 \times 15 = 180$, we obtain

$$22.5 = 27P_e/180.$$

Finally, by multiplying both sides by 180 and dividing by 27, we get the final answer

$$P_e = (22.5)(180)/27 = 150.$$

7. Using the data you generated in the preceding exercise, plot the market demand and supply curves in the space provided there. Once you've completed your graphs, locate the equilibrium market price. What is that price according to your graphs? ____________ Is it the same price you obtained by solving the demand and supply equations? ____________ It should be, so if it is not, go back and see what you did wrong.) What is the equilibrium quantity? ____________ Is it the same as you would get if you plugged your answer for equilibrium price into the market demand and market supply curves? ____________ (It should be.)

8. Annual market demand and market supply for tons of California cumquats are given, respectively, by the following equations

$$Q^D = 500 - P/8$$

$$Q^S = P/2 - 500.$$

Without plotting graphs for demand or supply, answer the following questions.

a. In equilibrium, the price of California cumquats will be $____________. The quantity of cumquats bought and sold will be ____________ tons.

b. If market price were $1,200, quantity demanded would be ____________ tons and quantity supplied would be ____________ tons. There would be (excess demand/excess supply) equal to ____________ tons of cumquats per year.

c. If market price were $2,000, quantity demanded would be ____________ tons and quantity supplied would be ____________ tons. There would be (excess demand/excess supply) equal to ____________ tons of cumquats per year.

15-MINUTE PRACTICE TEST

Set a timer, giving yourself just 15 minutes to answer all of the following questions. To see what you *really* know and remember, take the test at least a day *after* you've read the chapter in the text and completed the exercises in this study guide.

Multiple Choice: Circle the letter in front of the single best answer.

1. In economics, a "market" is
   a. a geographic location where buyers and sellers trade with each other.
   b. virtually always defined locally, rather than nationally or internationally.
   c. virtually always defined nationally, rather than locally or internationally.
   d. defined only *after* an exchange actually takes place.
   e. a group of buyers and sellers with the potential to trade.

2. A perfectly competitive market is one in which
   a. buyers and sellers never actually meet each other.
   b. no buyer or seller can influence the price of the product being traded.
   c. a few very large firms directly compete with each other for customers.
   d. there are no limits to the tricks sellers can play to drive their rivals out of business.
   e. all of the above.

3. Which of the following would cause a rightward shift of the demand curve in the market for eggs in St. Louis?
   a. A technological advance in the egg-producing industry
   b. An increase in the number of firms in the egg-producing industry
   c. An increase in the price of chicken feed
   d. An increase in the price of powdered eggs, a substitute for fresh eggs
   e. None of the above

4. If used books are an inferior good, then a decrease in income will cause a
   a. rightward shift of the demand curve for used books.
   b. leftward shift of the demand curve for used books.
   c. rightward shift of the supply curve for used books.
   d. leftward shift of the demand curve for used books.
   e. shift in both the demand and the supply curves for used books.

5. If the price of oranges is expected to rise, then
   a. the demand curve for oranges will shift rightward.
   b. the demand curve for oranges will shift leftward.
   c. the supply curve for oranges will shift leftward.
   d. both *a* and *c*.
   e. both *b* and *c*.

6. Which of the following would shift the supply curve for a good leftward?
   a. A rise in the price of a complement
   b. A rise in the price of an input used in producing the good
   c. A cost-saving technological advance in producing the good
   d. All of the above
   e. None of the above

7. If there is an excess supply of a good, we can generally expect
   a. the price of the good to rise.
   b. the price of the good to fall.
   c. the demand curve to shift rightward.
   d. the supply curve to shift leftward.
   e. both *c* and *d*.

8. A rise in the price of a substitute for a good will cause
   a. the equilibrium price of the good to increase and the equilibrium quantity to decrease.
   b. the equilibrium price of the good to decrease and the equilibrium quantity to increase.
   c. both the equilibrium price and the equilibrium quantity of the good to increase.
   d. both the equilibrium price and the equilibrium quantity of the good to decrease.
   e. no change in either the equilibrium price or equilibrium quantity of the good.

9. Which of the following is *not* included among the four key steps that economists use to solve problems?
   a. Identify Goals and Constraints.
   b. Graph the Equations.
   c. Find the Equilibrium.
   d. What Happens when Things Change.
   e. Characterize the Market.

10. In the market for potatoes, a rise in the price of beef (a complement) and a rise in the wage paid to farm labor (an input) would cause
    a. both the equilibrium price and equilibrium quantity to rise.
    b. both the equilibrium price and equilibrium quantity to fall.
    c. a decrease in the equilibrium quantity, and an ambiguous effect on the equilibrium price.
    d. an increase in the equilibrium price, and an ambiguous effect on the equilibrium quantity.
    e. none of the above.

True/False: For each of the following statements, circle T if the statement is true or F if the statement is false.

T F 1. The law of demand tells us that, for most goods, a rise in income will cause an increase in quantity demanded.

T F 2. If people want to buy more of a good at any price, sellers will want to sell more of the good, so the supply curve will shift.

T F 3. A change in the expected future price of a good will cause both the supply curve and the demand curve for the good to shift.

T F 4. A "change in supply" refers to a movement along the supply curve.

T F 5. A rightward shift in the demand curve for cotton shirts will cause a rise in both the equilibrium price and equilibrium quantity of cotton shirts.

T F 6. A rise in the price of *rayon* shirts will cause a decrease in the equilibrium price and quantity of *cotton* shirts.

T F 7. The *first* key step of the four-step procedure is: Find the Equilibrium.

T F 8. The *last* key step of the four-step procedure is to ask: What Happens When Things Change?

CHAPTER 4

WHAT MACROECONOMICS TRIES TO EXPLAIN

SPEAKING ECONOMICS

Fill in each blank with the appropriate word or phrase from the list provided in the word bank. (For a challenge, fill in as many blanks as you can *without* using the word bank.)

_______________________ 1. Fluctuations in real GDP around its long-term growth trend.

_______________________ 2. A period of increasing real GDP.

_______________________ 3. The point at which real GDP reaches its highest level during a period of rising real GDP.

_______________________ 4. A period of declining real GDP.

_______________________ 5. The point at which real GDP reaches its lowest level during a recession.

_______________________ 6. An unusually severe recession.

_______________________ 7. The process of combining different things into a single category.

Word Bank

aggregation
business cycles
depression
expansion
peak
recession
trough

CHAPTER HIGHLIGHTS

Fill in the blanks with the appropriate words or phrases. If you have difficulty, review the chapter and then try again.

1. Economists—and society at large—agree on three important macroeconomic goals: rapid economic growth, full employment, and ____________________.

2. Economists monitor economic growth by keeping track of ____________________.

3. One measure economists use to keep track of employment is the ____________________.

4. In a typical business cycle, when output rises we are in the ____________________ phase, which continues until we reach a ____________________. Then, as output falls we enter a ____________________, and when output hits bottom, we are in a ____________________.

5. Macroeconomics makes extensive use of ____________________, the process of combining different things into a single category and treating them as a whole.

IMPORTANT CONCEPTS

Write a brief answer below each of the following items.

1. List the three important macroeconomic goals about which there is widespread agreement.

   a.

   b.

   c.

2. What is the difference between an *expansion* and a *peak*?

3. What are the two types of disagreements that can arise on macroeconomics issues?

   a.

   b.

10-MINUTE PRACTICE TEST

Set a timer, giving yourself just ten minutes to answer all of the following questions. To see what you *really* know and remember, take the test at least a day *after* you've read the chapter in the text and completed the exercises in this study guide.

Multiple Choice: Circle the letter in front of the single best answer.

1. Which of the following is *not* a generally agreed-upon macroeconomic goal?
   a. Rapid economic growth
   b. High employment
   c. Low inflation
   d. Stable prices
   e. Zero unemployment

2. Which of the following is a *macro*economic question?
   a. Why do English professors generally earn less than business professors?
   b. Which automobile company makes the best product: General Motors, Ford, or Toyota?
   c. Why are apartment rents higher in San Francisco than in New York?
   d. Why, in the late 1990s, has real GDP in the United States been growing more rapidly than real GDP in England, France or Germany?
   e. Which nation has the best medical care: the United States, Canada, Germany, or England?

3. A recession is a period during which real GDP
   a. doesn't change.
   b. decreases.
   c. hits bottom.
   d. rises.
   e. reaches a peak.

4. A trough is a period during which real GDP
   a. doesn't change.
   b. falls.
   c. hits bottom.
   d. rises.
   e. reaches a peak.

5. A period of rising real GDP is called a(n)
   a. recession.
   b. inflation.
   c. peak.
   d. expansion.
   e. trough.

6. An inflation rate of zero means that the price level is
   a. falling, but very slowly.
   b. falling rapidly.
   c. not changing.
   d. rising, but slowly.
   e. rising rapidly.

7. In the United States, the goal of high employment
   a. is a good goal, but one that has never been written into law.
   b. is embodied in a law that calls for an unemployment rate of 4 percent.
   c. has virtually always been attained.
   d. has never been attained.
   e. is none of the above.

8. The British economist who originated modern macroeconomics by taking on the classical economists was named
   a. Milton Friedman.
   b. Robert Hall.
   c. John Maynard Keynes.
   d. Maynard G. Krebs.
   e. Sir Robert Denver.

True/False: For each of the following statements, circle T if the statement is true or F if the statement is false.

T F 1. When economists study output, employment, or inflation in small countries like Estonia or the Bahamas, they are practicing *micro*economics.

T F 2. In any period during which real GDP rises, output per person and the average standard of living automatically rise as well.

T F 3. The unemployment rate in the United States never reaches zero, even when the economy is doing well.

T F 4. The United States has never experienced double-digit inflation.

T F 5. While high unemployment is costly to society, high inflation is not.

CHAPTER 5

PRODUCTION, INCOME, AND EMPLOYMENT

SPEAKING ECONOMICS

Fill in each blank with the appropriate word or phrase from the list provided in the word bank. (For a challenge, fill in as many blanks as you can *without* using the word bank.)

______________________ 1. The total value of all final goods and services produced for the marketplace during a given year, within the country's borders.

______________________ 2. A good used up in producing a final good.

______________________ 3. A good sold to its final user.

______________________ 4. A measure of a process that takes place over a period of time.

______________________ 5. A measure of an amount that exists at a moment in time.

______________________ 6. Measuring GDP by adding the value of goods and services purchased by each type of final user.

______________________ 7. The part of GDP purchased by households as final users.

______________________ 8. The total value of all goods that will provide useful services in future years.

______________________ 9. The sum of business plant and equipment purchases, new home construction, and inventory changes.

______________________ 10. Total investment spending minus depreciation.

______________________ 11. Spending by federal, state, and local governments on goods and services.

______________________ 12. Funds the government gives to people or organizations, but not as payment for goods or services.

______________________ 13. Total exports minus total imports.

______________________ 14. The revenue a firm receives minus the cost of the intermediate goods it buys.

______________________ 15. Measuring GDP by summing revenue minus the cost of intermediate goods at all firms in the economy.

____________________ 16. Payments to the owners of resources that are used in production.

____________________ 17. Measuring GDP by summing the factor payments made by all firms in the economy.

____________________ 18. A variable measured without adjusting for the dollar's changing value.

____________________ 19. A variable adjusted for changes in the dollar's value.

____________________ 20. Goods and services that are produced, but not for sale in a market.

____________________ 21. Joblessness experienced by people who are between jobs or who are just entering or reentering the labor market.

____________________ 22. Joblessness related to the time of year, such as job loss caused by changes in weather or tourist patterns.

____________________ 23. Joblessness arising from mismatches between workers' skills and employers' requirements or between workers' locations and employers' locations.

____________________ 24. Joblessness arising from changes in production over the business cycle.

____________________ 25. A situation in which there is no cyclical unemployment.

____________________ 26. The level of output the economy could produce if operating at full employment.

____________________ 27. Those people who have a job or who are looking for one.

____________________ 28. The fraction of the labor force that is without a job.

____________________ 29. Individuals who would like a full-time job, but who are working only part time.

____________________ 30. Individuals who would like a job, but have given up searching for one.

Word Bank

capital stock
consumption
cyclical unemployment
discouraged workers
expenditure approach
factor payments
factor payments approach
final good
flow variable
frictional unemployment
full employment
government purchases
gross domestic product (GDP)
intermediate good
involuntary part-time workers
labor force
net exports
net investment
nominal variable
nonmarket production
potential output
private investment
real variable
seasonal unemployment
stock variable
structural unemployment
transfer payments
unemployment rate
value added
value-added approach

CHAPTER HIGHLIGHTS

Fill in the blanks with the appropriate words or phrases. If you have difficulty, review the chapter and then try again.

1. The nation's ____________________ (abbreviated GDP) is the total value of all ____________________ goods and services produced for the marketplace during a given year, within ____________________.

2. To avoid overcounting ____________________ products when measuring GDP, we add up the value of ____________________ goods and services only. The value of all ____________________ products is automatically included in the value of the ____________________ goods they are used to create.

3. Gross domestic product is a ____________________ variable: It measures a process—production—over a period of time.

4. In the ____________________ approach to measuring GDP, we add up the value of the final goods and services purchased by each type of final user.

5. Consumption is the part of GDP purchased by ____________________.

6. Private investment is the sum of (1) business purchases of ____________________ and ____________________; (2) new ____________________ construction; and (3) changes in business firm's ____________________.

7. Total investment during the year is the sum of ____________________ investment and ____________________ investment.

8. ____________________ payments represent money redistributed from one group of citizens (taxpayers) to another (the poor, the unemployed, the elderly). While ____________________ are included in government budgets as spending, they are not payments for currently produced goods and services, and so are not included as part of government ____________________ and not included in GDP.

9. To properly account for output sold to, and bought from, foreigners, we must include ____________________ exports—the difference between exports and ____________________.

10. A firm's value added is the revenue it receives for its output, minus the cost of all the ____________________ that it buys.

11. In the value-added approach, GDP is the sum of the values added by all ____________________ in the economy.

12. In any year, the value added by a firm is equal to the total ____________________ payments made by that firm.

13. In the factor payments approach, GDP can be measured by summing all of the factor payments made by all ____________________ in the economy. Equivalently, it can be measured by adding up all of the income—wages and salaries, rent, interst and ____________________—earned by all ____________________ in the economy.

14. GDP—the total output of the economy—is equal to the total ____________________ earned in the economy.

15. When a variable is measured over time with no adjustment for the dollar's changing value, it is called a ____________________ variable. When a variable is adjusted for the dollar's changing value, it is called a ____________________ variable.

16. Since our economic well-being depends, in large part, on the goods and services we can buy, it is important to translate ____________________ values—which are measured in ____________________ dollars—to real values—which are measured in ____________________ power.

17. ____________________-term changes in real GDP are fairly accurate reflections of the state of the economy. A significant ____________________-term drop in real GDP virtually always indicates a decrease in production, rather than a measurement problem.

18. In macroeconomics, full employment is achieved when __________________ unemployment has been reduced to zero. But the overall unemployment rate at full employment is greater than zero, because there are still positive levels of __________________, __________________, and __________________ unemployment.

19. When there is cyclical unemployment, the nation *produces* less output, and so some group or groups within society must __________________ less output.

IMPORTANT CONCEPTS

Write a brief answer below each of the following items.

1. State the entire definition of gross domestic product. (Come as close as you can without looking at the text or the end-of-chapter answers.)

2. What are the three different approaches to measuring GDP?

   a.

   b.

   c.

3. For each of the following transactions, state *yes* if it would be counted in the expenditure approach to GDP, and *no* if it would not. If *yes*, state which category of spending the transaction would contribute to (C, I, G or NX). If *no*, briefly state why not.

   a. ______________ Due to high crime in your area, your local police department hires two new police officers.

   b. ______________ You go to the ATM machine and withdraw $100 and put it in your wallet.

   c. ______________ A pick-pocket steals your wallet.

   d. ______________ You buy a new wallet at Macy's to replace the wallet the pick-pocket took.

   e. ______________ You sell your favorite videotape, *Terminator 12*, to a friend.

   f. ______________ You purchase a new computer to keep track of business at the poster store you own and manage.

   g. ______________ Your poster store sells $1,000 worth of posters to a German retail poster outlet located in Berlin.

   h. ______________ During the year, your store's inventory of unsold posters increases by 100 posters.

4. Identify each of the following as either a *stock* variable or a *flow* variable.

   a. ______________ Your income

   b. ______________ The total income of everyone in the nation

   c. ______________ The funds in your bank account

   d. ______________ The value of your house

   e. ______________ The nation's capital stock

   f. ______________ Real GDP

   g. ______________ Investment spending

   h. ______________ Consumption spending

5. What are the four types of unemployment?

SKILLS AND TOOLS

For the following items, follow the directions, write the correct answer in the blank, or circle the correct answer.

1. Having applied for a job at the Commerce Department's Bureau of Economic Analysis, you are given the following hypothetical data to study before your interview. Figures are total value in billions of dollars.

Household spending on:		
services	=	$3,008
nondurable goods	=	$1,776
durable goods	=	$706
Business spending on plant and equipment	=	$815
Wear and tear on factory equipment	=	$200
Inventory changes	=	$9
New homes constructed	=	$397
Existing homes which were destroyed	=	$123
State and Local Government spending on:		
consumption	=	$540
investment	=	$113
Federal Government spending on:		
consumption	=	$691
investment	=	$132
Depreciation of government assets	=	$245
Transfer payments	=	$2,936
Imports	=	$855
Exports	=	$961

You just *know* you're going to get some questions on this, so to get ready you ask yourself:

a. What is the total value of consumption spending in this economy?

____

b. What is the total value of private investment spending in this economy?

____

c. What is the total value of government purchases in this economy?

____

d. What is the total value of net exports in this economy? ________________

e. Using the expenditure approach, what is GDP for this economy?

____

f. Which entries in the table are not counted as part of the economy's GDP?

____

2. The tiny island nation of Kuruma has two types of final goods: cars and food. Rubber is the only material used in making tires, and tires and steel are the only materials needed to make cars. Consumers buy cars from the dealer, who buys them from the manufacturer. Food in Kuruma is raised on farms and sold to consumers through supermarkets.

The government has collected firm-level data to help keep track of all this activity, but its information is incomplete. Here is what is has:

	Firm	Cost of Intermediate Goods	Revenue	Value Added
Cars	Rubber Company	$0	$0.75	____
	Tire Company	____	$1.50	____
	Steel Company	$0	____	$2.00
	Car Manufacturer	____	$4.00	____
	Car Dealer	____	____	$0.50
Food	Farmer	____	$0.75	$0.75
	Supermarket	____	____	$0.25

a. Complete the table.

b. What is the GDP of Kuruma? ________________

3. There are only two firms in the economy of Gyroland: Summertime Farming (which makes sandwich ingredients) and Savory Sandwiches. Information on revenue and costs for these two firms is provided in the table.

Summertime Farming		**Savory Sandwiches**	
Total Revenue	$1,400	Total Revenue	$1,950
Costs		Costs	
wages to farmhands	$380	sandwich ingredients	$350
interest on loans	$115	wages to workers	$550
rent	$50	interest on loans	$200
		rent	$100

a. What is the total factor payment to labor in this economy? ________________

b. What is the total factor payment to capital in this economy? ________________

c. What is the total factor payment to land in this economy? ________________

d. What is the total profit in this economy? ________________

e. Using the factor-payment approach, what is the GDP of Gyroland?

____

f. Explain briefly why GDP is *not* equal to the sum of total sales revenue at the two firms. (Hint: does all of this revenue result from the sale of *final* goods?)

4. The employment status of residents in a friendly country is given below. This country defines its terms and follows procedures established by the Bureau of Labor Statistics (BLS) in the United States.

Category		**Population in millions**
Under 16		55.0
Military		8.0
Institutionalized		4.0
Not in Labor Force		
	Discouraged Workers	0.5
	Full-time Students (age 16 and above)	33.0
	All Others	30.0
Employed		
	Involuntarily Part-time Workers	4.5
	All Others	137.0
Unemployed		7.0

a. What is the size of the civilian noninstitutionalized population? ________________ What is the size of the labor force? ________________ What is the current unemployment rate? ________________

For each of parts (b) through (g), make all requested comparisons to the situation described in the preceding table.

b. If there is a baby boom and the number of individuals under 16 increases by 15 million, the size of the labor force will (increase/remain unchanged/decrease). The size of the labor force will then be ________________.

c. If full-time college students are drafted into the military, the size of the labor force will (increase/remain unchanged/decrease). The unemployment rate will (increase/remain unchanged/decrease).

d. If the number of unemployed individuals decreases by two million and the number of discouraged workers increases by two million, the size of the labor force will (increase/remain unchanged/decrease). The unemployment rate will (increase/remain unchanged/decrease) and will be ____________________.

e. If three million unemployed individuals decide to stop looking for work, the size of the labor force will (increase/remain unchanged/decrease). The unemployment rate will (increase/remain unchanged/decrease) and will be ____________________.

f. If seven million unemployed individuals find part-time employment, but really want full-time employment, the number of unemployed individuals will (increase/remain unchanged/decrease) and the unemployment rate will be ____________________.

g. If cuts in defense spending force two million military personnel out of the army to look for work, the size of the labor force will (increase/remain unchanged/ decrease). If the two million former military personnel are unable to find work, the unemployment rate will (increase/remain unchanged/decrease) and will be ____________________.

15-MINUTE PRACTICE TEST

Set a timer, giving yourself just 15 minutes to answer all of the following questions. To see what you *really* know and remember, take the test at least a day *after* you've read the chapter in the text and completed the exercises in this study guide.

Multiple Choice: Circle the letter in front of the single, best answer.

1. Fill in the blank: GDP is the total value of ____________________ produced for the marketplace during a given year, within the nation's borders.
   a. all goods
   b. all goods and services
   c. all final goods
   d. all final goods and services
   e. all final and intermediate goods and services

2. Which of the following is a flow variable?
   a. GDP
   b. Income
   c. Investment spending
   d. All of the above
   e. None of the above

3. Which of the following would be considered "private investment" in GDP?
   a. A computer printer purchased by a student
   b. A computer printer purchased by a law firm
   c. A computer printer purchased by the St. Louis police department
   d. All of the above
   e. None of the above

4. Net investment is equal to
   a. private investment.
   b. private investment plus government investment.
   c. private investment plus government investment minus depreciation.
   d. private investment plus government investment minus consumption spending.
   e. private investment minus government investment.

5. If Americans buy $500 billion worth of foreign goods and services, and foreigners buy $200 billion worth of American goods and services, then net exports for the United States are equal to
   a. –$700 billion.
   b. –$300 billion.
   c. $200 billion.
   d. $300 billion.
   e. $700 billion.

6. In the expenditure approach, GDP is equal to
   a. C + I + G.
   b. C + I + G + exports.
   c. C + I + G + imports.
   d. C + I + G + exports + imports.
   e. C + I + G + exports – imports.

7. When nominal GDP has increased in the United States, we know that
   a. U.S. output of goods and services has increased.
   b. the U.S. price level has increased.
   c. the U.S. price level has decreased.
   d. both U.S. output of goods and services *and* the price level have increased.
   e. either U.S. output of goods and services *or* the price level have increased.

8. One potential *problem* with the way GDP is measured is that it excludes
   a. nonmarket production.
   b. intermediate products.
   c. goods and services that are not sold during the year.
   d. all of the above.
   e. none of the above.

9. The economy is considered at "full employment" when
   a. the unemployment rate is zero.
   b. structural unemployment is zero.
   c. frictional unemployment is zero.
   d. cyclical unemployment is zero.
   e. none of the above.

10. The unemployment rate in the United States is defined as the number of unemployed divided by
   a. the U.S. population.
   b. the U.S. population over the age of 16.
   c. the number of employed.
   d. the number of employed minus the number of unemployed.
   e. the number of employed plus the number of unemployed.

True/False: For each of the following statements, circle T if the statement is true or F is the statement is false.

T F 1. While short-term changes in real GDP can give a misleading picture of economic activity, long-term changes in real GDP give a fairly accurate picture.

T F 2. U.S. GDP measures the production of goods and services by Americans, regardless of which country they reside in when they produce those goods and services.

T F 3. Goods that are not sold during the year are included as part of that year's investment in calculating GDP.

T F 4. When investment is greater than depreciation, net investment is positive and the capital stock grows.

T F 5. In the expenditure approach to GDP, government purchases include all spending on goods, services and transfer payments by government agencies.

T F 6. Structural unemployment is considered a *micro*economic problem.

T F 7. Discouraged workers are people who used to work, but no longer want a job.

T F 8. In the United States, one step in computing the unemployment rate is to count all those who apply for, and receive, unemployment insurance.

CHAPTER 6

THE MONETARY SYSTEM, PRICES, AND INFLATION

SPEAKING ECONOMICS

Fill in each blank with the appropriate word or phrase from the list provided in the word bank. (For a challenge, fill in as many blanks as you can *without* using the word bank.)

____________________ 1. A common unit for measuring how much something is worth.

____________________ 2. Anything acceptable as payment for goods and services.

____________________ 3. The central bank and national monetary authority of the United States.

____________________ 4. Anything that serves as a means of payment by government declaration.

____________________ 5. The average dollar price of goods and services in the economy.

____________________ 6. A series of numbers used to track a variable's rise or fall over time.

____________________ 7. A measure of the price level that tracks the cost of a fixed market basket of goods purchased by a typical household.

____________________ 8. The percentage change in the price level from one period to the next.

____________________ 9. A falling price level.

____________________ 10. Adjusting the value of some payment in proportion to a price index in order to keep the real payment unchanged.

____________________ 11. A variable measured in current dollars.

____________________ 12. A variable measured in terms of purchasing power.

____________________ 13. A measure of the average price level of all final goods and services included in GDP.

____________________ 14. The annual percent increase in a lender's dollars from making a loan.

____________________ 15. The annual increase in a lender's purchasing power from making a loan.

Word Bank

Consumer Price Index
deflation
Federal Reserve System
fiat money
GDP price index
index
indexation
inflation rate
means of payment
nominal interest rate
nominal variable
price level
real interest rate
real variable
unit of value

CHAPTER HIGHLIGHTS

Fill in the blanks with the appropriate words or phrases. If you have difficulty, review the chapter and then try again.

1. When we measure change in the macroeconomy, we usually care not about the number of dollars we are counting, but the purchasing power those dollars represent. Thus, we translate ____________________ values into real values, using the formula:

   real value = ____________________ value/price index) × ____________________

2. The ____________________ price index measures the prices of all goods and services that are included in U.S. GDP, while the ____________________ price index measures the prices of all goods and services bought by U.S. households.

3. Inflation can redistribute purchasing power from one group to another, but it cannot, by itself, decrease the ____________________ real income in the economy.

4. Inflation can shift ____________________ away from those who are awaiting future payments specified in dollars and toward those who are obligated to make such payments.

5. Over any period, the percentage change in a real value is approximately equal to the percentage change in the associated nominal value minus ____________________.

6. If inflation is fully ____________________, and if both parties to a contract take it into account, then inflation will *not* redistribute purchasing power.

7. When inflationary expectations are ____________________, purchasing power is shifted between those obliged to make future payments and those waiting to be paid. An inflation rate ____________________ than expected harms those awaiting payment and benefits the payers; an inflation rate ____________________ than expected harms the payers and benefits those awaiting payment.

8. When people must spend time and other ____________________ coping with inflation, they pay an opportunity cost, that is, they sacrifice the goods and services those resources could have produced instead.

9. Although the BLS has partially fixed the problem, the CPI still suffers from substitutijon bias. That is, the CPI still overestimates the relative importance of the goods whose prices are rising ____________________ and underestimates the relative importance of goods whose prices are rising or rising ____________________. The result is an ____________________-estimate of the inflation rate.

10. Because the CPI excludes many new products that lower the cost of living when they come on the market, it ____________________-estimates the inflation rate.

11. The CPI still fails to recognize that, in many cases, prices rise because of improvements in quality, not because the cost of living has risen. This causes the CPI to ____________________-estimate the inflation rate.

12. The CPI omits reductions in the prices people pay from more frequent shopping at discount stores, so the CPI ____________________-estimates the inflation rate.

13. When a payment is indexed, and the price index overstates inflation, inflation causes the real payment to ____________________, shifting purchasing power toward those who are indexed and away from the rest of society.

IMPORTANT CONCEPTS

Write a brief answer below each of the following items.

1. What is the key difference between *commodity* money and *fiat* money?

2. List two types of costs of inflation.

   a.

   b.

3. List three sources of bias in the CPI (your text discusses four). For each source of bias, state whether it causes the CPI to overestimate or underestimate the true rise in the price level.

   a.

   b.

   c.

SKILLS AND TOOLS

1. The Weather Bureau recorded the daily temperature in Middletown, New York, and prepared the following table of monthly average temperature in degrees Fahrenheit.

	Average Temperature (Degrees F)	**Temperature Index (May = 100)**
January	33	______
February	30	______
March	42	______
April	56	______
May	70	______
June	78	______
July	84	______
August	88	______
September	79	______
October	75	______
November	63	______
December	45	______

   a. Compute a temperature index from the data in the table. Let the month of May be the base period; that is, construct your index so that it has a value of 100 for the month of May. Enter your index numbers in the in the blank column.

b. From May to June, the temperature index (increased/decreased) from ____________________ to ____________________. From this we conclude that the temperature in August was ____________________ percent (higher/lower) than it was in May.

c. In November, the temperature index had a value of ____________________. This means the temperature in November was ____________________ percent (higher/lower) than it was in May.

d. Compared to the month of May, in what month(s) was the temperature approximately:

57% lower? ____________________

7% higher? ____________________

20% lower? ____________________

2. The Civil War had a dramatic impact on consumer prices in the United States. The table below reports estimates of a price index like the CPI for the years 1855 through 1880.

Year	CPI (1860 = 100)
1855	104
1856	102
1857	105
1858	99
1859	100
1860	100
1861	106
1862	121
1863	151
1864	189
1865	196
1866	191
1867	178
1868	171
1869	164
1870	157
1871	147
1872	147
1873	144
1874	137
1875	132
1876	129
1877	129
1878	120
1879	120
1880	123

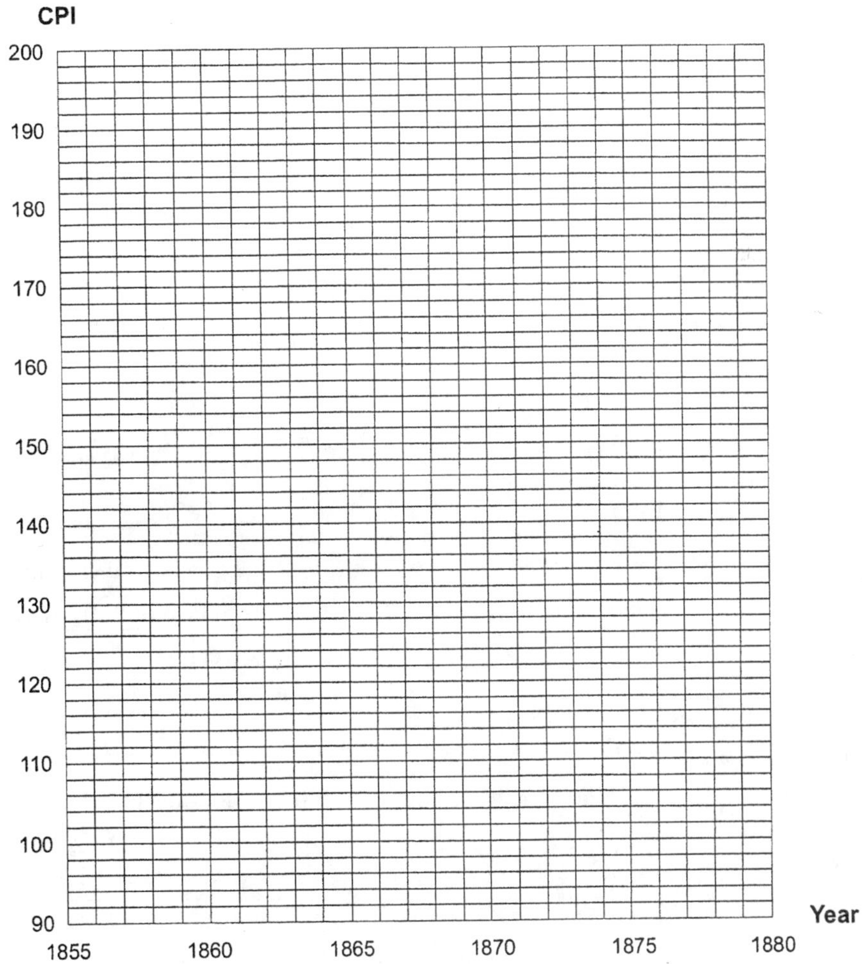

a. Plot the CPI from 1855 to 1880 on the grid provided.

b. Between 1860 and 1865, the CPI (increased/decreased) from ____________________ to ____________________. By 1865 prices were ____________________ percent (higher/lower) than they had been in 1860—a mere five years earlier. From 1865 to 1880, prices (increased/decreased) rapidly. Nonetheless, by 1880, prices were still approximately ____________________ percent (higher/lower) than they had been in 1860.

c. Copy the necessary CPI data from the table and compute the annual rate of inflation between the indicated years to complete the table.

Remember: The inflation rate is the *percentage change* in the price level over the year. So, for example, to compute the rate of inflation between 1863 and 1864, subtract the CPI in 1863 from the CPI in 1864, divide by the CPI in 1863, then multiply by 100.

Inflation Rate, 1863 to 1864 $= \dfrac{CPI_{1864} - CPI_{1863}}{CPI_{1863}} \times 100$

$= \dfrac{189 - 151}{151} \times 100$

$= 25.2\%$

Year	CPI	Inflation Rate	Year	CPI	Inflation Rate
1860	____		1865	____	
		____			____
1861	____		1866	____	
		____			____
1862	____		1867	____	
		____			____
1863	____		1868	____	
		25.2 %			____
1864	____		1869	____	
		____			____
1865	____		1870	____	

d. Between 1860 and 1865, the country experienced (inflation/deflation) in every year. During those war years, the rate of (inflation/deflation) varied from a low of ____________________ between the years ____________________ and ____________________, to a high of ____________________ between the years ____________________ and ____________________.

e. After the war, from 1865 to 1870, the country experienced (inflation/deflation) in every year. The country experienced the greatest rate of (inflation/deflation) between the years ____________________ and ____________________.

3. Nominal GDP, real GDP and the GDP price index in the United States between 1989 and 1999 are reported below. Nominal GDP is in billions of dollars. Real GDP is in billions of chained (1996) dollars.

Year	Nominal GDP	GDP Price Index	Real GDP
1989	5,489.1	83.3	6,591.8
1990	5,803.2	86.5	6,707.9
1991	5,986.2	89.7	6,676.4
1992	6,318.9	91.9	6,880.0
1993	6,642.3	94.1	7,062.6
1994	7,054.3	96.0	7,347.7
1995	7,400.5	98.1	7,543.8
1996	7,813.2	100.0	7,813.2
1997	8,318.4	102.0	8,159.5
1998	8,781.5	103.2	8,508.9
1999	9,268.6	104.7	8,856.5

a. Carefully examine nominal GDP and the GDP price index over the period 1989 to 1999. We can see from the table that nominal GDP (increased some years and decreased other years/increased every year/decreased every year) over the period. At the same time, the price level (increased some years and decreased other years/increased every year/ decreased every year).

b. On the grid below, plot nominal GDP and real GDP between 1989 and 1999. Be sure to label your graphs.

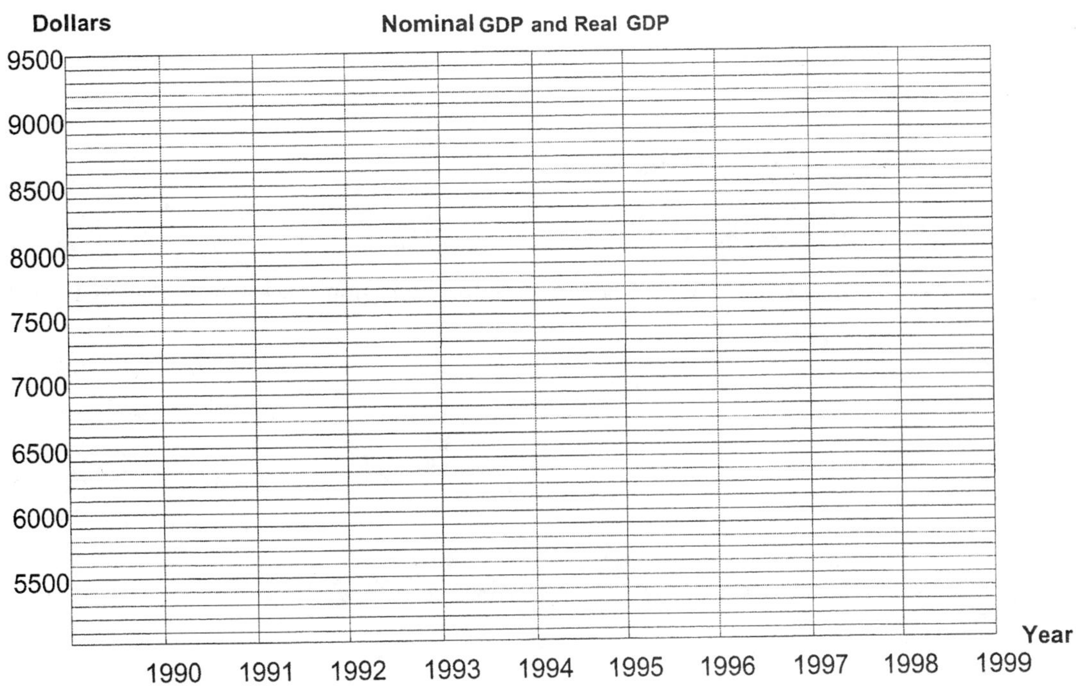

c. From a close examination of the table and graph, we can see that real GDP (did/did not) increase in every year over the period 1989 to 1999. From 1990 to 1991, real GDP (increased/decreased) from ________________ to ________________. Over the same period, nominal GDP (increased/decreased) from ________________ to ________________ and the price index (increased/decreased) from ________________ to ________________. Because real GDP (increased/decreased) while nominal GDP (increased/decreased) we can deduce that between 1990 and 1991 prices (increased/decreased) by a (greater/smaller) percentage than nominal GNP (increased/decreased).

4. The prime bank interest rate, commonly called the *prime rate*, is the interest rate banks charge their best and most credit-worthy customers. Data on the nominal prime, the real prime, and the rate of inflation are presented below.

Year	Prime Bank Interest Rate (Nominal)	Inflation Rate	Prime Bank Interest (Real)
1991	8.5%	3.1%	____
1992	6.3%	____	3.4%
1993	____	2.7%	3.3%
1994	7.1%	2.7%	____
1995	8.8%	____	6.3%
1996	____	3.3%	5.0%
1997	8.4%	____	6.7%
1998	8.4%	1.6%	____
1999	____	2.7%	5.3%
2000	9.2%	____	5.8%
2001	6.9%	1.6%	____

a. Complete the table.

b. Plot both the nominal prime rate and the real prime rate on the grid provided. Remember to label your graphs.

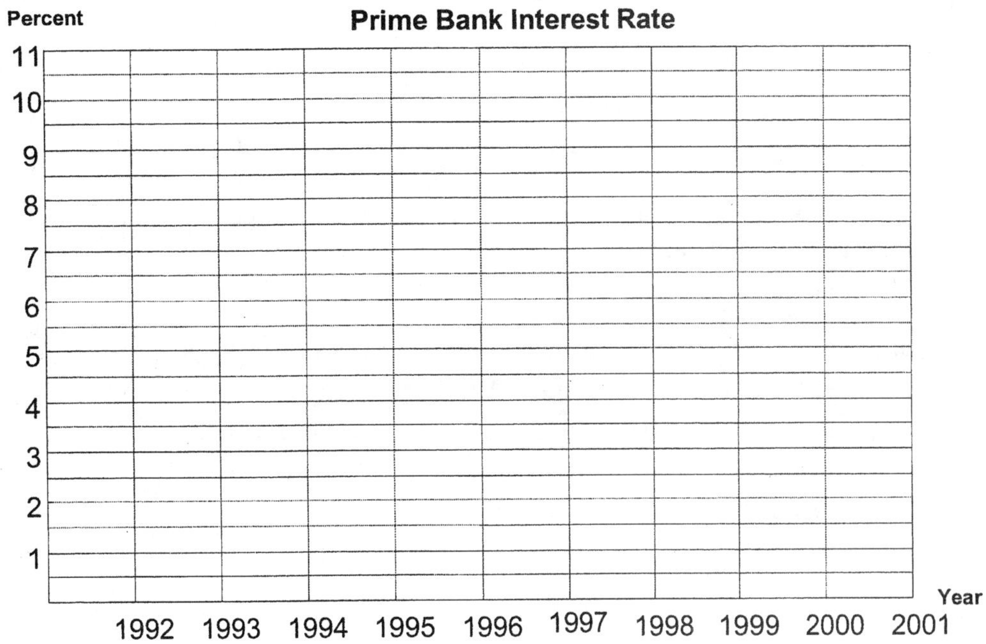

15-MINUTE PRACTICE TEST

Set a timer, giving yourself just 15 minutes to answer all of the following questions. To see what you *really* know and remember, take the test at least a day *after* you've read the chapter in the text and completed the exercises in this study guide.

Multiple Choice: Circle the letter in front of the single best answer.

1. The paper currency that is now in use in the United States is an example of
   a. commodity money.
   b. fiat money.
   c. constitutional money.
   d. all of the above.
   e. none of the above.

2. The consumer price index tracks the average level of prices of all
   a. goods and services produced in the United States.
   b. final goods and services produced in the United States.
   c. final goods and services produced in the United States, plus imports into the United States.
   d. final goods and services produced by Americans, regardless of where they reside.
   e. goods and services purchased by consumers, whether they are produced in the United States or not.

3. Which of the following goods is *not* included in U.S. GDP, even though its price *is* included in the CPI?
   a. A new computer produced in the U.S. and purchased by an American household
   b. A new computer produced in the U.S. and purchased by an American corporation
   c. A second-hand computer purchased in the U.S. in a previous year, and now purchased by an American household
   d. A second-hand computer purchased in the U.S. in a previous year, and now purchased by a resident of Bulgaria.
   e. All of the above

4. Which of the following statements about inflation and the price level is true?
   a. When the price level is rising, the inflation rate must be rising as well.
   b. When the inflation rate is positive, the price level must be rising.
   c. When the inflation rate is falling, the price level *can* not be rising.
   d. When the inflation rate is zero, the price level must be zero as well.
   e. All of the above.

5. If your nominal wage rises from \$5 to \$7.50, while the price level rises from 100 to 150, then your real wage
   a. rises by 50%.
   b. rises by 25%.
   c. rises by 20%.
   d. does not change.
   e. falls.

6. If the nominal interest rate is 7 percent, and the annual inflation rate is 3 percent, then the real interest rate is
   a. –4%.
   b. –3%.
   c. 3%.
   d. 4%.
   e. 10%.

7. Inflation will redistribute purchasing power away from lenders and toward borrowers when
   a. the actual inflation rate turns out to be greater than expected.
   b. the actual inflation rate turns out to be smaller than expected.
   c. inflationary expectations are accurate.
   d. the inflation rate is higher than normal.
   e. the inflation rate is lower than normal.

8. Which of the following problems has caused the CPI to *overestimate* the rate of inflation?
   a. Substitution bias
   b. New technologies
   c. Quality changes
   d. All of the above
   e. None of the above

9. Which of the following is a change planned by the BLS to help eliminate the substitution bias of the CPI?
    a. A larger number of goods and services in the CPI
    b. A larger number of households in the CPI survey
    c. More frequent updates of the typical consumer's market basket
    d. Better estimates of the quality of goods and services
    e. None of the above

10. Which groups gain from the overstatement of inflation by the CPI?
    a. Workers with fixed nominal wages
    b. Recipients of social security payments
    c. Foreigners
    d. All Americans
    e. None of the above

True/False: For each of the following statements, circle T if the statement is true or F if the statement is false.

T F 1. Over a period during which prices are rising, the inflation rate must be rising as well.

T F 2. In the United States today, the dollar is accepted as payment for goods and services because the dollar is "backed" by the gold held in Fort Knox.

T F 3. If the price index rises over the year from 200 to 230, then the rate of inflation for the year is 30%.

T F 4. If your real wage is rising at the same time as the price level is rising, then your nominal wage must be rising as well.

T F 5. When inflation is correctly anticipated, it is less likely to redistribute purchasing power between borrowers and lenders.

T F 6. An example of the "resource cost" of inflation is when someone must re-tag a store's merchandise with new prices.

T F 7. In the United States, the CPI is reported and calculated once each year.

T F 8. In the United States, over the past twenty years, the CPI has risen about as often as it has fallen, and is now back pretty much where it started.

CHAPTER 7

THE CLASSICAL LONG-RUN MODEL

SPEAKING ECONOMICS

Fill in each blank with the appropriate word or phrase from the list provided in the word bank. (For a challenge, fill in as many blanks as you can *without* using the word bank.)

____________________ 1. A macroeconomic model that explains the long-run behavior of the economy.

____________________ 2. Adjustment of prices until quantities supplied and demanded are equal.

____________________ 3. Indicates how many people will want to work at various wage rates.

____________________ 4. Indicates how many workers firms will want to hire at various wage rates.

____________________ 5. The relationship showing how much total output can be produced with different quantities of labor, with land, capital, and technology held constant.

____________________ 6. A diagram that shows how goods, resources, and dollar payments flow between households and firms.

____________________ 7. The idea that total spending will be sufficient to purchase the total output produced.

____________________ 8. Government tax revenues minus transfer payments.

____________________ 9. The portion of after-tax income that households do not spend on consumption goods.

____________________ 10. Income earned, but not spent, by households during a given year.

____________________ 11. Spending from sources other than households.

____________________ 12. Business purchases of plant and equipment.

____________________ 13. A market in which households make their savings available to borrowers.

____________________ 14. The excess of government purchases over net taxes.

______________________ 15. The excess of net taxes over government purchases.

______________________ 16. The total amount that the federal government owes.

______________________ 17. Indicates the level of household saving at various interest rates

______________________ 18. Indicates the level of investment spending firms plan at various interest rates.

______________________ 19. Indicates the amount of government borrowing at various interest rates.

______________________ 20. Indicates the total amount of borrowing at various interest rates.

______________________ 21. A change in government purchases or net taxes designed to change total spending and total output.

______________________ 22. A decline in one sector's spending caused by an increase in some other sector's spending.

______________________ 23. A dollar-for-dollar decline in one sector's spending caused by an increase in some other sector's spending.

Word Bank

aggregate production function
budget deficit
budget surplus
circular flow
classical model
complete crowding out
crowding out
fiscal policy
government demand for funds curve
(household) saving
injections
investment demand curve
labor demand curve
labor supply curve
leakages
loanable funds market
market clearing
national debt
net taxes
planned investment spending
Say's law
supply of funds curve
total demand for funds curve

CHAPTER HIGHLIGHTS

Fill in the blanks with the appropriate words or phrases. If you have difficulty, review the chapter and then try again.

1. While Keynes's ideas and their further development help us understand economic fluctuations—movements in output around the long-run trend—the _______________ model has proven more useful in explaining the long-run trend itself.

2. A critical assumption in the classical model is that ____________________: The price in every market will adjust until quantity supplied and quantity demanded are equal.

3. In order to earn income so we can buy goods and services, we must supply labor and other ____________________ to firms.

4. The labor supply curve slopes ____________________ because—as the wage rate ____________________—more and more individuals are better off working than not working. Thus, a ____________________ in the wage rate increases the number of people in the economy who want to work—to supply their labor.

5. As the wage rate ____________________, each firm in the economy will find that—to maximize profit—it should employ fewer workers than before. When all firms behave this way together, a ____________________ in the wage rate will decrease the quantity of labor demanded in the economy. This is why the economy's labor demand curve slopes ____________________.

6. In the ____________________ view, the economy achieves full employment on its own.

7. The aggregate production function shows the total output the economy can produce with different quantities of ____________________, holding constant the amounts of land and capital and the current state of ____________________.

8. In the classical, long-run view, the economy reaches its ____________________ output level automatically.

9. In a simple economy with just households and firms, in which households spend all of their income, total spending must be equal to total ____________________.

10. _______________'s law states that by producing goods and services, firms create a total demand for goods and services equal to what they have produced.

11. Total spending will equal total output if and only if total leakages in the economy are equal to total ____________________; that is, only if the sum of saving and ____________________ is equal to the sum of investment spending and ____________________.

12. When government purchases of goods and services (G) are greater than net taxes (T), the government runs a budget ____________________ equal to ____________________. When government purchases of goods and services (G) are less than net taxes (T), the government runs a budget ____________________ equal to ____________________.

13. ____________________ and ____________________ governments, like the federal government, can run deficits and surpluses, requiring them to participate in the loanable funds market. In our classical model, we aggregate all of these levels of government together and refer only to *the government*. When the government runs a budget ____________________, it demands loanable funds equal to its ____________________. When the government runs a budget ____________________, it supplies loanable funds equal to its ____________________.

14. The quantity of funds supplied to the financial market depends positively on the ____________________. This is why saving, or the supply of funds curve, slopes upward.

15. When the interest rate ____________________, investment spending and the business borrowing needed to finance it rise. The investment demand curve slopes ____________________.

16. The government sector's deficit and, therefore, its demand for funds are independent of the ____________________.

17. As the interest rate decreases, the quantity of funds demanded by business firms ____________________, while the quantity demanded by the government ____________________. Therefore, the total quantity of funds demanded ____________________.

18. As long as the ____________________ market clears, Say's law holds even in a more realistic economy with saving, taxes, investment, and a government deficit.

19. Fiscal policy is a change in ____________________ purchases or in ____________________ designed to change total spending in the economy and thereby influence the levels of employment and ____________________.

20. Crowding out is a (an) ____________________ in one sector's spending caused by a (an) ____________________ in some other sector's spending.

21. In the ____________________ model, a rise in government purchases completely crowds out ____________________ sector spending, so total spending remains unchanged.

22. If the government increases its purchases, it just removes funds from the ____________________ market that would have been spent by ____________________ or by households. Thus, an increase in government purchases has no impact on total spending and no impact on total output or total employment.

IMPORTANT CONCEPTS

Write a brief answer below each of the following items.

1. What two words describe the key critical assumption in the classical model? Briefly, what does this assumption mean?

2. Which *two* graphs are necessary to determine the equilibrium level of output in the classical model?

   a.

   b.

3. Which single graph is necessary to determine the equilibrium interest rate in the classical model?

4. List the two types of leakages and the two types of injections in the macroeconomy.

Leakages: a.

b.

Injections: a.

b.

5. Suppose the government increases G, its purchases of goods and services. In the classical view, how is each of the following variables affected? In each case, write increase, decrease, no change, or ambiguous.

a. real output ______________

b. employment ______________

c. interest rate ______________

d. (real) household saving ______________

e. (real) business investment ______________

SKILLS AND TOOLS

1. Classica's northern neighbor, Upper Classica, is a large economy. Labor supply depends on the real wage, and that relationship is graphed below. Labor demand depends on the real wage, too, and it is given by the equation

$$L^D = 300 - 20W$$

where W is the real hourly wage and L^D is millions of workers demanded.

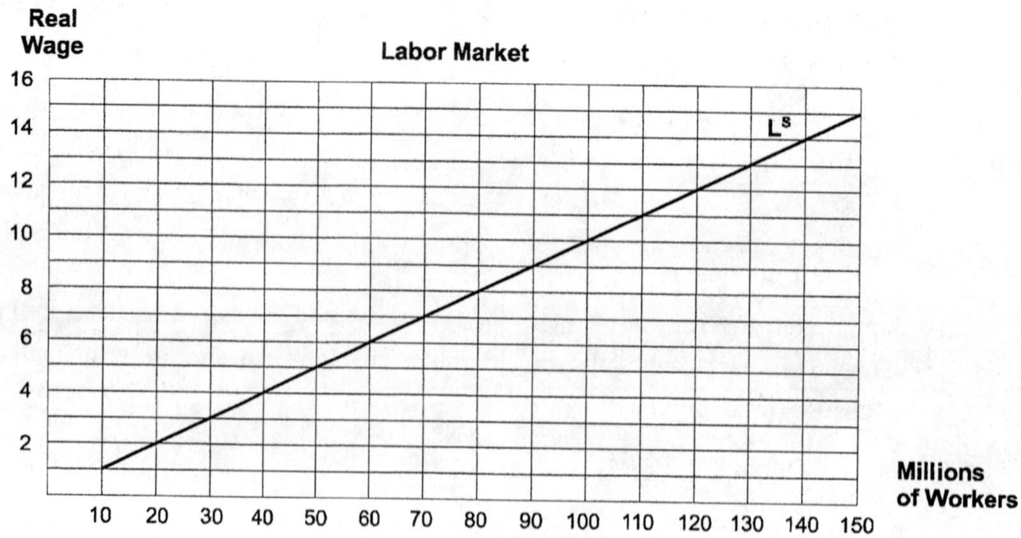

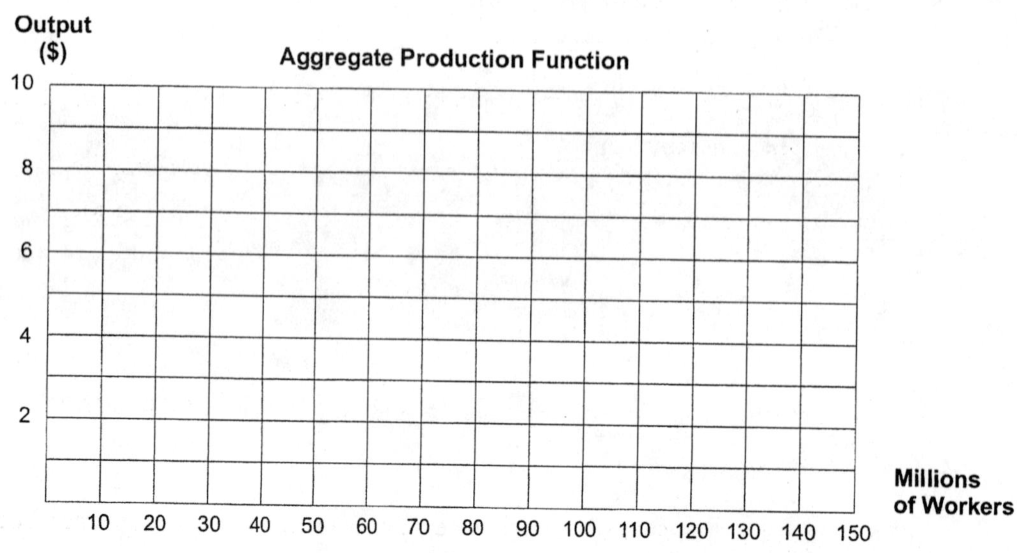

a. Graph Upper Classica's labor demand curve in the appropriate panel.

b. If the real wage in this economy were \$12, firms would want to hire ______________ million workers, while a total of ______________ million workers would be willing to work. Because there is (excess demand/equilibrium/excess supply) in the labor market at a wage of \$12, wages will have a tendency to (rise above/remain at/fall below) \$12 in this economy.

c. If the real wage in this economy were \$8, firms would want to hire ______________ million workers, while a total of ______________ million workers would be willing to work. Because there is (excess demand/equilibrium/excess supply) in the labor market at a wage of \$8, wages will have a tendency to (rise above/remain at/fall below) \$8 in this economy.

d. If the real wage in this economy were \$10, firms would want to hire ______________ million workers, while a total of ______________ million workers would be willing to work. Because there is (excess demand/ equilibrium/excess supply) in the labor market at a wage of \$10, wages will have a tendency to (rise above/remain at/fall below) \$10 in this economy.

e. Given the current state of its technology, and its stocks of capital and land, the aggregate production function in Upper Classica is

$$Y = \frac{\sqrt{L}}{2}$$

where Y is total real output (in trillions of dollars) and L is total employment. Plot this production function in the appropriate panel of the grid provided.

f. What is the full-employment output level in Upper Classica? ______________

2. In the economy of Upper Classica, described in the previous problem, the supply of savings from households, S, depends on the interest rate according to the equation

$$S = \frac{r-1}{2}.$$

where r is the interest rate measured in percentage points (e.g. seven percent is 7 rather than decimal 0.07).

The demand for funds arises from (1) the business sector's investment spending and (2) the government sector's budget deficit.

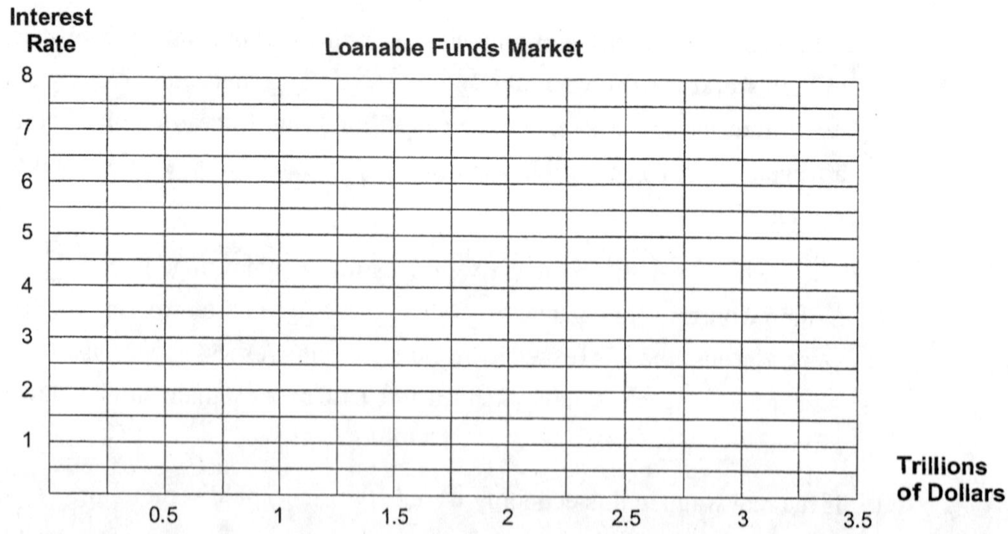

a. Plot the supply of funds curve on the grid provided. Label this curve *Supply*.

b. Businesses in Upper Classica are like business in most countries. As the interest rate falls, their planned investment spending (rises/falls/remains unchanged). To finance their investment spending, businesses (demand/supply) funds in the loanable funds market. In fact, business borrowing to finance investment in Upper Classica is given by the following equation:

$$I = 3.0 - (1/2)r.$$

Because the slope of this relationship is (negative/zero/positive), we can see that borrowing to finance investment spending will increase as the interest rate (decreases/remains unchanged/increases).

c. In Upper Classica, government purchases (G) are always \$1.5 trillion. Net taxes (T) are \$1.0 trillion. Because government purchases exceed net taxes, the government budget (surplus/deficit) will be _______________ trillion dollars per year. We can write this as follows:

$$G - T = \_\_\_\_\_\_\_\_\_\_\_\_\_\_.$$

To finance this (surplus/deficit), the government will (demand/supply) funds in the loanable funds market. Specifically, the government will (lend/borrow) loanable funds in the amount of _______________ trillion dollars, no matter what the interest rate may be.

d. To obtain the total demand for funds, we must (add/subtract) business firms' demand and the government's demand for funds. From the information in parts (b) and (c), we can determine that the total demand for funds in Upper Classica is given by the equation:

Total Demand for Funds = ______________ .

Plot the total demand for funds on the grid provided, and label your graph *Demand*.

e. From the graph, we can see that if the interest rate in Upper Classica is 6%, there will be (excess demand/equilibrium/excess supply) in the loanable funds market. According to the classical model, we should expect the interest rate to (rise above/remain unchanged at/fall below) this level. If the interest rate is 3%, there will be (excess demand/equilibrium/excess supply) in the loanable funds market. We should then expect the interest rate to (rise above/remain unchanged at/fall below) this level. In Upper Classica, the loanable funds market will be in equilibrium when the interest rate is ______________ percent.

f. When the interest rate is at its equilibrium level in the loanable funds market, the total demand for funds will be ______________ trillion dollars. Of this, the government (surplus/deficit) will be the amount G – T= ______________, and investment demand will be I^p = ______________ trillion dollars. At this same interest rate, the total supply of funds will be ______________ trillion dollars, and of this, household saving will be the amount S = ______________ trillion dollars.

g. Review the preceding parts of this problem, then complete the following table to describe the spending flows in Upper Classica. (Hint: Consumption must be what is left of total income after subtracting net taxes and household saving.)

Flows in the Economy of Upper Classica
(Trillions of Dollars)

Total Output		5.0
Total Income		______
Consumption Spending	(C)	______
Investment Spending	(I^p)	______
Government Spending	(G)	______
Net Taxes	(T)	______
Household Saving	(S)	______

h. When, as in part (f), the total quantity of funds supplied equals the total quantity of funds demanded, leakages out of the income-spending stream will (exceed/equal/fall below) total injections. Total leakages, or the sum (S+T / I^P+G / I+T), amount to _______________ trillion dollars in Upper Classica. Total injections, or the sum (S+T / I^P+G/ I^P+T), amount to _______________ trillion dollars. Thus, at the interest rate that clears the loanable funds market, the economy of Upper Classica (does/does not) satisfy Say's Law.

3. Policy makers in Upper Classica are not satisfied with things the way they are. Some people have suggested that the government should increase its spending above its current level of $1.5 trillion. On the grid below, copy the demand and supply of funds curves you plotted in the previous problem. Then answer the following questions.

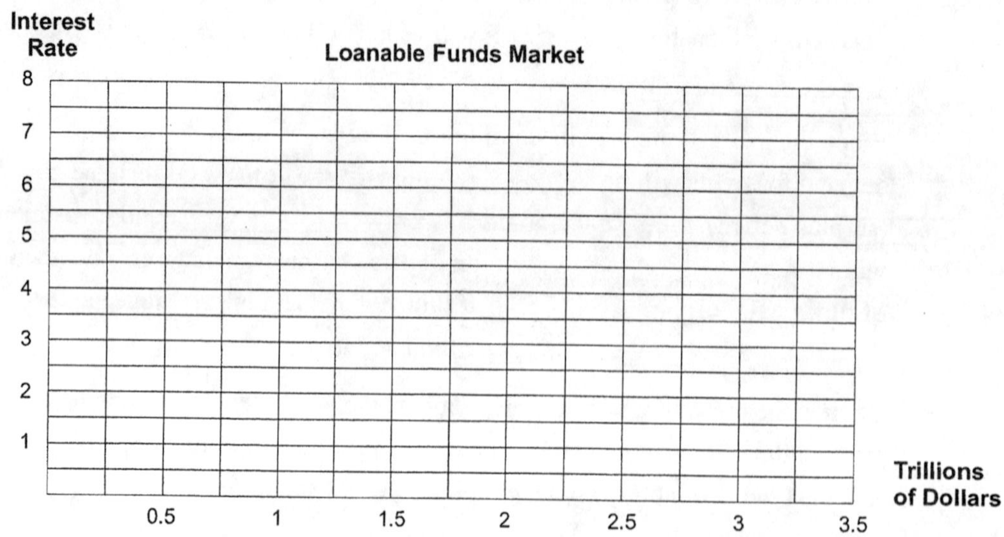

a. Suppose the government decides to increase its purchases by $1 trillion. This will cause the (demand curve/supply curve) for funds to shift (leftward/rightward) by an amount just equal to _______________ trillion dollars at every level of the interest rate. With this in mind, plot the new (demand/supply) curve.

b. After the increase in government purchases, the equilibrium interest rate will (rise/fall) to _______________ percent. This (increase/decrease) in the equilibrium interest rate will cause households to (increase/decrease) saving and to (increase/decrease) consumption spending. It will also cause investment spending by firms to (increase/decrease).

c. From a careful reading of the graph, we can see that the (increase/decrease) in the equilibrium interest rate causes household saving to (increase/decrease) by exactly _______________ trillion dollars, and so causes consumption spending to (increase/decrease) by exactly _______________ trillion dollar(s). At the same time, investment spending by businesses (increases/decreases) by exactly _______________ trillion dollar(s). From this we can see that the original $1 trillion increase in government spending caused spending elsewhere in the economy to (increase/decrease) by (a larger amount/the same amount/a smaller amount). Thus, the original increase in government spending (did/did not) result in complete crowding out.

15-MINUTE PRACTICE TEST

Set a timer, giving yourself just 15 minutes to answer all of the following questions. To see what you *really* know and remember, take the test at least a day *after* you've read the chapter in the text and completed the exercises in this study guide.

Multiple Choice: Circle the letter in front of the single best answer.

1. According to the classical view, which of the following statements is true?
   a. Fiscal policy cannot change real output or employment.
   b. Fiscal policy can change output but not employment.
   c. Fiscal policy can change employment but not output.
   d. All of the above.
   e. None of the above.

2. The key critical assumption in the classical model is that
   a. fiscal policy is ineffective.
   b. output and income are equal.
   c. the government is running a budget deficit.
   d. the budget deficit does not depend on the interest rate.
   e. markets clear.

3. Say's law tells us that
   a. markets clear.
   b. total spending is equal to total output.
   c. total income is equal to total output.
   d. the budget deficit is equal to household saving.
   e. investment spending is equal to household saving.

4. The government's budget deficit is equal to
   a. government purchases minus total taxes.
   b. government purchases plus total taxes.
   c. government purchases minus the difference between total taxes and transfer payments.
   d. government purchases minus transfer payments.
   e. government purchases plus investment spending minus total taxes.

5. Which of the following is a "leakage" in the macroeconomy?
   a. Household saving
   b. Consumption spending
   c. Investment spending
   d. Government spending
   e. None of the above

6. The total demand for funds curve slopes downward because a rise in the interest rate causes
   a. government borrowing to decrease.
   b. business borrowing to decrease.
   c. both government borrowing and business borrowing to decrease.
   d. household saving to increase.
   e. consumption spending to decrease.

7. When the government is running a budget deficit, the loanable funds market will clear when household saving plus net taxes is equal to
   a. investment spending plus the government's budget deficit.
   b. investment spending plus government purchases.
   c. consumption spending plus the budget deficit.
   d. consumption spending plus investment spending plus government spending.
   e. consumption spending

8. When the government is running a budget surplus, the loanable funds market will clear when household saving plus the budget surplus is equal to
   a. net taxes.
   b. investment spending.
   c. government purchases.
   d. investment spending plus government purchases.
   e. investment spending plus net taxes.

9. In the classical view, if government purchases rise (and there is no other fiscal change),
   a. employment.
   b. the interest rate rises.
   c. the real wage rises.
   d. output rises.
   e. all of the above.

10. According to the classical model, to ensure that the economy reaches its potential output level, the government
    a. must run a budget deficit.
    b. must run a budget surplus.
    c. must run a balanced budget.
    d. must set its purchases equal to private investment spending.
    e. need not worry about its fiscal policy.

True/False: For each of the following statements, circle T if the statement is true or F if the statement is false.

T F 1. The classical model takes a short-run view of the economy, while the Keynesian model takes a more long-run view.

T F 2. According to the classical view, the economy needs the government's help in achieving full employment.

T F 3. The aggregate production function tells us how much output can be produced with different amounts of capital and land, and a fixed amount of labor.

T F 4. "Net taxes" are equal to the government's total tax revenue minus government transfer payments.

T F 5. Investment spending and government purchases play the role of "injections" in the macroeconomy.

T F 6. In the classical model, an increase in government spending—with no other change—will shift the total demand for funds curve rightward.

T F 7. The key conclusions of the classical model do not hold if the government is running a budget surplus rather than a budget deficit.

T F 8. In the classical model, an increase in government purchases causes household saving to increase, and household consumption spending to decrease.

CHAPTER 8

ECONOMIC GROWTH AND RISING LIVING STANDARDS

SPEAKING ECONOMICS

Fill in each blank with the appropriate word or phrase from the list provided in the word bank. (For a challenge, fill in as many blanks as you can *without* using the word bank.)

_______________________ 1. Total output (real GDP) per person.

_______________________ 2. Total output (real GDP) per worker.

_______________________ 3. The total capital stock divided by total employment.

_______________________ 4. A tax on the profits earned by corporations.

_______________________ 5. A reduction in taxes for firms that invest in certain favored types of capital.

_______________________ 6. A tax on profits earned when a financial asset is sold at more than its acquisition price.

_______________________ 7. A tax on the part of their incomes that households spend.

_______________________ 8. Skills and knowledge possessed by workers.

_______________________ 9. The invention or discovery of new inputs, new outputs, or new production methods.

_______________________ 10. A government grant of exclusive rights to use or sell a new technology.

Word Bank

average standard of living
capital gains tax
capital per worker
consumption tax
corporate profits tax
human capital
investment tax credit
patent protection
productivity (or labor productivity)
technological change

CHAPTER HIGHLIGHTS

Fill in the blanks with the appropriate words or phrases. If you have difficulty, review the chapter and then try again.

1. Achieving a higher rate of growth in the ____________________ run generally requires some sacrifice in the ____________________ run.

2. When output grows faster than ____________________, GDP per capita—which we call the average standard of living—will ____________________. When output grows more slowly than ____________________, GDP per capita, or the average standard of living, will ____________________.

3. Growth in employment can arise from an increase in labor supply (a ____________________ shift in the labor supply curve) or an increase in the labor demand (a ____________________ shift in the labor demand curve).

4. A cut in tax rates increases the reward for working, while a cut in benefits to the needy increases the hardship for not working. Either policy can cause a greater rightward shift in the economy's labor ____________________ curve than would otherwise occur and speed the growth in employment and output.

5. Government policies that help increase the skills of the workforce or that subsidize employment more directly shift the economy's labor ____________________ curve to the right, increasing employment and output.

6. When employment increases, while the capital stock remains constant, the amount of capital available to the average worker will ____________________, and labor productivity will ____________________.

7. If the capital stock grows faster than ____________________, then capital per worker will rise, and labor productivity will increase along with it. But if the capital stock grows more slowly than ____________________, then capital per worker will fall, and labor productivity will fall as well.

8. Reducing business ____________________ or providing specific investment incentives can shift the investment curve ____________________, thereby speeding growth in physical capital, and increasing the growth rate of living standards.

9. Government can alter the tax and transfer system to increase incentives for ____________________. If successful, these policies would make more funds available for investment, speed growth in the capital stock, and speed the rise in living standards.

10. A shrinking budget deficit or a ____________________ budget surplus tends to ____________________ interest rates and ____________________ investment, thus speeding the growth in the capital stock.

11. Government investment in new capital and in the maintenance of existing capital makes an important contribution to economic growth. Thus, the impact of deficit reduction on economic growth depends on which government programs are cut. Shrinking the deficit by cutting government ____________________ will not stimulate growth as much as would cutting other types of government spending.

12. An increase in ____________________ capital works much like an increase in physical capital to increase output: It causes the production function to shift ____________________, raises productivity, and increases the average standard of living.

13. Many pro-growth policies—policies that increase employment or increase investment in physical capital—are also effective in promoting investment in ____________________ capital.

14. The faster the rate of technological change, the greater the growth rate of productivity, and the faster the rise in living standards. The rate of technological change in an economy depends largely on firms' total spending on ____________________. Policies that increase ____________________ spending will increase the pace of technological change.

15. Government policy is constrained by the reactions of private decision makers. As a result, policymakers face ____________________: Making progress toward one goal often requires some sacrifice of another goal.

16. Promoting economic growth involves unavoidable ____________________: It requires some groups, or the nation as a whole, to give up something else that is valued. In order to decide how fast we want our economy to grow, we must consider growth's ____________________ as well as its benefits.

17. Properly targeted tax ____________________ can increase the rate of economic growth, but will force us to either redistribute the tax burden or cut government programs.

18. Greater investment in physical capital, human capital, and R&D will lead to faster economic growth and higher living standards in the future, but we will have fewer ____________________ goods to enjoy in the present.

19. A (an) ____________________ in the fraction of the population with jobs or a (an) ____________________ in working hours will increase output and raise living standards, but also require us to sacrifice time previously spent in nonmarket activities.

20. We can achieve greater worker safety, a cleaner environment, and other social goals, but we may have to sacrifice some economic ____________________ along the way. Alternatively, we can achieve greater economic ____________________, but we will have to compromise on other things we care about.

21. In order to have rising living standards, a nation's stock of capital must not only grow, but grow faster than its ____________________.

22. The poorest LDCs are too poor to take advantage of the trade-off between producing ____________________ goods and producing ____________________ goods in order to increase their living standards. Since they cannot tolerate a decrease in the production of ____________________ goods below current levels, they cannot produce enough ____________________ goods to keep up with their rising populations.

IMPORTANT CONCEPTS

Write a brief answer below each of the following items.

1. Each of the different methods of promoting economic growth can be illustrated as a curve shift (or more-rapid-than-otherwise curve shift) in one of the three classical market diagrams: the labor market, the production function, or the loanable funds market. For each growth-promoting change listed below, state (1) which diagram would be most directly affected, (2) which curve shifts or shifts more rapidly as a result of the change; and (3) the direction of the shift. (You may want to draw diagrams to help with your answer.)

   a. an increase in population with no change in the labor force participation rate

   b. an increase in the labor force participation rate with no change in population

   c. a cut in the tax rate on wages

d. increased spending on educating and training the workforce

e. reduction in the corporate profits tax rate

f. reduction in the capital gains tax

g. decrease in the budget deficit

h. increase the budget surplus

i. more rapid technological change

2. List three different types of costs society may have to pay for faster economic growth (the text discusses four types of costs):

   a.

   b.

   c.

3. List three characteristics of many less-developed countries that help explain their low growth rates.

   a.

   b.

   c.

SKILLS AND TOOLS

1. Upper Classica's neighbor to the north, Northern Classica, (called No. Classica for short) is in long-run economic equilibrium. Data from the economy's aggregate production function is provided in the table.

Real Output ($ Trillions)	Employment (Millions)
0	0
9	20
16	40
21	60
24	80
25	100

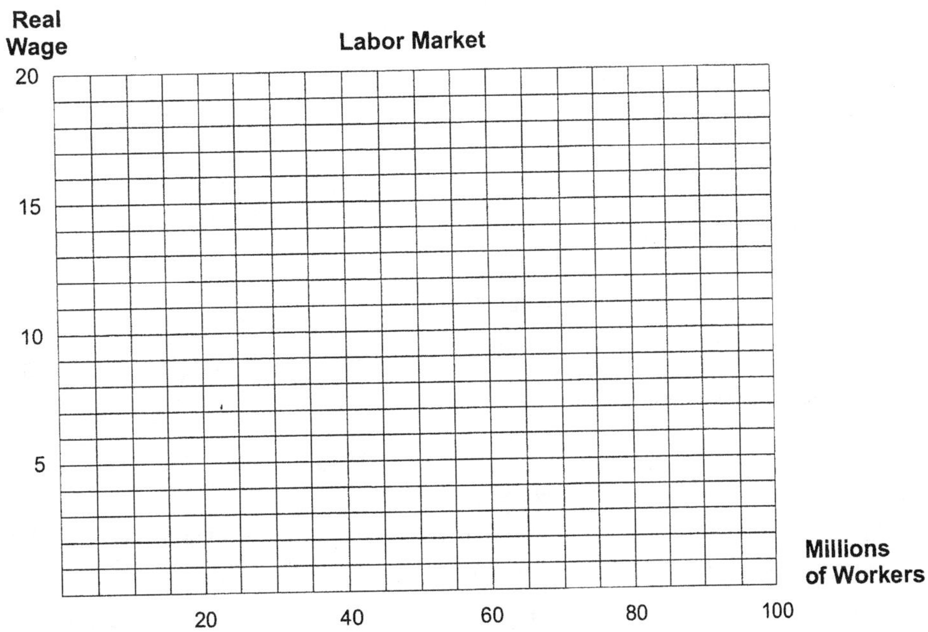

a. Plot the aggregate production function for No. Classica on the following page.

b. Labor demand in No. Classica is given by the equation

$$L^D_1 = 90 - 5W$$

where W is the real wage and L^D_1 is the number of workers (in millions) demanded.

Plot the labor demand curve above.

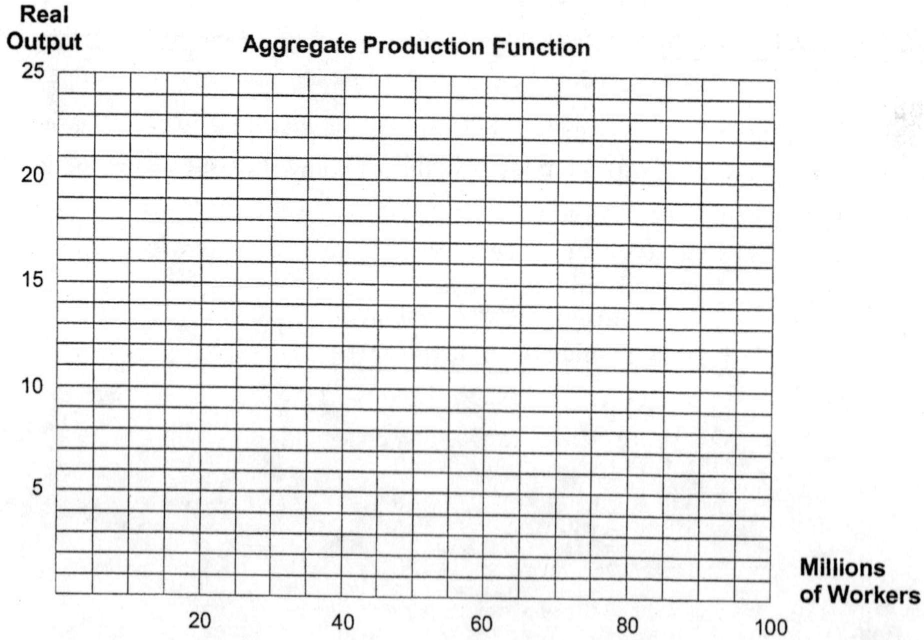

c. Labor supply in No. Classica is given by the equation

$$L^S_1 = 10W - 60.$$

Plot the labor supply curve in the appropriate panel.

d. Given the information in parts (a) through (c), the equilibrium real wage in No. Classica is _______________ dollars. The equilibrium level of employment is _______________ million workers, and potential output is _______________ trillion dollars. Labor productivity is _______________.

e. Large segments of No. Classica's labor force have been under-educated and under-skilled for years. To improve the situation, the government instituted a crash program of guaranteed student loans. It reasoned that better-educated workers would be more productive and so more attractive employees to the country's businesses. If the government is right and the policy succeeds, it will shift the labor demand curve to the (right/left). Suppose that the policy *is* successful and that businesses now want to hire exactly 30 million more workers than they did before at every level of the real wage. Plot the new labor demand curve in No. Classica.

f. After successful implementation of the policy in (e), the equilibrium real wage in No. Classica is _______________ dollars. The equilibrium level of employment is _______________ million workers, and full-employment real output is _______________ trillion dollars. Labor productivity is _______________. Compared to the economy's original equilibrium described in part (d), this policy targeting labor demand has (increased/decreased) the real wage, (increased/decreased) employment, and (increased/decreased) real output in No. Classica. Labor productivity has (increased/decreased).

g. Suppose the government now decides that too few people are in the labor force. To change that, the government decides to institute a broad range of policies to increase the reward for working, and to increase the hardship of not working. If successful, such policies as these will shift the labor supply curve to the (right/left). Suppose that the policies are *so* successful that now, at every real wage, there are 60 million more workers willing to work than there were before. Plot the new labor supply curve in No. Classica.

h. After successful implementation of the policy in (g), the equilibrium real wage in No. Classica is ______________ dollars. The equilibrium level of employment is ______________ million workers, and real output is ______________ trillion dollars. Labor productivity is ______________. Compared to the economy's previous equilibrium described in part (f), this policy targeting labor supply has (increased/decreased) the real wage, (increased/decreased) employment, and (increased/decreased) real output in No. Classica. Labor productivity has (increased/decreased).

i. To assess the combined effects of the policies directed at labor demand and labor supply, we may compare the economy's final equilibrium described in part (f), to its original equilibrium described in part (d). Making that comparison, we see that as a result of both policies combined, the real wage in No. Classica has (increased/decreased) from ______________ to ______________, while employment has (increased/decreased) from ______________ to ______________. At the same time, real output has (increased/decreased) from ______________ to ______________, and labor productivity has (increased/decreased) from ______________ to ______________. Ordinarily, this (increase/decrease) in labor productivity will be associated with a(n) (increase/decrease) in the average standard of living in No. Classica.

2. The economy of Duplicata has many similarities with No. Classica. The economy's labor demand curve, labor supply curve, and aggregate production function are all graphed on the following pages. In the graphs, the real wage is in dollars per hour, employment is in millions of workers, and real output is in trillions of dollars.

   a. When Duplicata is in long run economic equilibrium, what is:

      The equilibrium real wage? ______________

      The equilibrium level of employment? ______________

      Potential output? ______________

      Labor productivity? ______________

The government recently announced a range of plans to stimulate investment and so increase the economy's capital stock. The Ministry of Economics has predicted that, if successful, the economy's aggregate production function would no longer be described by the graph in the lower panel. Instead, they predict that the new aggregate production function will be described by data in the following table.

Real Output ($ Trillions)	Employment (Millions)
0	0
13	20
20	40
24	60
25	80

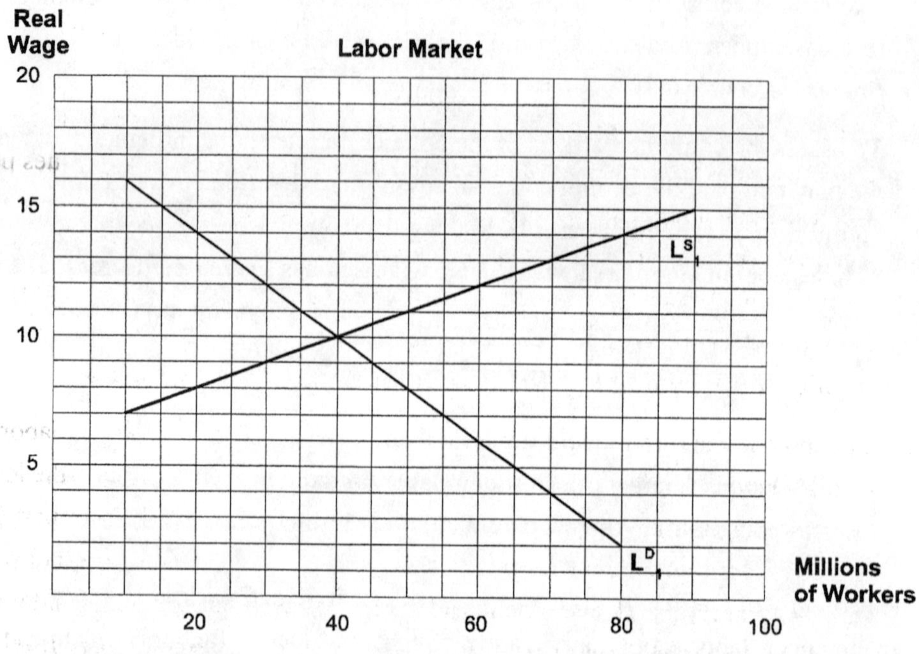

b. Plot the new aggregate production function for Duplicata on the following page.

c. If labor demand and labor supply remain as depicted, while the aggregate production function shifts as predicted in part (b), the equilibrium real wage will (rise/be unaffected/fall), employment will (rise/be unaffected/fall), real output will (rise/be unaffected/fall), and labor productivity will (rise/be unaffected/fall). Specifically, the equilibrium real wage will be _______________, employment will be _______________, and real output will be _______________. Labor productivity will be _______________.

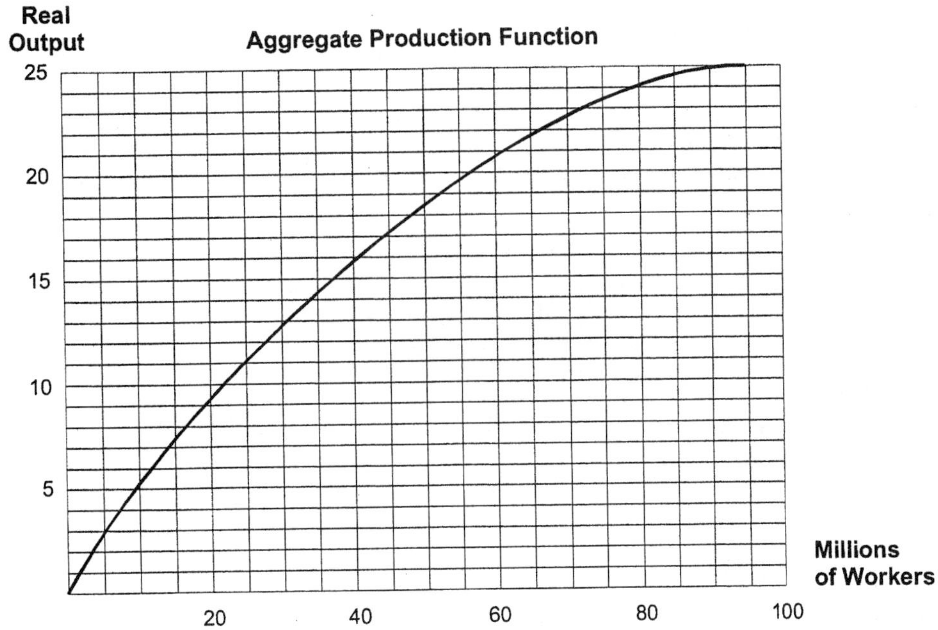

d. The new government promised to expand employment, as well as investment, but it is concerned that labor productivity might decline. If the government pursues policies that increase labor supply, employment will (increase/remain unchanged/decrease) and the real wage will (increase/remain unchanged/decrease). If it pursues policies that increase labor demand, employment will (increase/remain unchanged/decrease) and the real wage will (increase/remain unchanged/decrease). Either way, along the new aggregate production function, labor productivity will (increase/remain unchanged/decrease).

e. The government has thought this all out and determined that as long as labor productivity falls no lower than the level it was when the government took office—the level you described in part (a)—it can get either policy in part (d) adopted. From part (a), we note that labor productivity was originally at ______________. To keep labor productivity at *exactly* that level, the government could increase labor demand until it intersected the labor supply curve L^S_1 at a wage of ______________ and employment level of ______________. Alternatively, it could increase labor supply until it intersected labor demand curve L^D_1 at a wage of ______________ and employment level of ______________. Either way, labor productivity would remain at a level of ______________.

15-MINUTE PRACTICE TEST

Set a timer, giving yourself just 15 minutes to answer all of the following questions. To see what you *really* know and remember, take the test at least a day *after* you've read the chapter in the text and completed the exercises in this study guide.

Multiple Choice: Circle the letter in front of the single best answer.

1. A nation's standard of living is best measured by its
   a. real GDP.
   b. real GDP per capita.
   c. output per worker.
   d. capital per worker.
   e. investment per capita.

2. Which of the following policies promotes growth by directly shifting the labor supply curve rightward?
   a. A decrease in the budget deficit
   b. A decrease in the corporate profits tax rate
   c. A cut in income tax rates
   d. A cut in the capital gains tax rate
   e. Tax incentives for firm spending on R & D

3. As employment rises along a given aggregate production function,
   a. output falls.
   b. productivity falls.
   c. labor force participation falls.
   d. all of the above.
   e. none of the above.

4. Which of the following directly causes the aggregate production function to shift upward?
   a. An increase in human capital
   b. An increase in physical capital
   c. Technological change
   d. All of the above
   e. None of the above

5. Productivity increases when
   a. investment increases.
   b. the capital stock increases.
   c. the capital stock increases faster than the population.
   d. the capital stock increases faster than employment.
   e. the labor force increases faster than the population.

6. Which of the following would tend to increase the pace of technological change?
   a. A decrease in the life span of patents
   b. Decreasing the capital gains tax rate
   c. Increasing the budget deficit
   d. Imposing a special tax on household saving
   e. Imposing a special tax on R & D

7. Which of the following policies would shift the demand for funds curve rightward in the loanable funds market, and at the same time promote more rapid economic growth?
   a. An increase in the budget deficit
   b. A decrease in the budget deficit
   c. An investment tax credit
   d. Imposing a special tax on income from wages
   e. None of the above

8. The "budgetary costs" of economic growth refers to the
   a. part of the government's budget devoted to growth-enhancing projects.
   b. part of business firms' budgets devoted to growth enhancing projects.
   c. part of households' budgets devoted to increasing their income in the future.
   d. fact that many growth-enhancing policies require decreases in tax rates and tax revenue
   e. myth that only government, and not the private sector, contributes to economic growth.

9. The "consumption cost" of economic growth refers to the
   a. increased pollution caused by rising living standards.
   b. increased use of oil and other scarce natural resources as living standards rise.
   c. need to cut back on government spending in order to promote economic growth.
   d. need to shift resources into the consumption-goods sector in order to promote growth.
   e. sacrifice of consumption goods needed to increase production of capital goods to promote growth.

10. Which of the following enables a less developed country to make use of a combination of consumption and capital goods beyond its PPF?
    a. Foreign assistance
    b. Shifting resources away from producing consumption goods and toward producing capital goods
    c. Decreasing the growth rate of the population
    d. Technological change
    e. A rightward shift of the labor supply curve

True/False: For each of the following statements, circle T if the statement is true or F if the statement is false.

T F 1. Economic growth is an example of a "free lunch": higher growth gives society benefits, with no associated cost.

T F 2. When output grows more slowly than the population, real GDP per capita—which we call the average standard of living—will fall.

T F 3. Increases in employment, with a constant capital stock, tend to raise productivity.

T F 4. An investment tax credit promotes economic growth primarily by inducing firms to hire more workers, thus moving the economy along its aggregate production function.

T F 5. A decrease in the budget deficit promotes economic growth primarily by lowering interest rates, which increases investment and speeds growth in the capital stock.

T F 6. Technological change is one of those things that just "happens," and there is virtually nothing the government can do to speed it up.

T F 7. One way to speed growth in real GDP is to pass more laws and create more regulations to promote worker safety, a clean environment, and other social goals.

T F 8. Less developed countries with very low growth rates typically suffer from a poor infrastructure and very low population growth rates.

CHAPTER 9

ECONOMIC FLUCTUATIONS

SPEAKING ECONOMICS

Fill in each blank with the appropriate word or phrase from the list provided in the word bank. (For a challenge, fill in as many blanks as you can *without* using the word bank.)

________________________ 1. A period during which real GDP exceeds full-employment GDP.

________________________ 2. A situation in which a market does not clear—quantity supplied is not equal to quantity demanded.

________________________ 3. A change in spending that ultimately affects the entire economy.

Word Bank

boom
disequilibrium
spending shock

CHAPTER HIGHLIGHTS

Fill in the blanks with the appropriate words or phrases. If you have difficulty, review the chapter and then try again.

1. Because sudden, large shifts in the ____________________ curve and in the ____________________ curve are unlikely to occur, and because they could not accurately describe the facts of booms and recessions, the classical model cannot explain fluctuations through shifts in the ____________________ and ____________________ curves.

2. We cannot explain the facts of ____________________ -run economic fluctuations with a model in which the labor market always ____________________. This is why the classical model, which assumes that the labor market always ____________________, does a poor job of explaining the economy in the ____________________ run.

3. At every point along the labor supply curve, the wage rate tells us the ____________________ of working for the last worker to enter the labor force.

4. At every point along the labor demand curve, the ____________________ tells us the benefit obtained by some firm from the last worker hired.

5. At the ____________________ level of employment, all opportunities for mutually beneficial trade in the labor market have been exploited.

6. During a recession, the labor market is in disequilibrium, and the benefit from hiring another worker is ____________________ than the opportunity cost to that worker.

7. In recessions, there are incentives to ____________________ the level of employment, because the benefit to firms from additional employment is ____________________ than the opportunity cost to workers. These incentives help explain why recessions do not last forever.

8. In booms, there are incentives to ____________________ the level of employment, because the benefit to firms from some who have been hired is ____________________ than the opportunity cost to those workers. These incentives help explain why booms do not last forever.

9. When a positive shock causes a boom, firms operate—temporarily—at ____________________-normal rates of utilization. As a consequence, employment rises above its normal, full-employment level.

10. Over time, firms that have experienced an increase in demand will return to ____________________ utilization rates, and employment will fall back to its normal, full-employment level.

11. When an adverse shock causes a recession, firms operate—temporarily—at ____________________ -normal rates of utilization. As a consequence, employment drops below its normal, full-employment level.

12. Over time, firms that have experienced a decrease in demand will return to ____________________ utilization rates, and employment will rise back to its normal, full-employment level.

IMPORTANT CONCEPTS

Write a brief answer below each of the following items.

1. A leftward shift of the labor supply curve would cause a decrease in employment and output. In spite of this, we cannot attribute real world recessions to such shifts. List two reasons why not.

   a.

   b.

2. In a recession, which is greater: the opportunity cost of working for the next worker to be hired, or the benefit to some firm from hiring one more worker? Which is greater in a boom?

3. Briefly, how do your answers to the previous question help explain why booms and recessions do not last forever?

SKILLS AND TOOLS

For each item, follow the instructions, write the correct answer in the blank, or circle the correct answer.

1. Upandown is an economy often buffeted by shocks. Right now, however, things are pretty quiet. Labor demand and labor supply in Upandown are given by the equations

$$L^S = 10W$$

$$L^D = 240 - 10W$$

where W is the hourly real wage in dollars and L^D and L^S are millions of workers demanded and supplied, respectively.

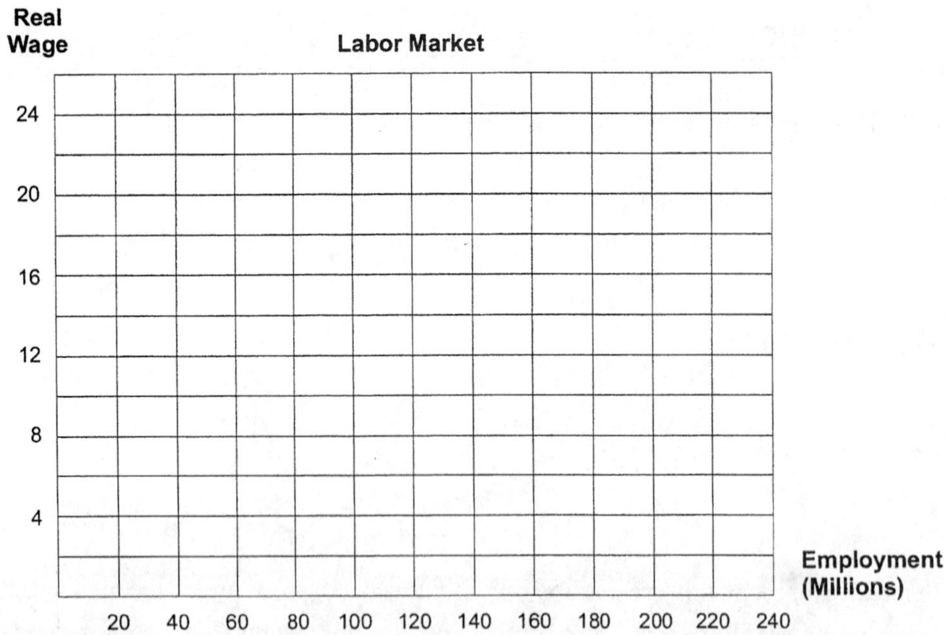

a. Plot the labor demand and labor supply curves in Upandown. In the long run, we should expect to see a prevailing equilibrium wage of _______________ per hour and equilibrium employment of _______________ million workers.

Recently, one of those financial doomsday books, *Day of Reckoning*, has soared to number one on the best-seller lists. The author's dire predictions of economic disaster have been the talk of worried executives in board rooms around the country, and many have already cut back on their production and hiring plans. As a result, total employment in Upandown has declined to 80 million workers.

b. When employment is 80 million, the labor market is in (equilibrium/ disequilibrium). The typical firm in Upandown is operating at a rate of utilization that is (above/just equal to/below) what is normal for that firm. The economy of Upandown is (in a boom/in long run equilibrium/in a recession).

c. Some of the people have begun to worry that things will never get back to normal. But those who study the labor market carefully have made some important observations. They note that with 80 million workers employed, the opportunity cost of working for that 80-millionth worker is _______________ dollars per hour. At the same time, the benefit obtained by some firm from hiring that worker is _______________ dollars per hour. Because under current condition the benefit to some firms from hiring additional workers (exceeds/equals/is exceeded by) the opportunity cost of working for those workers, mutually beneficial changes in employment (are/are not) possible. Over time, we would therefore expect to see firms (increase/keep steady/decrease) the number of workers they hire. As a result, employment in Upandown should (rise above/remain stable at/fall below) 80 million workers.

d. As these changes occur, the benefit firms derive from hiring additional workers will (increase/remain unchanged/decrease) while the opportunity cost of working for additional workers will (increase/remain unchanged/decrease). In the long run, we should expect to see total employment in Upandown at the level of _______________ million workers, and the wage at the level of _______________ dollars per hour. Under these conditions, the benefit to some firm of hiring an additional worker will be _______________ dollars per hour, while the opportunity cost of working for the last worker employed will be _______________ dollars per hour. Under these conditions, additional employment (would/would not) result in mutual gain for firms and workers. The labor market would again be in (equilibrium/disequilibrium) and the economy of Upandown would once again be in (a recession/long run equilibrium/a boom).

2. Labor demand and labor supply in Upandown are still given by the equations at the beginning of the previous problem. In what follows, refer to the graph you plotted there.

   a. From that graph, we know that in the long run, we should expect to see a prevailing equilibrium wage of _______________ per hour and equilibrium employment of _______________ million workers.

   Just when things seemed finally back to normal in Upandown, the government announced an immediate major increase in military spending to counter growing threats from the country's disgruntled neighbor, Downenout. Very quickly, employment grew to 160 million workers.

   b. When employment is at 160 million, the labor market is in (equilibrium/disequilibrium). The typical firm in Upandown is operating at a rate of utilization that is (above/just equal to/below) what is normal for that firm. The economy of Upandown is (in a boom/in long run equilibrium/in a recession).

   c. People had never seen employment so high, and many thought it would stay that high forever. Once again, however, those who study the labor market carefully were able to make some important observations. First, they noted that in order to have attracted 160 million workers into the workforce, the real wage firms pay had to have (risen/fallen) from _______________ dollars to _______________ dollars per hour. With the wage at that level, the opportunity cost of working for that last 160-millionth worker would be _______________ dollars per hour, while the benefit obtained by some firm from that worker is _______________ dollars per hour. Because under current conditions the benefit to some firm from the last worker hired (exceeds/equals/is exceeded by) the wage the firm must pay to attract that worker, firms have an incentive to (hire more workers/keep employment steady/let some workers go). Over time, we would therefore expect to see firms (increase/keep steady/decrease) the number of workers they employ. As a result, employment in Upandown should (rise above/remain stable at/fall below) 160 million workers.

d. In the long run, we should expect to see total employment in Upandown at the level of ______________ million workers, and the wage at the level of ______________ dollars per hour. Under these conditions, the benefit to some firm of hiring an additional worker will be ______________ dollars, while the opportunity cost of working for the last worker employed will be ______________ dollars. Under these conditions, the labor market would again be in (equilibrium/disequilibrium) and the economy of Upandown would once again be in (a recession/long run equilibrium/a boom).

10-MINUTE PRACTICE TEST

Set a timer, giving yourself just ten minutes to answer all of the following questions. To see what you *really* know and remember, take the test at least a day *after* you've read the chapter in the text and completed the exercises in this study guide.

Multiple Choice: Circle the letter in front of the single best answer.

1. A boom is a period during which output
   a. is rising.
   b. is recovering from a recession.
   c. exceeds full-employment output.
   d. is falling.
   e. hits bottom during a recession.

2. Real world recessions can be explained by
   a. shifts in labor demand.
   b. shifts in labor supply.
   c. changes in the labor market equilibrium.
   d. all of the above.
   e. none of the above.

3. At each level of employment, the labor supply curve tells us the
   a. opportunity cost of working for the last worker hired.
   b. benefit to some firm from the last worker hired.
   c. difference between the last worker's opportunity cost of working and the benefit he/she provides to some firm.
   d. equilibrium level of employment in the labor market.
   e. level of employment that a firm would hire during "normal" utilization.

4. The classical model cannot explain booms and recessions because it assumes that
   a. spending shocks can push the economy away from equilibrium.
   b. markets always clear.
   c. the labor supply curve slopes upward and the labor supply curve slopes downward.
   d. there is only one type of labor in the economy.
   e. neither the labor supply curve nor the labor demand curve can shift.

5. In a recession, the last worker hired
   a. has an opportunity cost of working greater than the benefit he/she provides for some firm.
   b. has an opportunity cost of working less than the benefit he/she provides for some firm.
   c. has an opportunity cost of working equal to the benefit he/she provides for some firm.
   d. has an opportunity cost of working greater than the wage that he/she is paid.
   e. provides a benefit to some firm that is smaller than the wage that he/she is paid.

6. In the real world, booms seem to be caused by
   a. sudden rightward shifts in the labor supply curve.
   b. sudden rightward shifts in the labor demand curve.
   c. spending shocks.
   d. all of the above.
   e. none of the above.

True/False: For each of the following statements, circle T if the statement is true or F if the statement is false.

T F 1. During recessions, employment is unusually low and the unemployment rate is unusually high.

T F 2. A leftward shift in the labor demand curve would occur if fewer people wanted to work at any given wage.

T F 3. The classical model makes assumptions about the economy that make sense in the short run, but not the long run.

T F 4. In a boom, the opportunity cost of working for the last worker hired is greater than the benefit that worker provides to some firm.

T F 5. During a recession, firms typically operate at below-normal rates of labor utilization.

CHAPTER 10

THE SHORT-RUN MACRO MODEL

SPEAKING ECONOMICS

Fill in each blank with the appropriate word or phrase from the list provided in the word bank. (For a challenge, fill in as many blanks as you can *without* using the word bank.)

_________________________ 1. A macroeconomic model that explains how changes in spending can affect real GDP in the short run.

_________________________ 2. The part of household income that remains after paying taxes.

_________________________ 3. A positively-sloped relationship between real consumption spending and real disposable income.

_________________________ 4. The part of consumption spending that is independent of income; also, the vertical intercept of the consumption function.

_________________________ 5. The amount by which consumption spending rises when disposable income rises by one dollar.

_________________________ 6. Shows aggregate consumption spending at each level of income or GDP.

_________________________ 7. The sum of spending by households, business firms, the government and foreigners on final goods and services produced in the U.S.

_________________________ 8. In the short-run macro model, the level of output at which output and spending are equal.

_________________________ 9. The amount by which equilibrium real GDP changes as a result of a one-dollar change in autonomous consumption, investment, government purchases or net exports.

_________________________ 10. Forces that reduce the size of the expenditure multiplier and diminish the impact of spending shocks.

Word Bank

aggregate expenditure (AE)
automatic stabilizers
autonomous consumption spending
consumption function
consumption-income line
disposable income
equilibrium GDP
expenditure multiplier
marginal propensity to consume (MPC)
short-run macro model

CHAPTER HIGHLIGHTS

Fill in the blanks with the appropriate words or phrases. If you have difficulty, review the chapter and then try again.

1. In the short run, the relationship between ____________________ and ____________________ goes both ways: ____________________ depends on ____________________, and ____________________ depends on ____________________.

2. The marginal propensity to consume (MPC) is (1) the slope of the ____________________ function; (2) the change in consumption divided by the change in ____________________ income; or (3) the amount by which consumption spending rises when ____________________ income rises by one dollar.

3. The MPC is always greater than ____________________ and less than ____________________.

4. When the government collects a fixed amount of taxes from households, the line representing the relationship between consumption and income shifts downward by the amount of the tax times the ____________________. The slope of this line, however, is unaffected by taxes, and is equal to the ____________________.

5. When a change in ____________________ causes consumption spending to change, we move along the consumption-income line. When a change in ____________________ causes consumption spending to change, the line will shift.

6. In the short-run macro model, we define investment spending as ____________________ and equipment purchases by business firms, and ____________________ construction. ____________________ investment is treated as unintentional and undesired, and is therefore excluded from our definition of investment spending.

7. In the simple, short-run macro model of this chapter, ____________________ spending, ____________________ purchases, and ____________________ are all regarded as given values, determined by forces ____________________ of the model.

8. Aggregate expentirue is the sum of spending by households, ____________________, the government, and the ____________________ sector on ____________________ goods and services produced in the United States. Or, in symbols, AE = ____________________ .

9. When income increases, aggregate expenditure will rise by the ____________________ times the change in income.

10. When aggregate expenditure is less than GDP, output will ____________________ in the future. Thus, any level of output at which aggregate expenditure is less than GDP cannot be the ____________________ GDP.

11. When aggregate expenditure is greater than GDP, output will ____________________ in the future. Thus, any level of output at which aggregate expenditure exceeds GDP cannot be the ____________________ GDP.

12. In the short-run, equilibrium GDP is the level of output at which ____________________ and ____________________ are equal.

13. The change in inventories during any period will always equal ____________________ minus ____________________.

14. A ____________________ line is a translator line: It allows us to measure any horizontal distance as a vertical distance instead.

15. At any output level at which the aggregate expenditure line lies below the ____________________ line, aggregate expenditure is less than GDP. If firms produce any of these output levels, their ____________________ will grow, and they will ____________________ output in the future.

16. At any output level at which the aggregate expenditure line lies above the ____________________ line, aggregate expenditure exceeds GDP. If firms produce any of these output levels, their ____________________will decline, and they will ____________________ their output in the future.

17. ____________________ GDP is the output level at which the aggregate expenditure line intersects the ____________________ line. If firms produce this output level, their inventories will not change, and they will be content to continue producing the same level of output in the future.

18. In the short-run macro model, cyclical unemployment is caused by insufficient ____________________. As long as ____________________ remains low, production will remain low, and unemployment will remain high.

19. In the short-run macro model, the economy can overheat because ____________________ is too high. As long as ____________________ remains high, production will exceed potential output, and unemployment will be unusually low.

20. The expenditure multiplier is the number by which a change in spending (e.g., investment spending) must be multiplied to get the change in ____________________.

21. For any value of the MPC, the formula for the expenditure multiplier is ____________________.

22. Just as increases in spending cause equilibrium GDP to ____________________ by a multiple of the change in spending, decreases in spending cause equilibrium GDP to ____________________ by a multiple of the change in spending.

23. Changes in investment, government purchases, net exports or autonomous consumption lead to a ____________________ effect on GDP. The expenditure ____________________ is what we multiply the initial change in spending by in order to get the change in equilibrium GDP.

24. An increase in ____________________ consumption spending, investment spending, government purchases or ____________________ will shift the ____________________ line upward by the increase in spending, causing equilibrium GDP to rise. The increase in GDP will equal the initial increase in spending times the ____________________ multiplier.

25. An automatic ____________________ reduces the size of the expenditure multiplier and therefore ____________________ the impact of spending shocks on the economy. As a result, the economy is ____________________ stable.

26. In the long run, the expenditure multiplier has a value of ____________________: No matter what the change in spending or taxes, output will return to ____________________, so the change in equilibrium GDP will be ____________________.

27. In the long run, an increase in the desire to save leads to faster economic growth and rising living standards. In the short run, however, it can cause a (an) ____________________ that pushes output ____________________ its potential.

IMPORTANT CONCEPTS

Write a brief answer below each of the following items.

1. List the four components of aggregate expenditure used in this chapter's short-run macro model.

   a.

   b.

   c.

   d.

2. Give the mathematical formulas for each of the following:

   a. The relationship between consumption (C) and disposable income (DI):

   b. The formula for the expenditure multiplier:

   c. The special formula for the tax multiplier (if you've read Appendix 2 of this chapter):

3. List five different changes that could cause equilibrium GDP to *decrease*.

   a.

   b.

   c.

   d.

   e.

4. If the MPC were equal to zero, and government spending increased by $100 billion, would equilibrium GDP increase? If yes, by how much. If no, why not?

SKILLS AND TOOLS

1. Data on income (GDP), disposable income, and consumption spending are presented below. All figures are in billions of dollars.

Income or GDP ($ Billions)	Tax Collections ($ Billions)	Disposable Income ($ Billions)	Consumption Spending ($ Billions)
______	______	2,000	2,500
______	______	2,500	2,750
4,000	______	______	3,000
______	______	3,500	3,250
5,000	______	4,000	3,500
5,500	______	______	3,750
______	______	5,000	4,000
______	______	5,500	4,250
7,000	______	______	4,500
7,500	______	______	4,750

a. Suppose taxes are $1,000 at every level of real income. Complete the table.

b. On the grid provided, plot the consumption-income line corresponding to these data.

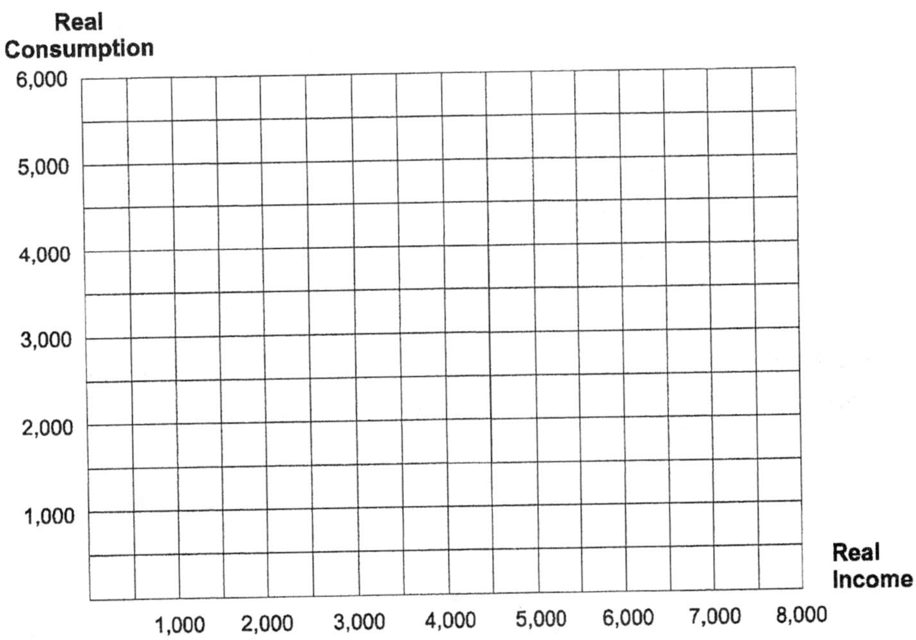

c. What is the marginal propensity to consume (MPC) in this economy? ____________

d. If taxes increase from $1,000 to $2,000 at every level of real income, then real disposable income will (increase/decrease) by ______________ dollars at every level of real income. Because the MPC in this economy is equal to ______________, this means that consumption spending will (increase/decrease) by exactly ______________ dollars at every level of real income. In the graph above, this means that an increase in taxes from $1,000 to $2,000 will cause the consumption-income line to shift (upward/downward) by exactly ______________ at every level of real income.

e. Plot the new consumption-income line when taxes are $2,000. What is the marginal propensity to consume equal to now? ______________

f. Following the increase in taxes just described, in order to restore the consumption-income line to its original position in part (b), there would have to be an (increase/decrease) in the interest rate, an (increase/decrease) in household wealth, or an (increase/decrease) in consumer optimism.

2. In the table below, consumption and income data have been carried forward from the previous problem.

a. If planned investment spending by businesses is fixed at $600 billion, government purchases are fixed at $400 billion, and net exports are fixed at $250 billion, complete the table.

Income or GDP ($ Billions)	Consumption Spending ($ Billions)	Investment Spending ($ Billions)	Government Purchases ($ Billions)	Net Exports ($ Billions)	Aggregate Expenditure ($ Billions)
3,000	2,500	____	____	____	____
3,500	2,750	____	____	____	____
4,000	3,000	____	____	____	____
4,500	3,250	____	____	____	____
5,000	3,500	____	____	____	____
5,500	3,750	____	____	____	____
6,000	4,000	____	____	____	____
6,500	4,250	____	____	____	____
7,000	4,500	____	____	____	____
7,500	4,750	____	____	____	____

b. At any level of GDP, aggregate expenditure, or *AE*, is equal to the sum ______________. When aggregate expenditure exceeds GDP, output will tend to (rise/remain constant/fall). When aggregate expenditure is less than GDP, output will tend to (rise/remain constant/fall). Output will remain constant, and the economy will have achieved its short run equilibrium GDP, when aggregate expenditure (exceeds/equals/is exceeded by) GDP.

c. On the grid provided, plot the "45-degree line," or translator line, along which GDP and real aggregate expenditure are equal to each other. Then, using the data from part (a), plot the economy's aggregate expenditure line.

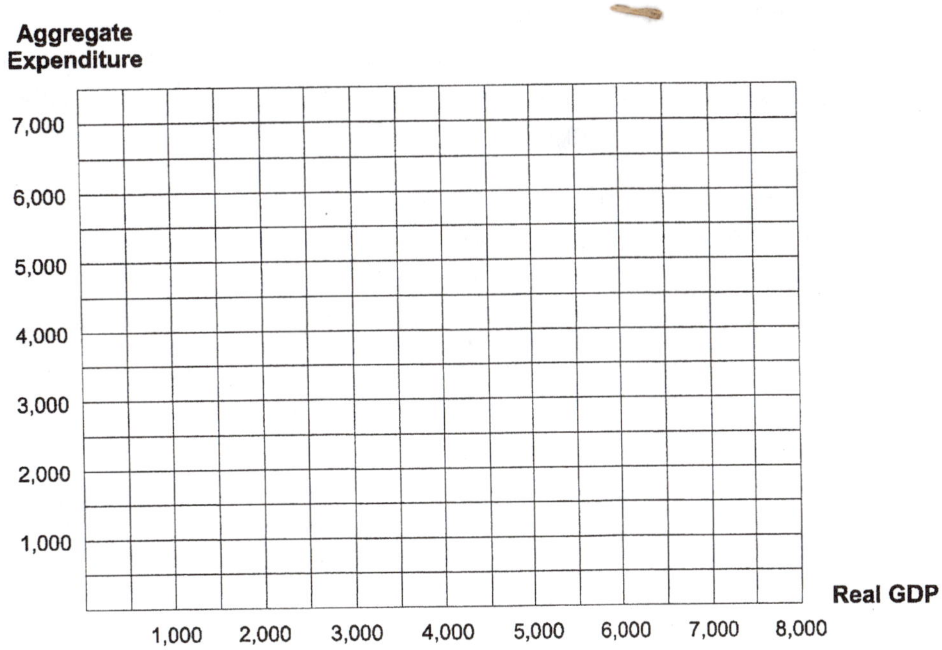

d. The equilibrium GDP in this economy (is/is not) equal to $2,500 billion. When real GDP is $2,500 billion, aggregate expenditure is _______________ billion. Because aggregate expenditure is (greater than/equal to/less than) GDP, firms are producing (more output than/as much output as/less output than) they are selling. As a result, the change in firms' inventories is equal to _______________ billion dollars. Over time, this means that firms will (increase their output/keep their output constant/decrease their output) and GDP will (rise/remain constant/fall).

e. The equilibrium GDP in this economy (is/is not) equal to $4,500 billion. When real GDP is $4,500 billion, aggregate expenditure is _______________ billion. Because aggregate expenditure is (greater than/equal to/less than) GDP, firms are producing (more output than/as much output as/less output than) they are selling. As a result, the change in firms' inventories is equal to _______________ billion dollars. Over time, this means that firms will (increase their output/keep their output constant/decrease their output) and GDP will (rise/remain constant/fall).

f. The equilibrium GDP in this economy (is/is not) equal to $6,500 billion. When real GDP is $6,500 billion, aggregate expenditure is _______________ billion. Because aggregate expenditure is (greater than/equal to/less than) GDP, firms are producing (more output than/as much output as/less output than) they are selling. As a result, the change in firms' inventories is equal to _______________ billion dollars. Over time, this means that firms will (increase their output/keep their output constant/decrease their output) and GDP will (rise/remain constant/fall).

g. Suppose that (potential) full-employment output in this economy is $5,000 billion. Then the short-run equilibrium levels of output and employment are (above/the same as/ below) the long run equilibrium levels of output and employment. In this case, aggregate spending is (too high/just right/too low), and the economy will experience (over-heating/steady income/unemployment) in the short run. To achieve full-employment, the government could (increase/hold constant/decrease) government purchases in order to (increase/hold constant/decrease) aggregate expenditure and cause equilibrium GDP to (rise to/stay steady at/fall to) its full employment equilibrium level.

3. The aggregate expenditure line for some economy is plotted below. Axes measure billions of dollars.

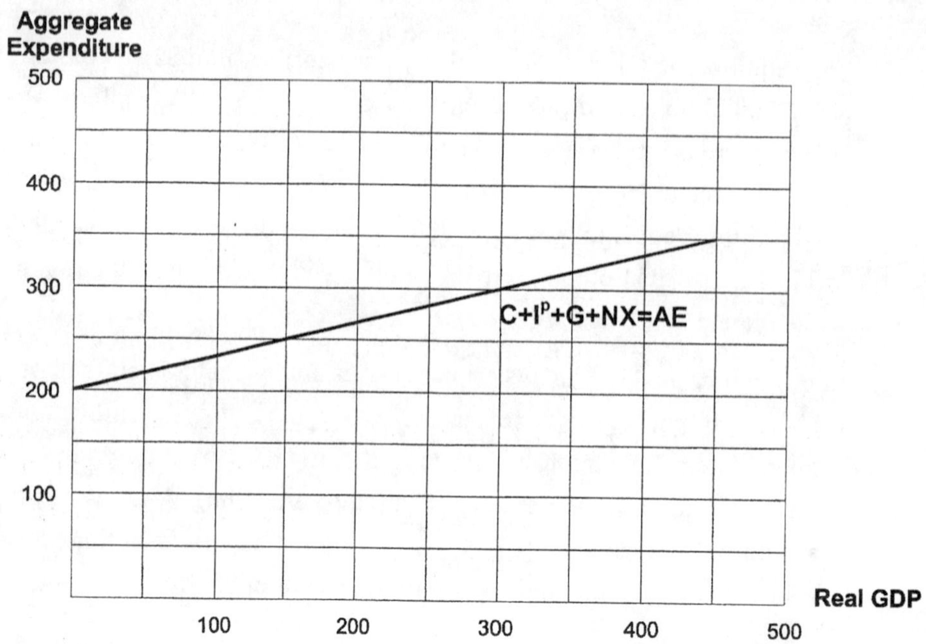

a. What is the value of the marginal propensity to consume in this economy?

____

b. What is the value of the expenditure multiplier in this economy? _______________

c. What is the short run equilibrium level of real GDP? ____________

d. If full employment output in this economy is $150 billion, investment would have to (increase/decrease) by ____________ dollars to bring equilibrium output to this level. Alternatively, government purchases would have to (increase/decrease) by ____________ to achieve the same result.

e. If either of the spending changes in part (d) occurred, the economy's aggregate expenditure line would (shift downward/shift upward) by exactly ____________ billion dollars at every level of real GDP. On the graph on the previous page, plot the aggregate expenditure line that would result.

4. You have been trying to collect information on the MPC and the short run expenditure multiplier in six different countries. You've been able to come up with only a few of the items you want, and you've arranged them in the table below. Note that the last three columns report the change in equilibrium GDP that results from changes in different kinds of expenditure.

			Change in Equilibrium GDP due to:			
Country	**MPC**	**Multiplier**	$\Delta I^P = +200$	$\Delta G = -100$	$\Delta a = +400$	$\Delta NX = -150$
1	0.40	____	____	____	____	–250
2	____	2.00	____	–200	800	____
3	0.60	____	500	–250	____	____
4	____	____	800	____	1,600	–600
5	____	____	____	–500	2,000	____
6	____	____	2,000	____	4,000	____

a. Complete the table.

b. Suppose we know that in Country 4, short run equilibrium output is $1,000 billion and potential output is $1,400 billion. Then in order to increase output to its full employment level, the government could (increase/decrease) government purchases by ____________ billion dollars. Because the expenditure multiplier in Country 4 is ____________, this change in spending will cause equilibrium real output to rise by ____________ billion dollars.

c. Suppose we know that in Country 5, short run equilibrium output is $1,000 billion and potential output is $800 billion. Then in order to decrease output to its full employment level, the government could (increase/decrease) government purchases by ____________ billion dollars. Because the expenditure multiplier in Country 1 is ____________, this change in spending will cause equilibrium real output to fall by ____________ billion dollars.

(This question refers to material found in Appendix 1 to the chapter.)

5. Consumption spending (C), investment spending (I^P), government purchases (G), and taxes (T) are given by the following equations:

$$C = 85 + (1/2)\,Y_D$$
$$I^P = 55$$
$$G = 75$$
$$T = 30.$$

All figures are in billions of dollars.

a. In the consumption function given above, the term Y_D stands for _______________. If Y stands for total income or GDP, Y_D is calculated by (adding/subtracting) the amount of (C/I^P/G/T/Y) from (C/I^P/G/T/Y).

b. What is the equation for the consumption-income line? _______________

c. What is the equation for aggregate expenditure, AE? _______________

d. What is the value of equilibrium GDP? _______________

e. What is the MPC in this economy? _______________

f. What is the value of the expenditure multiplier? _______________

g. Suppose that investment spending rises to $70 billion. What will be the resulting equilibrium GDP? _______________

(This question refers to material found in Appendix 2 to the chapter.)

6. The equation for aggregate expenditures in an economy is

$$AE = 5{,}000 + 0.5Y$$

Where AE is aggregate expenditure ($C + I^P + G + NX$) and Y is GDP, both in billions of dollars.

a. What is the MPC in this economy ? _______________

b. What is the expenditure multiplier in this economy? _______________

c. What is the tax multiplier in this economy? _______________

d. What is equilibrium GDP in this economy? _______________

e. Potential output in this economy is $12,000 billion. To bring equilibrium GDP to this full-employment level, the government could (increase/decrease) taxes by _______________ billion dollars. Alternatively, the government could (increase/decrease) government purchases by _______________ billion dollars, instead.

15-MINUTE PRACTICE TEST

Set a timer, giving yourself just 15 minutes to answer all of the following questions. To see what you *really* know and remember, take the test at least a day *after* you've read the chapter in the text and completed the exercises in this study guide.

Multiple Choice: Circle the letter in front of the single, best answer.

1. Disposable income is equal to
   a. income plus taxes.
   b. income minus taxes.
   c. income plus saving minus taxes.
   d. consumption plus government purchases minus taxes.
   e. consumption plus saving minus taxes.

2. If the MPC in an economy equals 0.8, and disposable income falls by \$100, consumption spending will fall by
   a. \$0.80.
   b. \$8.00.
   c. \$20.00.
   d. \$80.00.
   e. \$500.00.

3. Which of the following will cause the consumption-income line to shift upward?
   a. An increase in income
   b. An increase in taxes
   c. An increase in government spending
   d. All of the above
   e. None of the above

4. The increase in inventories during the year is equal to
   a. C + I + G + NX.
   b. AE – I.
   c. AE – (C + I + G + NX).
   d. GDP – AE.
   e. C + I + G + NX – GDP.

5. In the short-run macro model, if the MPC equals 0.9 and investment spending rises by \$200 billion, then equilibrium GDP will rise by
   a. \$20 billion.
   b. \$180 billion.
   c. \$90 billion.
   d. \$1,000 billion.
   e. \$2,000 billion.

6. In the short-run macro model, a rise in autonomous consumption (a) causes
   a. a movement rightward along the consumption-income line.
   b. equilibrium real GDP to increase by an amount equal to the rise in autonomous consumption.
   c. equilibrium real GDP to increase by a multiple of the rise in autonomous consumption.
   d. equilibrium real GDP to decrease by an amount equal to the rise in autonomous consumption.
   e. no change in equilibrium real GDP.

7. Automatic stabilizers are
   a. well-timed government policy changes that help keep the economy stable at full employment.
   b. forces in the economy that increase the size of the expenditure multiplier.
   c. spending shocks that move in the opposite direction of, and help to neutralize, other spending shocks.
   d. actions taken by foreign governments that help stabilize our own economy.
   e. none of the above.

8. In the short-run macro model, an increase in saving has the effect of
   a. speeding economic growth.
   b. increasing consumption.
   c. increasing investment.
   d. increasing government spending.
   e. causing a recession.

9. In the short-run macro model, cyclical unemployment is caused by insufficient
   a. labor supply.
   b. labor demand.
   c. spending.
   d. saving.
   e. taxes.

10. If the MPC were equal to zero, the expenditure multiplier would be
   a. less than zero.
   b. zero.
   c. between zero and one.
   d. one.
   e. greater than one.

True/False: For each of the following statements, circle T if the statement is true or F if the statement is false.

T F 1. Autonomous consumption spending is represented graphically as the vertical intercept of the consumption function.

T F 2. An increase in disposable income causes the consumption function to shift upward.

T F 3. An increase in taxes causes the consumption-income line to shift downward.

T F 4. In the short-run macro model, an increase in autonomous consumption spending, investment spending, net exports, government purchases, or taxes will all cause equilibrium GDP to increase.

T F 5. When aggregate expenditure is less than GDP, the change in inventories is negative and GDP will increase in future periods.

T F 6. In the short-run macro model, an increase in government spending will cause an increase in employment.

T F 7. All else being equal, the larger the MPC, the larger will be the multiplier.

T F 8. As the economy adjusts to its new equilibrium after an increase in government spending, consumption spending rises.

CHAPTER 11

THE BANKING SYSTEM AND THE MONEY SUPPLY

SPEAKING ECONOMICS

Fill in each blank with the appropriate word or phrase from the list provided in the word bank. (For a challenge, fill in as many blanks as you can *without* using the word bank.)

____________________ 1. The property of being easily converted into cash.

____________________ 2. Currency and coins held outside of banks.

____________________ 3. Checking accounts that do not pay interest.

____________________ 4. A standard measure of the money supply, including cash in the hands of the public, checking account deposits, and travelers' checks.

____________________ 5. A measure of the money supply including cash in the hands of the public, checking accounts, travelers' checks, savings account balances, noninstitutional money market mutual fund balances, and small time deposits.

____________________ 6. A business firm that specializes in brokering between savers and borrowers.

____________________ 7. A financial statement showing assets, liabilities, and net worth at a point in time.

____________________ 8. An IOU issued by a corporation or government agency when it borrows funds.

____________________ 9. An IOU issued by a household or unincorporated business when it borrows funds.

____________________ 10. Vault cash plus balances held at the Fed.

____________________ 11. The minimum amount of reserves a bank must hold, depending upon the amount of its deposit liabilities.

____________________ 12. The minimum fraction of checking account balances that banks must hold as reserves.

____________________ 13. The difference between assets and liabilities.

____________________ 14. A nation's principal monetary authority.

____________________ 15. A group of Federal Reserve officials that establishes U.S. monetary policy.

____________________ 16. The interest rate the Fed charges on loans to banks.

____________________ 17. Purchases or sales of bonds by the Federal Reserve System.

____________________ 18. Reserves held beyond those required.

____________________ 19. The number by which a change in reserves is multiplied to determine the resulting change in demand deposits.

____________________ 20. An attempt by many of a bank's depositors to withdraw their funds.

____________________ 21. A situation in which depositors attempt to withdraw funds from many banks simultaneously.

Word Bank

balance sheet
banking panic
bond
cash in the hands of the public
central bank
demand deposit multiplier
demand deposits
discount rate
excess reserves
Federal Open Market Committee
financial intermediary
liquidity
loan
M1
M2
net worth
open market operations
required reserve ratio
required reserves
reserves
run on the bank

CHAPTER HIGHLIGHTS

Fill in the blanks with the appropriate words or phrases. If you have difficulty, review the chapter and then try again.

1. An asset is considered liquid if it can be converted to ____________________ quickly and at little cost. An illiquid asset, by contrast, can be converted to ____________________ only after a delay, or at considerable cost.

2. The money supply measure M1 consists of ____________________ in the hands of the public plus ____________________ deposits plus other ____________________ deposits plus ____________________ checks. In the text, it is assumed that the money supply consists of just two components: ____________________ in the hands of the public and ____________________ deposits.

3. One column of a bank's balance sheet lists the banks assets—anything of value that the bank ____________________. The other column lists the bank's liabilities—amounts that the bank ____________________.

4. The more funds a bank's customers hold in their checking accounts, the more the bank must hold as ____________________.

5. When the Fed wishes to increase or decrease the money supply, it buys or sells ____________________ bonds. These actions are called ____________________.

6. The demand deposit multiplier is the number by which we must multiply the injection of ____________________ to get the total change in demand deposits.

7. For any value of the required reserve ratio (RRR), the formula for the demand deposit multiplier is ____________________.

8. After an injection of reserves, the demand deposit multiplier stops working—and the money supply stops incr4easing—only when all the reserves injecfted are being held by banks as ____________________ reserves.

9. While other tools can affect the money supply, open market operations have two advantages over them: precision and ____________________. This is why open market operations remain the Fed's primary means of changing the money supply.

10. Most economists believe that if we want the freedom from banking panics provided by the ____________________, we must also accept the strict regulation and close monitoring of banks provided by the Fed and other agencies.

IMPORTANT CONCEPTS

Write a brief answer below each of the following items.

1. List the four components of the M1 measure of the money supply.

   a.

   b.

   c.

   d.

2. State whether each of the following would be listed on a bank's balance sheet, by writing *yes* or *no*. If *yes*, state whether the entry would occur on the assets side or the liabilities side of the balance sheet.

   a. ________________ The real estate and buildings in the bank's possession.

   b. ________________ Government bonds held by the bank.

   c. ________________ Mortgage loans the bank has made to private citizens.

   d. ________________ The income earned by the bank during the year.

   e. ________________ Checking accounts held by the bank's customers.

   f. ________________ Cash in the bank's vault.

   g. ________________ The bank's net worth.

3. The membership of the Fed's Board of Governors and its Federal Open Market Committee (FOMC) are not identical. What is the difference?

4. State briefly how each of the following helps determine the composition of the Federal Open Market Committee.

   a. The President of the United States

   b. The U.S. Senate

   c. The 5,000 member banks

SKILLS AND TOOLS

1. The following are data on the economy of Minnewaska:

Cash in the hands of the public	=	$402
Public's credit limit on all credit cards	=	$136
Demand deposits and all other checkable deposits	=	$693
Money market mutual funds	=	$618
Travelers' checks	=	$8
Large time deposits	=	$512
Small time deposits	=	$971
Public's stock market holdings	=	$1,069
Savings-type accounts	=	$256

   a. What is the value of M1 for this economy? ______________

   b. What is the value of M2 for this economy? ______________

   c. What entries in the table are not counted as part of the economy's money stock?

   ____

2. Minnewaska has a central bank which, by coincidence, also happens to be called "the Fed." One of its leading commercial banks, First Bank of Minnewaska, holds the demand deposits of 15,000 individuals. Each individual has placed $10,000 in the bank. The government has borrowed $55 million from the bank. The bank has $45 million in loans to private citizens and $20 million in loans to various companies on its books. First Bank of Minnewaska owns the property and building where it is located, and these have a total assessed value of $21 million. The bank holds $12 million in vault cash and has $18 million in its account at the Fed. First Bank of Minnewaska *always* stays loaned up (i.e. never holds excess reserves).

   a. Complete the balance sheet for First Bank of Minnewaska.

First Bank of Minnewaska

Assets	**Liabilities and Net Worth**
____________________	____________________
____________________	____________________
____________________	
____________________	
____________________	
____________________	
Total Assets ______	Total Liabilities plus Net Worth ______

   b. What is First Bank's net worth? ______________

   c. How much in reserves does First Bank hold? ______________ Since this bank always remains loaned up, we can assume that all reserves it holds are (excess/required) reserves. Thus, we can deduce that in Minnewaska the required reserve ratio is ______________.

3. Minnewaska's Fed has decided to buy a $5,000 government bond from SabreTooth Trading, a bond dealer. SabreTooth has received a check for $5,000 from the Fed and deposited it into its checking account at First Bank of Minnewaska.

   a. As a result of the Fed's action, reserves at First Bank of Minnewaska have (increased/decreased) by ______________ dollars. If the required reserve ratio is 0.2, this means that First Bank of Minnewaska has (excess reserves/deficient reserves) in the amount of ______________ dollars. Now, the bank (can make new loans/must call in loans) in the amount of ______________ dollars. This transaction alone causes the money supply of Minnewaska to (increase/decrease) by ______________ dollars.

b. Fill in the blanks to describe the impact of the transaction in part (a) upon First Bank of Minnewaska's balance sheet. Model your answer on similar tables in the text, using + to indicate an increase, and – to indicate a decrease.

Changes in First Bank of Minnewaska's Balance Sheet

Action	Changes in Assets	Changes in Liabilities
Fed buys $5,000 bond from Sabre-Tooth Trading, which deposits $5,000 check from Fed deposits into its checking account:	_______ in reserves	_______ in demand deposits
First Bank (lends out excess reserves/calls in loans) in amount of _______ dollars:	_______ in reserves _______ in loans	
The total effect on First Bank from beginning to end:	_______ in reserves _______ in loans	_______ in demand deposits

c. Suppose First Bank of Minnewaska lends its excess reserves to Cindy, who then deposits the proceeds into her checking account at *Bank Too!* of Minnewaska. As a result of this action, reserves at *Bank Too!* have (increased/decreased) by _______________ dollars. If the required reserve ratio is 0.2, *Bank Too!* now has (excess reserves/deficient reserves) of _______________ dollars. Now, the bank (can make new loans/must call in loans) of _______________ dollars. This transaction, alone, causes the money supply of Minnewaska to (increase/decrease) by _______________ dollars.

d. Fill in the blanks to describe the impact of the transaction in part (c) upon the following balance sheet for *Bank Too!*, using + to indicate an increase, and – to indicate a decrease.

Changes in *Bank Too!'s* Balance Sheet

Action	Changes in Assets	Changes in Liabilities
Cindy deposits _____ loan check into her checking account:	_______ in reserves	_______ in demand deposits
Bank Too! (lends out excess reserves/calls in loans) in amount of _______ dollars:	_______ in reserves _______ in loans	
The total effect on *Bank Too!* from beginning to end:	_______ in reserves _______ in loans	_______ in demand deposits

e. Assume that banks in Minnewaska always keep themselves fully loaned up (that is, they never hold excess reserves). Suppose, also, that anyone receiving a loan deposits the proceeds in one of Minnewaska's banks, and anyone paying off a loan withdraws the amount due from one of Minnewaska's banks. Still supposing that the required reserve ratio is 0.2, complete the following table to trace the impact of the Fed's action throughout the banking system. (Note that the last column indicates *cumulative* change, as in the text.)

Round	Change in Demand Deposits at This Bank	Change in Demand Deposits at All Banks
First Bank of Minnewaska	_______	_______
Bank Too!	_______	_______
Bank 3	_______	_______
Bank 4	_______	_______
Bank 5	_______	_______
Bank 6	_______	_______
Bank 7	_______	_______
Bank 8	_______	_______
...		
All Other Banks	_______	_______

f. As each bank in turn (makes new loans/calls in old loans) it (creates/extinguishes) demand deposits. In the end, the cumulative effect of all banks' actions, together, is a multiple (increase/decrease) in Minnewaska's money supply equal to ____________ times the original change in reserves

4. Always in the bond market, Minnewaska's Fed has just sold a $2,000 bond to SabreTooth Trading. To buy the bond, SabreTooth has withdrawn $2,000 from its checking account at First Bank of Minnewaska.

a. As a result of the Fed's actions reserves at First Bank of Minnewaska have (increased/decreased) by ____________ dollars. If the required reserve ratio is 0.2, this means that First Bank of Minnewaska has (excess reserves/deficient reserves) in the amount of ____________ dollars. Now, the bank (can make new loans/must call in loans) in the amount of ____________ dollars. This transaction alone causes the money supply to (increase/decrease) by ____________ dollars.

b. Fill in the blanks to describe the impact of the transaction in part (a) upon First Bank of Minnewaska's balance sheet. Model your answer on similar tables in the text, using + to indicate an increase, and – to indicate a decrease.

Changes in First Bank of Minnewaska's Balance Sheet

Action	Changes in Assets	Changes in Liabilities
Fed sells $2,000 bond to SabreTooth, which pays with $2,000 check drawn on its checking account at First Bank.	_______ in reserves	_______ in demand deposits
First Bank (lends out excess reserves/calls in loans) in amount of _______ dollars:	_______ in reserves _______ in loans	
The total effect on First Bank from beginning to end:	_______ in reserves _______ in loans	_______ in demand deposits

c. Assume that banks in Minnewaska always keep themselves fully loaned up. Suppose, also, that anyone receiving a loan deposits the proceeds in one of Minnewaska's banks, and anyone paying off a loan withdraws the amount due from one of Minnewaska's banks. Still supposing that the required reserve ratio is 0.2, complete the following table to trace the impact of the Fed's action throughout the banking system. (Note that the last column indicates *cumulative* change, as in the text.)

Round	Change in Demand Deposits at This Bank	Change in Demand Deposits at All Banks
First Bank of Minnewaska	_____	_____
Bank 2	_____	_____
Bank 3	_____	_____
Bank 4	_____	_____
Bank 5	_____	_____
Bank 6	_____	_____
Bank 7	_____	_____
Bank 8	_____	_____
...		
All Other Banks	_____	_____

d. As each bank in turn (makes new loans/calls in old loans) it (creates/extinguishes) demand deposits. In the end, the cumulative effect of all banks' actions, together, is a multiple (increase/decrease) in Minnewaska's money supply equal to _____________ times the original change in reserves

5. Information on banking systems in six different countries has been arranged in the table below. The last three columns report the eventual change in the country's money supply resulting from open market sales or purchases by the country's central bank in the amounts indicated. Assume that all commercial banks remain always fully loaned up, and that cash in the hands of the public does not change.

Country	*RRR*	Demand Deposit Multiplier	*Change in Money Supply due to Open Market:* *Sale of* $200	*Purchase of* $100	*Sale of* $400
1	0.1	_____	_____	_____	–4,000
2	0.2	_____	_____	_____	_____
3	_____	2.5	_____	_____	_____
4	_____	_____	–400	_____	–800
5	0.8	_____	_____	125	_____
6	_____	1.0	–200	_____	_____

a. Complete the table.

b. If the central bank in Country 2 wants to increase the money supply by $1000, it must (increase/decrease) reserves by the amount of ______________ dollars. One way to do this is through open market (sales/purchases). Alternatively, the central bank could achieve the same increase in the money supply by an appropriate (increase/decrease) in the required reserve ratio, or an appropriate (increase/decrease) in the discount rate. However, if the central bank chooses to use open market operations to increase the money supply by $1000, it will be required to (buy/sell) securities from the public in the amount of ______________ dollars.

c. If the central bank in Country 4 wants to decrease the money supply by $1,000, it must (increase/decrease) reserves by the amount of ______________ dollars. One way to do this is through open market (sales/purchases). Alternatively, the central bank could achieve the same decrease in the money supply by an appropriate (increase/decrease) in the required reserve ratio, or an appropriate (increase/decrease) in the discount rate. However, if the central bank chooses to use open market operations to decrease the money supply by $1,000, it will be required to (buy/sell) securities from the public in the amount of ______________ dollars.

15-MINUTE PRACTICE TEST

Set a timer, giving yourself just 15 minutes to answer all of the following questions. To see what you *really* know and remember, take the test at least a day *after* you've read the chapter in the text and completed the exercises in this study guide.

Multiple Choice: Circle the letter in front of the single, best answer.

1. Which of the following assets is the most liquid?
   a. Checking account funds
   b. Government bonds
   c. Money market funds
   d. Real estate
   e. Rare stamps

2. Which of the following assets are included in the M1 measure of the money supply?
   a. Checking account funds
   b. Cash in a bank's vault
   c. Reserves that banks hold at the Fed
   d. All of the above
   e. None of the above

3. Which of the following items would *not* be listed on a bank's balance sheet?
   a. The bank's net worth
   b. Property and buildings that the bank owns
   c. Loans the bank has made to others
   d. Government bonds in the bank's possession
   e. The bank's income during the year

4. If the required reserve ratio is 0.10, and a bank has $10 million in customer demand deposits, then its required reserves are
   a. $100,000.
   b. $90,000.
   c. $1 million.
   d. $9 million.
   e. $10 million.

5. Which of the following is a member of the Federal Open Market Committee?
   a. The President of the New York Federal Reserve Bank
   b. The U.S. Secretary of the Treasury
   c. The President of the United States
   d. The Majority Leader of the U.S. Senate
   e. All of the above

6. Which of the following would tend to *increase* the U.S. money supply?
   a. An increase in the discount rate
   b. A decrease in the required reserve ratio
   c. A sale of government bonds by the FOMC
   d. All of the above
   e. None of the above

7. When a bank makes a loan, the bank's balance sheet will immediately show
   a. an increase in both assets and liabilities.
   b. a decrease in both assets and liabilities.
   c. an increase in assets and a decrease in liabilities.
   d. an increase and a decrease in assets.
   e. an increase and a decrease in liabilities.

8. Under the simple assumptions of the chapter (that the public does not change its holdings of cash, and that banks do not hold excess reserves), if the required reserve ratio is 0.2, and the Fed purchases $10 million in government bonds, then the money supply will
   a. decrease by $2 million.
   b. decrease by $5 million.
   c. increase by $2 million.
   d. increase by $5 million.
   e. increase by $50 million.

9. One important reason that banking panics have been eliminated in the United States since the Great Depression is that
   a. banks are more free today than in the 1930s to lend as they see fit.
   b. all commercial banks are now strictly regulated by individual states, rather than loosely regulated by the Federal government.
   c. the FDIC insures customer deposits.
   d. the government stands ready to suspend all banking activity at a moment's notice.
   e. all of the above.

10. The most common method used by the Fed to change the money supply is
    a. changes in the discount rate.
    b. alterations of FDIC regulations.
    c. changes in the required reserve ratio.
    d. open market operations.
    e. sales and purchases of gold.

True/False: For each of the following statements, circle T if the statement is true or F if the statement is false.

T F 1. The M2 measure of the money supply contains all of the assets in M1, plus some additional assets.

T F 2. A bank's balance sheet lists, among other items, the bank's income and expenses during the year.

T F 3. The U.S. President selects all of the members of the Federal Open Market Committee.

T F 4. An important function of the Fed is to supervise and regulate commercial banks.

T F 5. When the Fed sells government bonds, the money supply decreases.

T F 6. If banks increase their holdings of excess reserves as the money supply expands, the demand deposit multiplier will be larger than 1/RRR.

T F 7. Most economists argue that FDIC protection alone cannot eliminate banking panics; we must also eliminate banking regulation.

T F 8. The number of bank failures in the United States has steadily increased through the twentieth century.

CHAPTER 12

THE MONEY MARKET AND THE INTEREST RATE

SPEAKING ECONOMICS

Fill in each blank with the appropriate word or phrase from the list provided in the word bank. (For a challenge, fill in as many blanks as you can *without* using the word bank.)

_______________ 1. At any point in time, wealth is fixed.

_______________ 2. A curve indicating how much money will be willingly held at each interest rate.

_______________ 3. A line showing the total quantity of money in the economy at each interest rate.

_______________ 4. The amount of money households and firms are holding minus the amount demanded at a particular interest rate.

_______________ 5. The amount of bonds households and firms want to hold minus the amount they are actually holding at a particular interest rate.

_______________ 6. The interest rate charged for loans of reserves among banks.

Word Bank

excess demand for bonds
excess supply of money
federal funds rate
money demand curve
money supply curve
wealth constraint

CHAPTER HIGHLIGHTS

Fill in the blanks with the appropriate words or phrases. If you have difficulty, review the chapter and then try again.

1. An individual's quantity of money demanded is the amount of _______________ that the individual chooses to hold as money, rather than as other assets.

2. When you hold money, you bear an opportunity cost—the _______________ you could have earned.

3. In the chapter, we assume that individuals choose how to divide their wealth between two assets: (1) money, which can be used as a ____________________ but earns no ____________________; and (2) bonds, which earn ____________________, but cannot be used as a ____________________.

4. The (economy-wide) demand for money is the amount of total ____________________ in the economy that all households and businesses, together, choose to hold as ____________________ rather than as bonds.

5. A change in the ____________________ moves us along the money demand curve. A change in money demand caused by something other than a change in ____________________ (such as real income or the price level) will cause the curve to shift.

6. Open market purchases of bonds inject reserves into the banking system, and shift the money ____________________ curve to the ____________________ by a multiple of the reserve injection. Open market sales have the opposite effect: They withdraw reserves from the system and shift the money ____________________ curve to the ____________________ by a multiple of the reserve withdrawal.

7. _______________ in the money market occurs when the quantity of money people are actually holding (quantity supplied) is equal to the quantity of money they want to hold (quantity demanded).

8. When there is an excess supply of money in the economy, there is also an excess ____________________ for bonds.

9. When the price of bonds rises, the interest rate ____________________; when the price of bonds falls; the interest rate ____________________.

10. If the Fed increases the money supply by ____________________ government bonds, the interest rate ____________________. If the Fed decreases the money supply by ____________________ government bonds, the interest rate ____________________. By controlling the money supply through purchases and sales of bonds, the Fed can also control the interest rate.

11. When the Fed increases the money supply, the interest rate ____________________, and spending on three categories of goods increases: plant and equipment, new housing, and consumer ____________________ (especially automobiles). When the Fed decreases the money supply, the interest rate ____________________, and these categories of spending fall.

12. An increase in government purchases, which by itself shifts the aggregate expenditure line ____________________, also sets in motion forces that shift it ____________________.

13. In the short run, an increase in government purchases causes real GDP to rise, but not by as much as it would have risen if the ____________________ had not increased.

14. When effects in the money market are included in the short-run macro model, an increase in government purchases causes the interest rate to ____________________ and crowds out some private ____________________ spending. It may also crowd out consumption spending.

15. Increases in government purchases, investment, net exports and autonomous consumption, as well as decreases in taxes, all shift the aggregate expenditure line upward. Real GDP rises, but so does the ____________________, so the rise in equilibrium GDP is smaller than would occur if the ____________________ remained constant.

16. Decreases in government purchases, investment, and autonomous consumption, as well as increases in taxes, all shift the aggregate expenditure line downward. Real GDP falls, but so does the ____________________, so the decline in equilibrium GDP is smaller than would occur if the ____________________ remained constant.

17. Our view of the interest rate depends on the time period we are considering. In the long run, we view the interest rate as determined in the market for ____________________, where household saving is lent to businesses and the government. In the short run, we view the interest rate as determined in the ____________________ market, where wealth holders adjust their wealth between money and bonds, and the Fed participates by controlling the money supply.

18. A general expectation that interest rates will rise (i.e., that bond prices will ____________________) in the future will cause the money demand curve to shift ____________________ in the present. This will cause the interest rate to ____________________ in the present.

IMPORTANT CONCEPTS

Write a brief answer below each of the following items.

1. In the chapter, households must allocate their wealth between two types of assets. What are they?

   a.

   b.

2. Each of the following events shifts either the money demand or the money supply curve. For each event, write (1) which curve shifts and (2) whether it shifts rightward or leftward.

   a. Income decreases

   b. The Fed sells government bonds to bond dealers

   c. The Fed lowers the required reserve ratio

   d. People *expect* the interest rate to rise in the near future

   e. People *expect* the Fed to increase the money supply in the near future

   f. The government reduces taxes

3. Suppose that neither consumption spending nor investment spending were influenced by changes in the interest rate. How would this affect the Fed's ability to change GDP by using monetary policy?

4. Suppose the Fed *decreases* the money supply. State whether each of the following will increase, decrease, or remain unchanged.

   a. GDP _______________

   b. The interest rate _______________

   c. The price of bonds _______________

   d. Investment spending _______________

   e. Consumption spending _______________

   f. The quantity of money demanded _______________

SKILLS AND TOOLS

For each of the following items, follow the instructions, write the correct answer in the blank, or circle the correct answer.

1. Suppose the demand for money is given by

$$M^d = 750 - 50r$$

where M^d is the quantity of money demanded (in billions of dollars) and r is the interest rate in percentage points.

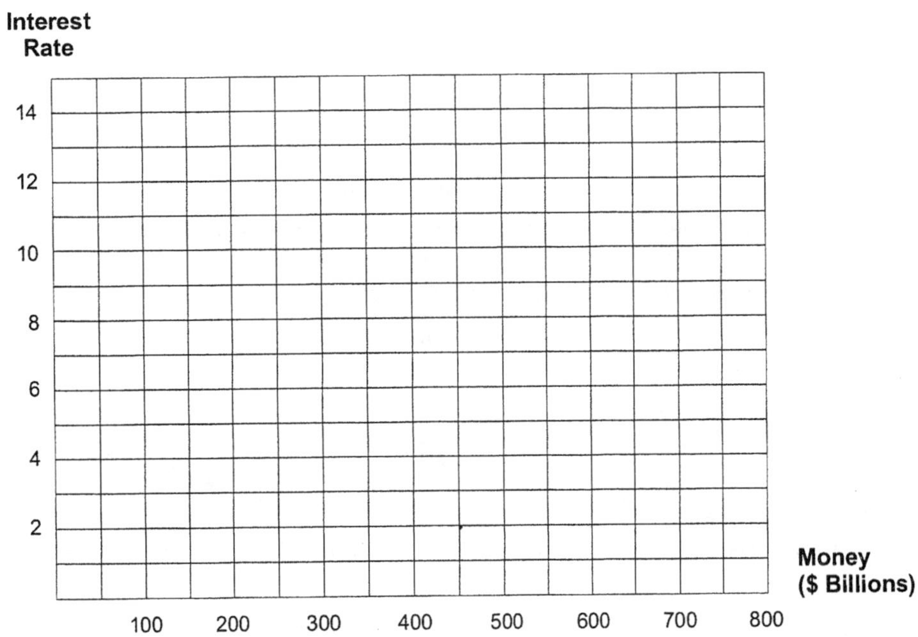

   a. Plot the money demand curve on the grid provided.

b. Plot the money supply curve if the Fed sets the money supply at $400 billion.

c. At an interest rate of 12%, the quantity of money demanded is (greater than/less than) the quantity of money supplied. There is (excess demand/excess supply) in the money market equal to dollars. This implies that when the interest rate is 12%, there is (excess demand/excess supply) in the bond market equal to _______________ billion dollars. In response, as people try to (buy more/sell more) bonds, the price of bonds will (rise/fall). As it does, the interest rate in the money market will (rise/fall).

d. At an interest rate of 4%, the quantity of money demanded is (greater than/less than) the quantity of money supplied. There is (excess demand/excess supply) in the money market equal to _______________ dollars. This implies that when the interest rate is 4%, there is (excess demand/excess supply) in the bond market equal to _______________ dollars. As people try to (buy more/sell more) bonds, the price of bonds will (rise/fall). As it does, the interest rate in the money market will (rise/fall).

e. The equilibrium interest rate is _______________ percent. At this rate of interest, the quantity of money people want to hold is (less than/equal to/greater than) the amount of money in circulation. At the same time, the bond market is in (equilibrium/disequilibrium). We can infer that the quantity of bonds people want to hold at the prevailing price of bonds is (greater than/equal to/less than) the quantity of bonds available.

2. The demand for money is

$$M^d = 650 - 50r$$

where M^d is the quantity of money demanded (in billions of dollars) and r is the interest rate in percentage points. The money supply has been set at

$$M^S{}_1 = \$250 \text{ billion.}$$

Suppose that all demand deposits are held in commercial banks, and that all commercial banks are subject to fractional reserve requirements where the required reserve ratio is

$$RRR = 0.5.$$

a. On the grid on the following page, plot the money demand and money supply curves. What is the equilibrium interest rate? _______________

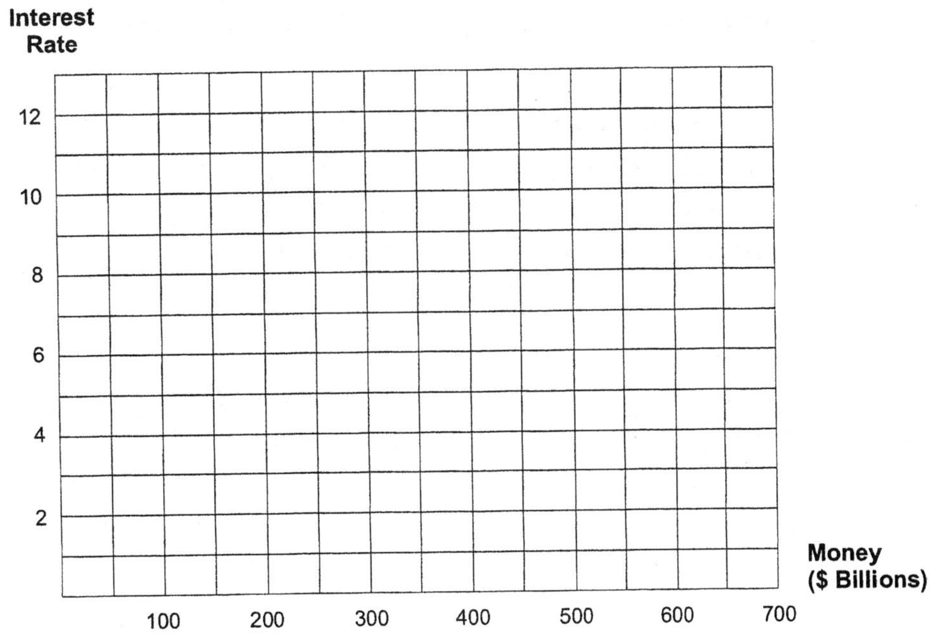

b. The Fed has decided it wants the interest rate to be 4%. To achieve that interest rate, the Fed must (increase/decrease) the money supply by ______________ billion, from its current level of M^S_1 = \$250 billion to a new level of ______________ billion dollars. If the Fed decides to use open market operations to change the money supply, it will have to (buy/sell) bonds. With $RRR = 0.5$ the demand deposit multiplier is ______________. Thus, to achieve an interest rate of 4% the Fed will have to (buy/sell) bonds in the amount ______________ billion.

c. Illustrate your answer to (b) by plotting the new money supply curve. Label your curve M^S_2.

d. Wait a minute. They changed their minds: the Fed would really rather the interest rate were 10%. To achieve that interest rate, the Fed must (increase/decrease) the money supply by ______________ billion, from its current level of M^S_1 = \$250 billion to a new level of ______________ billion. If the Fed decides to use open market operations to change the money supply, it will have to (buy/sell) bonds. With $RRR = 0.5$ the demand deposit multiplier is ______________. Thus, to achieve an interest rate of 10% the Fed will have to (buy/sell) bonds in the amount of ______________ billion.

e. Illustrate your answer to (d) by plotting the new money supply curve. Label your curve M^S_3.

3. In **Panel A**, the money market is in equilibrium at an interest rate of 6%. In **Panel B**, aggregate expenditure at an interest rate of 6% intersects the "45-degree" translator line where real GDP is $4,500 billion.

Panel A

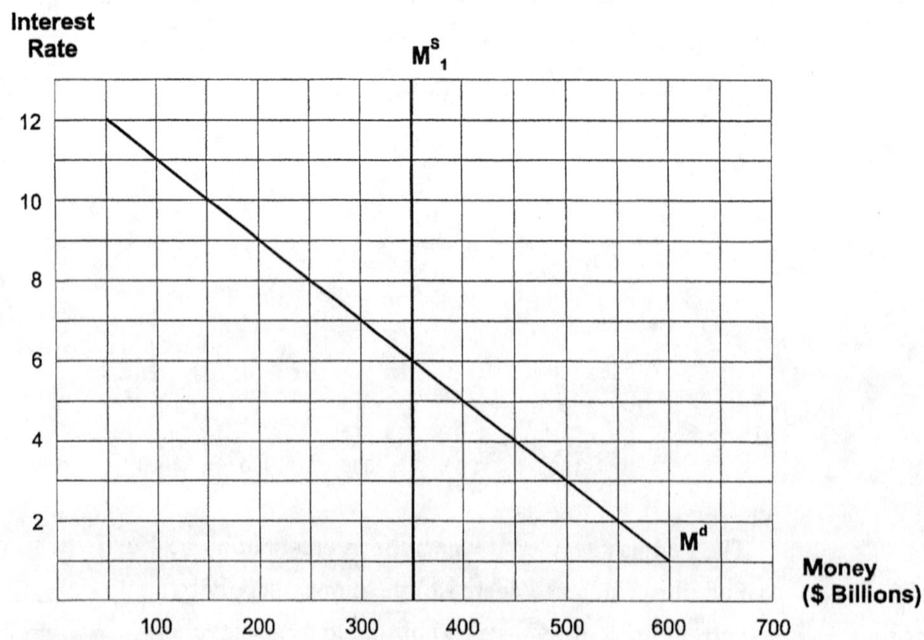

Panel B

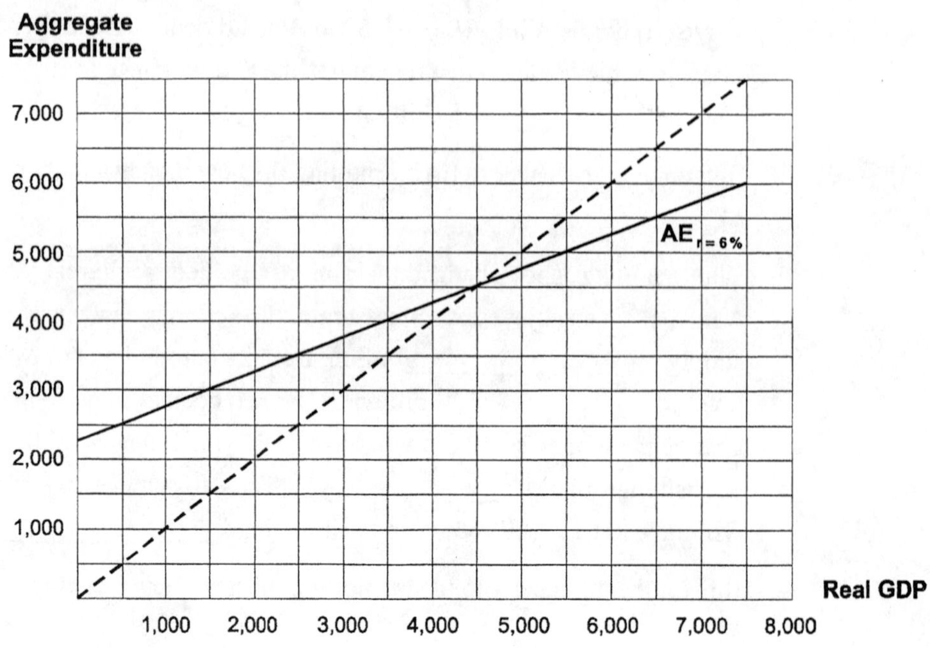

a. Suppose the Fed decides to reduce the money supply to $200 billion. As the money supply curve shifts (leftward/rightward), the equilibrium interest rate will (rise/fall) to ______________ percent. This (increase/decrease) in the equilibrium interest rate will tend to (increase/decrease) interest-sensitive spending such as (consumption/ consumption and planned investment/government purchases and planned investment). These spending changes will shift the aggregate expenditure line (upward/downward) in the Panel B. Equilibrium GDP will therefore (increase/decrease) by (the same amount as/a multiple of/a fraction of) that change in spending. This change in equilibrium GDP will, itself, cause further changes in the money market. Specifically, we would expect that this change in GDP will (increase/decrease) money (supply/demand), causing the equilibrium interest rate to (rise/fall).

b. Suppose that as a result of all the actions described in part (a), the new equilibrium interest rate is 7%. On the grid, illustrate this new equilibrium in the money market.

c. Suppose that as a result of all the actions described in part (a), and given the interest rate of 7% as in part (d), the new equilibrium GDP is $2,500. Illustrate this new equilibrium by drawing in an appropriate new aggregate expenditure line parallel to the line $AE_{r=6\%}$. Label the new line $AE_{r=7\%}$.

d. The Fed's monetary policy eventually caused short-run equilibrium GDP to fall from $4,500 billion to $2,500 billion. With a careful look at the diagrams, we can see that the Fed's action caused interest sensitive spending to (rise/fall) by ______________ billion from its original level.

4. In **Panel C**, the money market is in equilibrium at an interest rate of 8%. In **Panel D**, aggregate expenditure at an interest rate of 8% intersects the "45-degree" translator line where real GDP is $150 billion.

Panel C

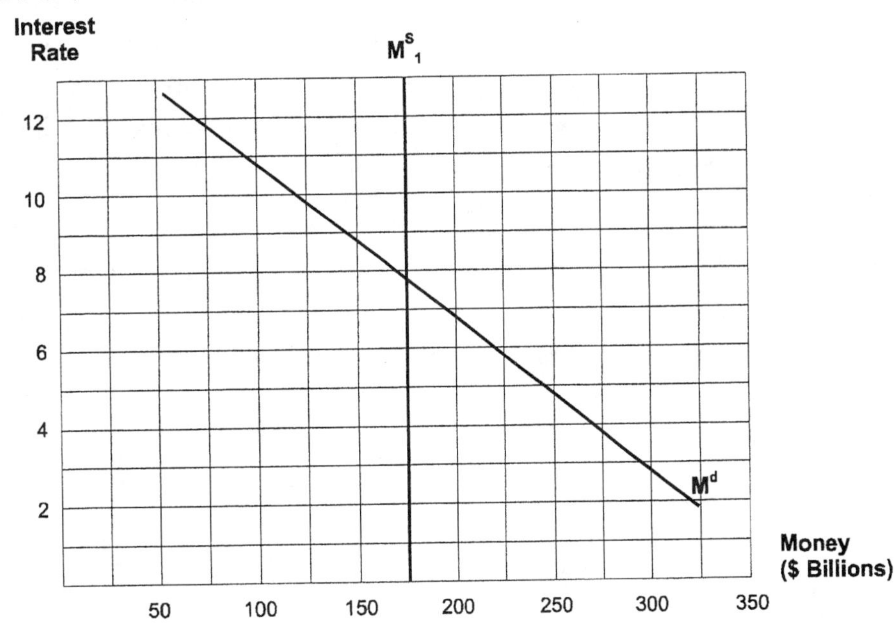

Panel D

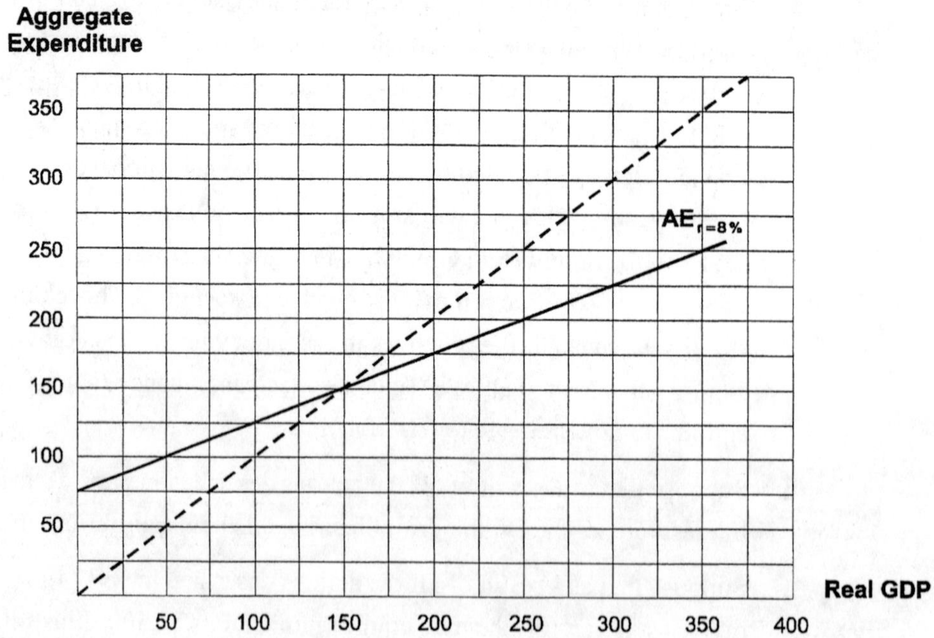

a. Suppose government purchases are increased by $75 billion. Assuming for the moment that this action has no impact whatsoever on the money market, the aggregate expenditure line in the Panel D would shift (upward/downward) by exactly ____________ billion at every level of real GDP. Equilibrium GDP would then rise from ____________ billion to ____________ billion. Draw in a dashed line to illustrate an *AE* curve consistent with the situation just described.

b. We know, however, that any change in GDP as described in part (a) will normally have an affect on the money market. In general, increases in GDP will (increase/decrease) money (demand/supply), shifting the money (demand/supply) curve (leftward/rightward). As a result, the interest rate will (rise/fall) in the money market. This change in the interest rate, all other thing equal, will cause a(n) (increase/decrease) in interest-sensitive spending. This would be reflected by a(n) (upward/downward) shift in the dashed *AE* line drawn in part (a).

c. Suppose that after all effects have been accounted for, the new short-run equilibrium level of GDP is $250 billion and the interest rate is 10 percent. Illustrate this in the Panel C with the appropriate shift in the money demand or money supply curve, and in the Panel D with an appropriate *AE* curve parallel to the one you drew for part (a).

d. From a careful look at the diagrams, we can see that the original $75 billion increase in government purchases caused the interest rate to (rise/fall) which, in turn, (crowded out/stimulated additional) private investment and consumption spending in the amount of _______________ billion. Had there been no affect on the money market, the $75 billion increase in government purchases would have increased equilibrium GDP from _______________ billion to _______________ billion. However, when we take account of the impact on the market and the equilibrium interest rate, equilibrium GDP rose, instead, from _______________ billion to _______________ billion. Thus, when we take account of the impact increased spending and income will have on the money market, we can see that fiscal policy (will still cause GDP to rise but by a smaller multiple of any given change in spending/cannot cause GDP to change at all).

15-MINUTE PRACTICE TEST

Set a timer, giving yourself just 15 minutes to answer all of the following questions. To see what you *really* know and remember, take the test at least a day *after* you've read the chapter in the text and completed the exercises in this study guide.

Multiple Choice: Circle the letter in front of the single best answer.

1. The opportunity cost of money is
   a. the time and trouble it takes to obtain money, such as the time it takes to go to an ATM machine and make a withdrawal.
   b. the risk that money can be lost or stolen.
   c. the interest that could have been earned if one's wealth were held in bonds, instead of money.
   d. the inconvenience of switching out of bonds and into money, and vice versa.
   e. all of the above.

2. The money demand curve slopes downward because a rise in the interest rate causes
   a. the Fed to decrease the quantity of money in circulation.
   b. bonds to become more attractive.
   c. the opportunity cost of holding money to decrease.
   d. investment spending to decrease.
   e. consumption spending to decrease.

3. The money supply curve
   a. slopes downward, because the Fed increases the money supply whenever the interest rate falls.
   b. slopes downward, because the Fed decreases the money supply whenever the interest rate falls.
   c. slopes upward, because a rise in the interest rate makes people want to hold more of their wealth in the form of money.
   d. slopes upward, because a rise in the interest rate makes people want to hold less of their wealth in the form of money.
   e. is vertical, because the Fed sets the money supply at whatever level it wants to.

4. If there is an excess demand for money, then
    a. there is also an excess supply of bonds.
    b. the interest rate is lower than its equilibrium value.
    c. the interest rate will rise.
    d. all of the above.
    e. none of the above.

5. Monetary policy works as follows: when the Fed purchases government bonds,
    a. the money supply decreases, the interest rate rises, and investment spending falls.
    b. the money supply increases, the interest rate rises, and investment spending falls.
    c. the money supply decreases, the interest rate falls, and investment spending rises.
    d. the money supply increases, the interest rate falls, and investment spending rises.
    e. the money supply decreases, the interest rate falls, and investment spending falls.

6. When we include the money market with the short-run macro model, an increase in government purchases causes
    a. GDP to increase.
    b. the interest rate to increase.
    c. the demand for money to increase.
    d. all of the above.
    e. none of the above.

7. When we add the money market to the short-run macro model,
    a. fiscal policy becomes completely ineffective in changing GDP.
    b. fiscal policy becomes less effective in changing GDP.
    c. monetary policy becomes completely ineffective in changing GDP.
    d. fiscal policy becomes even more effective in changing GDP.
    e. fiscal policy can change GDP, but not the interest rate.

8. If the Fed keeps the money supply unchanged, an increase in government purchases will cause
    a. the interest rate to rise.
    b. GDP to increase.
    c. investment spending to fall.
    d. all of the above.
    e. none of the above.

9. If people suddenly expect the interest rate to fall in the future, then currently,
    a. the money demand curve will shift leftward.
    b. the money supply curve will shift leftward.
    c. the price of bonds will fall.
    d. all of the above.
    e. none of the above.

10. If the Fed announces that it is about to dramatically decrease the money supply, then currently,
    a. the interest rate will fall.
    b. the money demand curve will shift leftward.
    c. the money supply curve will shift rightward.
    d. all of the above.
    e. none of the above.

True/False: For each of the following statements, circle T if the statement is true or F if the statement is false.

T F 1. The money demand curve is vertical because the Fed determines how much money is circulating in the economy.

T F 2. A rise in the interest rate causes the money demand curve to shift leftward.

T F 3. When there is an excess supply of money in the economy, there is also an excess supply of bonds.

T F 4. When bond prices rise, the interest rate falls.

T F 5. If the Fed keeps the money supply unchanged, a decrease in government purchases causes the interst rate to drop.

T F 6. Equilibrium in the money market occurs when the total quantity of money people are actually holding is equal to the total quantity of money that people want to hold.

T F 7. If the Fed sells government bonds, the interest rate will fall.

T F 8. When we include the effects of the money market, an increase in government purchases causes real GDP to rise by even more than when we ignore the money market.

CHAPTER 13

AGGREGATE DEMAND AND AGGREGATE SUPPLY

SPEAKING ECONOMICS

Fill in each blank with the appropriate word or phrase from the list provided in the word bank. (For a challenge, fill in as many blanks as you can *without* using the word bank.)

______________________ 1. A curve indicating equilibrium GDP at each price level.

______________________ 2. A curve indicating the price level consistent with firms' unit costs and markups for any level of output over the short run.

______________________ 3. A combination of price level and GDP consistent with both the AD and AS curves.

______________________ 4. Any event that causes the AD curve to shift.

______________________ 5. Any event that causes the AS curve to shift.

______________________ 6. The adjustment process through which price and wage changes return the economy to full-employment output in the long run.

______________________ 7. A vertical line indicating all possible output and price-level combinations at which the economy could end up in the long run.

______________________ 8. The combination of falling output and rising prices.

Word Bank

aggregate demand curve (AD) curve
aggregate supply (AS) curve
demand shock
long-run aggregate supply curve
self-correcting mechanism
short-run macroeconomic equilibrium
stagflation
supply shock

CHAPTER HIGHLIGHTS

Fill in the blanks with the appropriate words or phrases. If you have difficulty, review the chapter and then try again.

1. A rise in the price level causes a(n) ____________________ in equilibrium GDP. The aggregate demand (AD) curve tells us the equilibrium real GDP at any ____________________.

2. When a change in ____________________ causes equilibrium GDP to change, we move along the AD curve. Whenever anything other than ____________________ causes equilibrium GDP to change, the AD curve itself shifts.

3. The AD curve shifts rightward when government purchases, ____________________ spending, net exports or autonomous ____________________ spending increases, or when ____________________ decrease.

4. The AD curve shifts leftward when government purchases, ____________________ spending, net exports or autonomous ____________________ spending decreases, or when ____________________ increase.

5. A(n) ____________________ in the money supply shifts the AD curve rightward.
A(n) ____________________ in the money supply shifts the AD curve leftward.

6. In the chapter, it is assumed that a firm sets the price of its products as a markup over ____________________.

7. The average percentage ____________________ in the economy is determined by competitive conditions in the economy. The competitive structure of the economy changes very slowly, so the average percentage ____________________ should be somewhat stable from year to year.

8. In the short run, the price level ____________________ when there is an economy-wide increase in unit costs, and the price level ____________________ when there is an economy-wide decrease in unit costs.

9. For a year or so after a change in output, changes in the average nominal ____________________ are less important than other forces that change unit costs.

10. In the chapter, it is assumed that changes in output have no effect on the nominal ____________________ in the short run.

11. In the short run, a rise in real GDP, by causing unit costs to __________________, will also cause the price level to __________________. In the short run, a fall in real GDP, by causing unit costs to __________________, will also cause the price level to __________________.

12. The aggregate supply curve (or AS curve) tells us the __________________ consistent with firms' unit costs and their percentage markup at any level of __________________ over the short run.

13. When a change in __________________ causes the price level to change, we move along the AS curve. When anything other than a change in __________________ causes the price level to change, the AS curve itself shifts.

14. An event that causes the AD curve to shift is called a __________________. An event that causes the AS curve to shift is called a __________________.

15. When government purchases increase, the horizontal shift of the __________________ curve measures how much real GDP would increase if the price level remained constant. But because the price level rises, real GDP rises by __________________ than the horizontal shift in the __________________ curve.

16. A positive demand shock—one that shifts the AD curve __________________—causes both real GDP and the price level to __________________ in the short run. A negative demand shock—one that shifts the AD curve __________________—causes both real GDP and the price level to __________________ in the short run.

17. In the short run, we treat the wage rate as given. But in the long run, the wage rate can change. When output is above full employment, the wage rate will __________________, shifting the AS curve __________________. When output is below full employment, the wage rate will __________________, shifting the AS curve __________________.

18. If a demand shock pulls the economy away from full employment, changes in the wage rate and the price level will eventually cause the economy to correct itself and return to __________________ output.

19. Whenever a demand shock pulls the economy away from full employment, the __________________ mechanism will eventually bring it back. When output exceeds its full-employment level, wages will eventually __________________, causing a(n) __________________ in the price level and a(n) __________________ in real GDP until full employment is restored. When output is less than its full-employment level, wages will eventually __________________, causing a(n) __________________ in the price level and a(n) __________________ in real GDP until full employment is restored.

20. The self-correcting mechanism shows us that, in the ________________ run, the economy will eventually behave as the classical model predicts.

21. In the short run, a negative supply shock shifts the AS curve ________________, decreasing output and ________________ the price level. A negative supply shock causes stagflation in the short run. A positive supply shock shifts the AS curve ________________, increasing output and ________________ the price level.

22. In the long run, the economy self-corrects after a supply shock, just as it does after a demand shock. When output differs from its full-employment level, the wage rate changes, and the ________________ curve shifts until full employment is restored.

IMPORTANT CONCEPTS

Write a brief answer below each of the following items.

1. Indicate whether each of the following increases, decreases or remains the same as we move *rightward* along an AD curve.

   a. output ________________

   b. the price level ________________

   c. the money supply ________________

   d. the demand for money at any interest rate ________________

   e. the interest rate ________________

   f. investment spending ________________

   g. government purchases ________________

2. State whether each of the following increases, decreases or remains the same as we move *rightward* along an AS curve.

   a. output ________________

   b. the price level ________________

   c. the average percentage markup in the economy ________________

   d. the prices of inputs ________________

   e. firms' unit costs ________________

   f. the average nominal wage rate ________________

3. For each of the following, state which curve shifts (AD or AS) and in which direction (rightward, leftward, upward or downward).

   a. an increase in government purchases ______________

   b. an increase in taxes ______________

   c. an increase in the money supply ______________

   d. an increase in autonomous consumption spending ______________

   e. an increase in world oil prices ______________

   f. an increase in the average nominal wage ______________

   g. a decrease in firms' average percentage markup ______________

4. In the table below, identify the *short run* impact of each event on each variable by entering *increase*, *decrease*, or *no change*.

	Event		
Short run effect on:	**the money supply decreases**	**government purchases decrease**	**world oil prices decrease**
the price level	______	______	______
output	______	______	______
average nominal wage	______	______	______

5. In the table below, identify the *long run* impact of each event on each variable by entering *increase*, *decrease*, or *remains unchanged*. Assume that the economy begins at full-employment output. Remember to think only about *long run* effects in this table.

	Event		
Long run effect on:	**the money supply decreases**	**government purchases decrease**	**world oil prices decrease**
the price level	______	______	______
output	______	______	______
average nominal wage	______	______	______

SKILLS AND TOOLS

For each of the following items, follow the instructions, write the correct answer in the blank, or circle the correct answer.

1. The price level in the economy is 100 and the money supply is $550 billion. Money demand depends on the interest rate and is given by the equation

$$M^d = 1050 - 50r$$

where r is the interest rate in percentage points and M^d is billions of dollars demanded.

(a)
Money Market

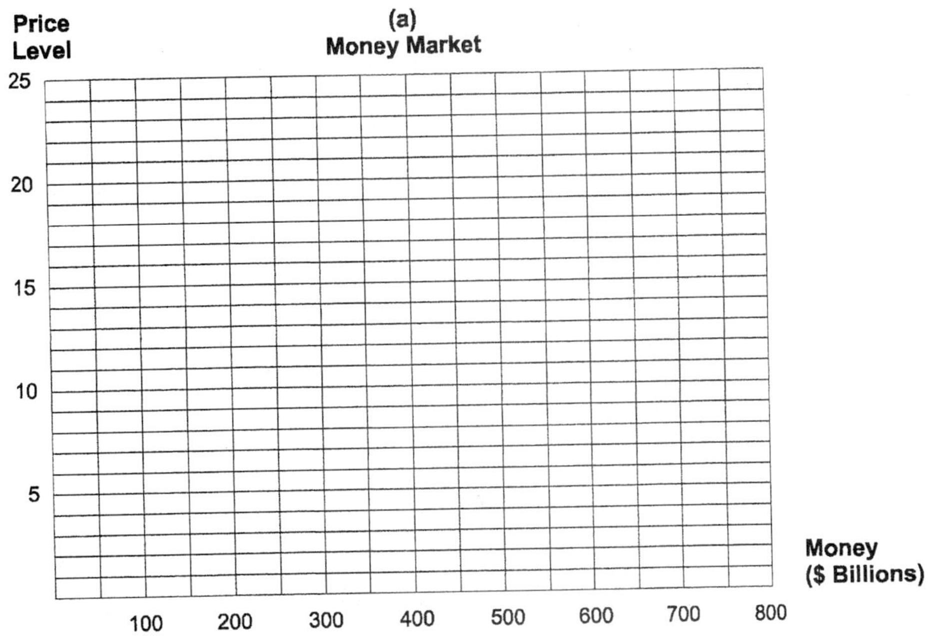

(b)
Aggregate Expenditure

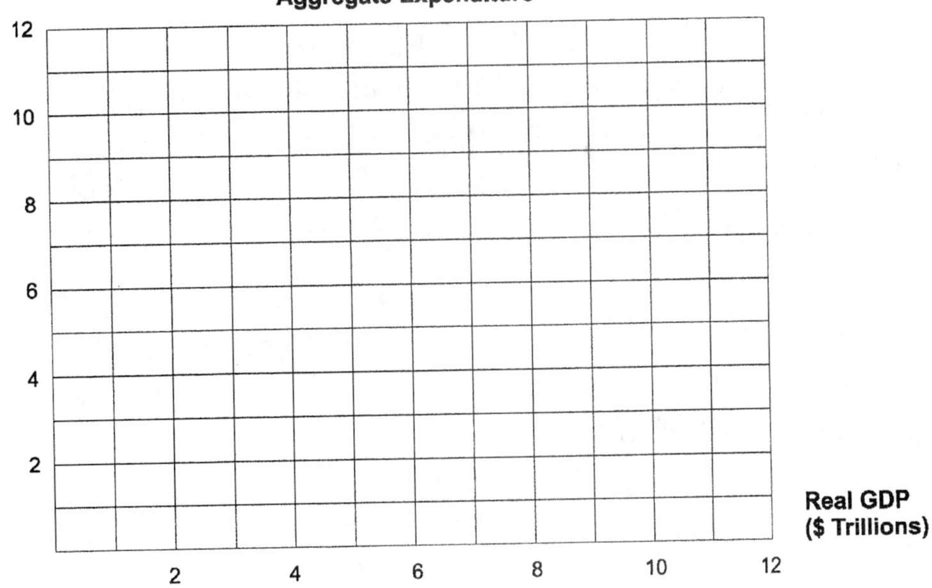

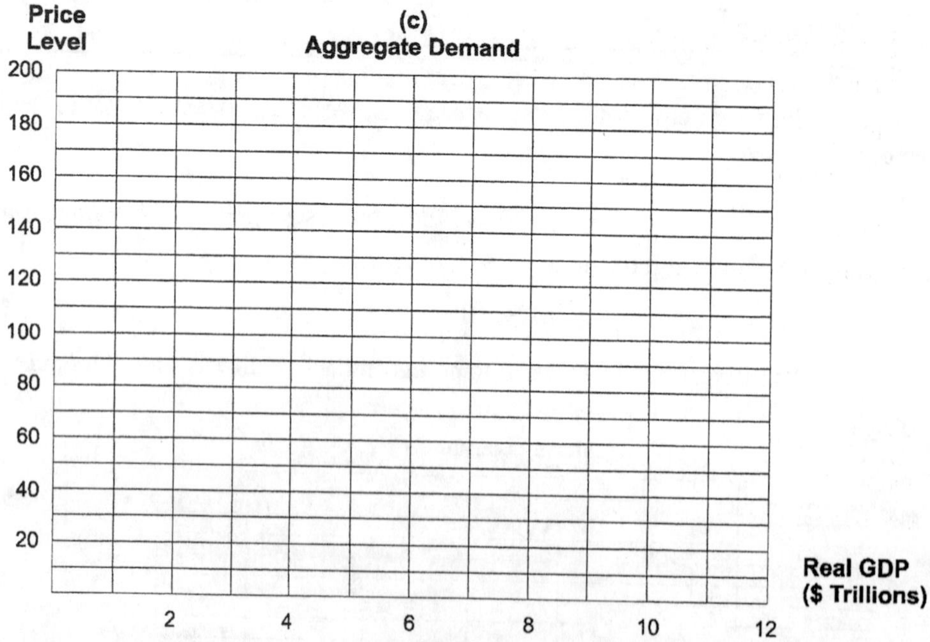

a. Plot money supply and money demand in panel (a), and label them M^S and $M^d_{P=100}$, respectively. The money market is in equilibrium when the interest rate is ________________.

b. At the interest rate from part (a), aggregate expenditure is given by the equation

$$AE = 3 + .5Y$$

where Y is the level of real GDP in trillions of dollars and AE is aggregate expenditure. Plot aggregate expenditure in panel (b) and label it $AE_{r=10\%}$.

c. At a price level of 100, equilibrium real GDP is ________________. Plot this point in panel (c) and label it *A*.

d. Suppose the price level increases to 130. In the money market, this will result in a (rightward/leftward) shift in the (money demand curve/money supply curve).

e. Suppose the shift described in part (d) is in the amount of $100 billion at every level of the interest rate. Plot the new money demand curve in panel (a) and label it $M^D_{P=130}$. The shift in the money demand curve will (increase/decrease) the interest rate to ________________ percent.

f. The new interest rate causes interest sensitive spending to (rise/fall) and causes the aggregate expenditure line to shift (upward/downward) at every level of real GDP.

g. Suppose the shift described in part (f) is in the amount of $1 trillion at every level of real GDP. Plot the new aggregate expenditure line in panel (b) and label it $AE_{r=12\%}$. Through the multiplier process, equilibrium real GDP will (increase/decrease) to ________________ trillion.

h. Looking back over questions (d) – (g), we can see that as the price level increases from 100 to 130, equilibrium real GDP (increases/decreases) from _______________ trillion to _______________ trillion. Plot the new point in panel (c) corresponding to a price level of 130 and label it *B*.

i. Suppose the price level decreases from 100 to 70. In the money market, this will result in a (rightward/leftward) shift in the (money demand curve/money supply curve).

j. Suppose the shift described in part (i) is in the amount of $100 billion at every level of the interest rate. Plot the new money demand curve in panel (a) and label it $M^D_{P=70}$. The shift in the money demand curve will (increase/decrease) the interest rate to _______________ percent.

k. The new interest rate causes interest sensitive spending to (rise/fall) and causes the aggregate expenditure line to shift (upward/downward) at every level of real GDP.

l. Suppose the shift described in part (k) is in the amount of $1 trillion at every level of real GDP. Plot the new aggregate expenditure line in panel (b) and label it $AE_{r=8\%}$. Though the multiplier process, equilibrium real GDP will (increase/decrease) to _______________ trillion.

m. Looking back over questions (i) – (l), we can see that as the price level decreases from 100 to 70, equilibrium real GDP (increases/decreases) from _______________ trillion to _______________ trillion. Plot the new point corresponding to a price level of 70 in panel (c) and label it *C*.

n. Connecting points *A*, *B*, and *C*, draw a curve in panel (c) that represents the *AD* curve for this economy.

2. The economy currently has an output of $7 trillion and a price level of 100.

   a. Plot this point in the grid on the following page and label it *A*.

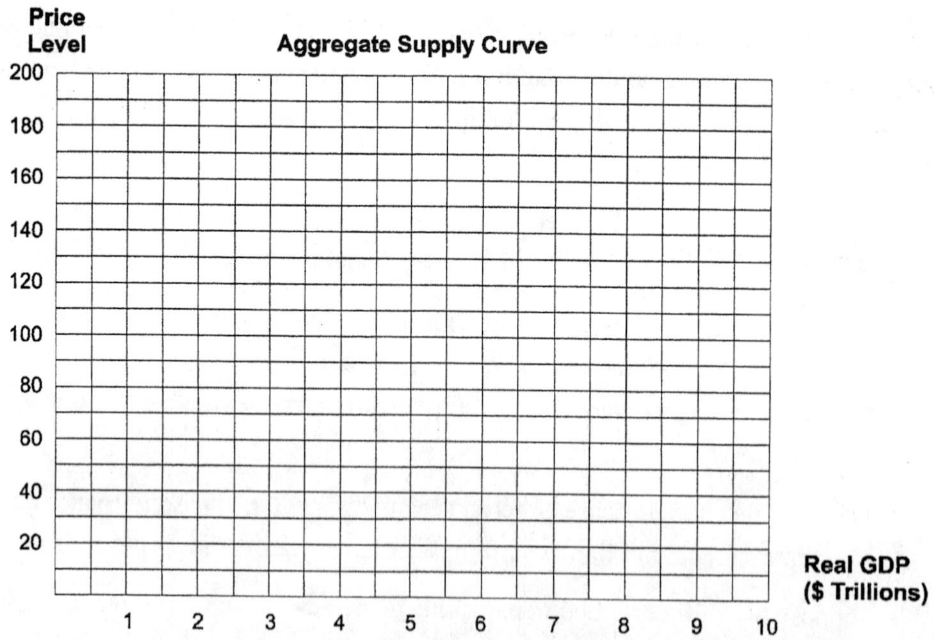

b. Suppose that the economy's real GDP increases from $7 trillion to $8.5 trillion. As a result of the increase in output, (greater/smaller) amounts of labor, capital, land, and raw materials are needed to produced each unit of output. As demand for these inputs (increases/decreases), the price of non-labor inputs will (increase/decrease). This causes unit costs to (increase/decrease). As long as the average percentage markup in the economy remains somewhat stable, the (rise/fall) in unit costs will lead firms to (raise/lower) their prices, and the price level will (increase/decrease).

c. Suppose the increase in real GDP described in part (b) changes the price level by 40. Plot the new point corresponding to a real GDP of $8.5 trillion in the space above and label it *B*.

d. Suppose that the economy's real GDP decreases from $7 trillion to $6 trillion. As a result of the decrease in output, (greater/smaller) amounts of labor, capital, land, and raw materials are needed to produced each unit of output. As demand for these inputs (increases/decreases), the price of non-labor inputs will (increase/decrease). This causes unit costs to (increase/decrease). As long as the average percentage markup in the economy remains somewhat stable, the (rise/fall) in unit costs will lead firms to (raise/lower) their prices, and the price level will (increase/decrease).

e. Suppose the decrease in real GDP described in part (d) changes the price level by 20. Plot the new point corresponding to a real GDP of $6 trillion in the space above and label it *C*.

f. Connecting points *A*, *B*, and *C*, draw a curve that represents the AS curve for this economy.

3. The full-employment output for some economy is \$6 trillion. Aggregate demand and aggregate supply depend on the price level, P, according to the following equations:

$$\text{Aggregate Demand: } AD = 16 - P/10$$

$$\text{Aggregate Supply: } AS = P/10 - 4.$$

a. In the space provided, plot the AD curve, the AS curve, and full-employment output for this economy. Label them AD_1, AS_1, and Y_{FE}, respectively.

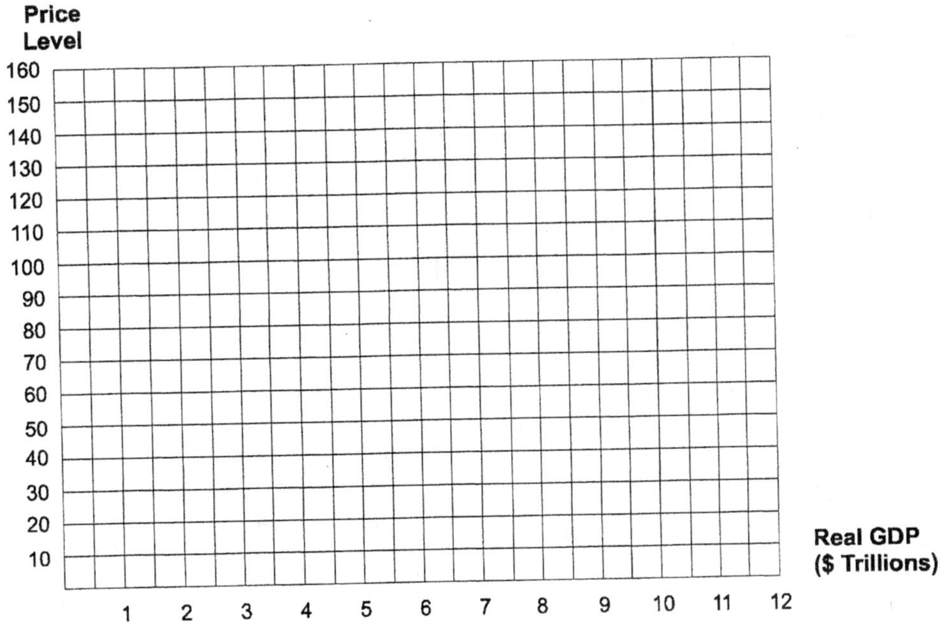

b. Is the economy in long-run equilibrium? (Yes/No). When the economy is in long-run equilibrium, the price level is ______________ and real GDP is ______________.

c. Suppose the Fed decreases the money supply through open market sales of bonds. This action will (increase/decrease) the interest rate, which will (increase/decrease) interest-sensitive consumption and investment spending. This results in an (increase/decrease) in real GDP and a (rightward/leftward) shift in the AD curve.

d. Suppose the shift described in part (c) is in the amount of \$4 trillion at every price level. Plot the new AD curve in the space above and label it AD_2.

e. As real GDP (increases/decreases), unit costs will (increase/decrease) and the price level will (increase/decrease). As a result, money demand will (increase/decrease) and the interest rate will (rise/fall). The new interest rate will cause interest-sensitive consumption and investment spending to (increase/decrease). Thus, overall, GDP will (increase/decrease) (more/less) than the original \$4 trillion shift in the AD curve.

f. In the new short-run equilibrium, real GDP is ______________ trillion and the price level is ______________.

g. In this short-run equilibrium, GDP is (above/below) its full-employment level. The unusually (high/low) unemployment rate drives the wage rate (up/down). As a result, the AS curve will shift (upward/downward) until a new long-run equilibrium is achieved. This will occur at a price level of _______________ and real GDP of _______________.

h. Plot the new AS curve described in part (g) and label it AS_2.

4. Copy onto the grid below the AD_1 curve, the AS_1 curve, and Y_{FE} from question (3).

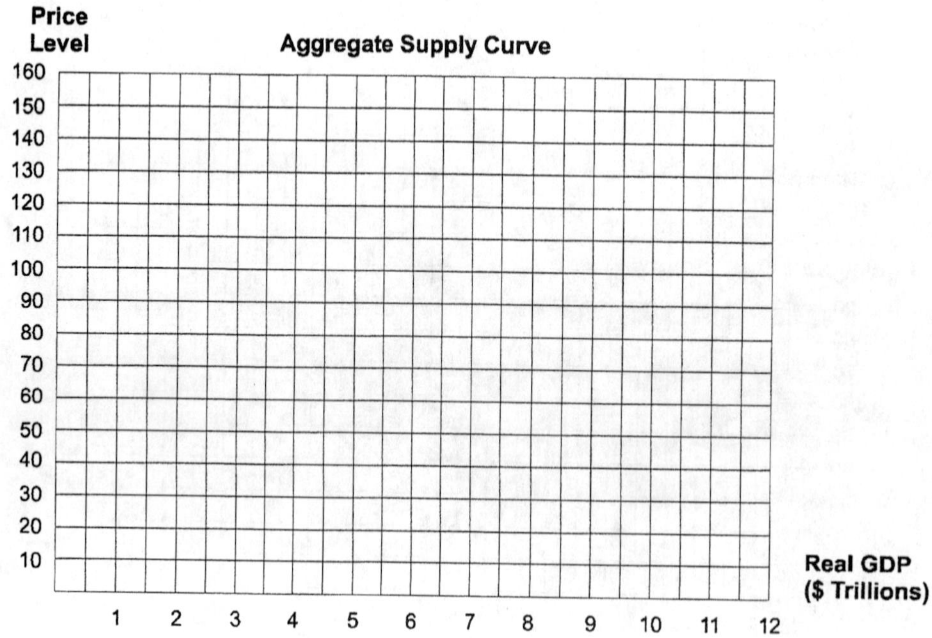

a. Suppose the economy experiences unusually good weather, resulting in bumper crop yields and falling agricultural prices. As a result, the price level will (increase/decrease) at every level of real GDP. This will shift the AS curve (upward/downward).

b. Suppose that the shift described in part (a) is in the amount of 20. Plot the new AS curve in the above grid and label it AS_2. The short-run equilibrium occurs at a price level of _______________ and real GDP of _______________.

c. Real GDP is now (above/below) the full-employment output for this economy. The unusually (high/low) unemployment rate drives the wage rate (up/down). As a result, the AS curve will shift (upward/downward) until a new long-run equilibrium is achieved. This occurs at a price level of _______________ and real GDP of _______________.

d. Plot the new *AS* curve described in part (c) and label it AS_3.

15-MINUTE PRACTICE TEST

Set a timer, giving yourself just 15 minutes to answer all of the following questions. To see what you *really* know and remember, take the test at least a day *after* you've read the chapter in the text and completed the exercises in this study guide.

Multiple Choice: Circle the letter in front of the single best answer.

1. At every point on the AD curve
   a. aggregate expenditure is equal to output.
   b. the demand for money is equal to the supply of money.
   c. the change in aggregate inventories is equal to zero.
   d. all of the above.
   e. none of the above.

2. A rise in the price level causes a
   a. rightward shift of the AD curve.
   b. leftward shift of the AD curve.
   c. movement rightward along the AD curve.
   d. movement leftward along the AD curve.
   e. leftward shift of the AD curve, as well as a movement leftward along the AD curve.

3. As we move rightward along the AD curve,
   a. the price level falls.
   b. the interest rate falls.
   c. investment spending increases.
   d. all of the above.
   e. none of the above.

4. According to the AS-AD model, the short-run effects of an increase in government spending include
   a. a rise in the interest rate.
   b. a fall in output.
   c. a fall in the price level.
   d. all of the above.
   e. none of the above.

5. According to the AS-AD model, the long-run effects of an increase in government spending include
   a. a drop in the interest rate.
   b. a rise in output.
   c. a rise in the price level.
   d. all of the above.
   e. none of the above.

6. The aggregate supply curve tells us
   a. the level of output at which aggregate expenditure equals output, for each possible price level.
   b. the price level consistent with firms' units costs and the average percentage markup, for each possible output level.
   c. the output level at which the demand for money is equal to the supply of money, for each possible price level.
   d. the output level at which investment spending is equal to household saving, for each possible price level.
   e. all of the above.

7. Which of the following would directly shift the AS curve upward?
   a. A decrease in the money supply
   b. An increase in the average nominal wage
   c. An increase in investment spending
   d. An increase in autonomous consumption spending
   e. An increase in output

8. Which of the following is an example of a positive demand shock?
   a. A decrease in the money supply
   b. An increase in world oil prices
   c. A decrease in world oil prices
   d. An increase in investment spending
   e. An increase in taxes

9. The long-run aggregate supply curve tells us that, in the long run,
   a. the higher the price level, the higher the level of output.
   b. the higher the level of output, the higher the interest rate.
   c. the greater the money supply, the lower the interest rate.
   d. demand shocks can affect the level of output, but not the price level.
   e. demand shocks can change the price level, but not the level of output.

10. In the short run, a negative supply shock—with no change in fiscal or monetary policy—will cause
    a. the price level to rise.
    b. output to fall.
    c. the interest rate to rise.
    d. all of the above.
    e. none of the above.

True/False: For each of the following statements, circle T if the statement is true or F if the statement is false.

T F 1. As we move rightward along the AD curve, output rises, firms units costs increase, and the price level rises.

T F 2. According to the aggregate demand curve, a rise in the price level causes a decrease in equilibrium real GDP.

T F 3. In the *short* run, a positive demand shock causes a rise in both the price level and real GDP.

T F 4. In the *long* run, a positive demand shock causes a rise in the price level, but no change in output.

T F 5. As the self-correcting mechanism brings the economy back to full employment after a positive demand shock, the average nominal wage in the economy falls.

T F 6. Stagflation occurs as part of the economy's self-correcting mechanism after a negative demand shock.

T F 7. The economy's aggregate supply curve can be obtained by summing up the supply curves for all the different products in the economy.

T F 8. If we wait long enough after a negative supply shock, the average nominal wage will fall and the economy will self correct back to full employment.

CHAPTER 14

INFLATION AND MONETARY POLICY

SPEAKING ECONOMICS

Fill in each blank with the appropriate word or phrase from the list provided in the word bank. (For a challenge, fill in as many blanks as you can *without* using the word bank.)

____________________ 1. The unemployment rate when there is no cyclical unemployment.

____________________ 2. When the Fed keeps the money supply constant regardless of shocks to the economy.

____________________ 3. When the Fed changes the money supply in response to economic shocks.

____________________ 4. The interest rate the Federal Reserve aims to achieve by adjusting the money supply.

____________________ 5. A curve indicating possible combinations of inflation and unemployment in the short run.

____________________ 6. A vertical line indicating that in the long run, unemployment must equal its natural rate, regardless of the rate of inflation.

Word Bank

active monetary policy
interest rate target
long-run Phillips curve
natural rate of unemployment
passive monetary policy
Phillips curve

CHAPTER HIGHLIGHTS

Fill in the blanks with the appropriate words or phrases. If you have difficulty, review the chapter and then try again.

1. When the unemployment rate is below the natural rate, GDP is ____________________ than potential output. The economy's self-correcting mechanism will then create inflation. When the unemployment rate is above the natural rate, GDP is ____________________ than potential output. The self-correcting mechanism will then put downward pressure on the price level.

2. To deal with money demand shocks, the Fed sets an interest rate target and changes the ____________________ as needed to maintain the target. In this way, the Fed can achieve its goals of ____________________ stability and full employment simultaneously.

3. To maintain full employment and ____________________ stability after a spending shock, the Fed must change its interest rate target. A positive spending shock requires a(n) ____________________ in the target; a negative spending shock requires a(n) ____________________ in the target.

4. When the Fed raises its interest rate target, stock and bond prices tend to ____________________; when it lowers its target, stock and bond prices tend to ____________________.

5. Good news about the economy sometimes leads to expectations that the Fed—fearing inflation—will ____________________ its interest rate target. This is why good economic news sometimes causes stock and bond prices to ____________________. Similarly, bad news about the economy sometimes leads to expectations that the Fed—fearing recession—will ____________________ its interest rate target. This is why bad economic news sometimes causes stock and bond prices to ____________________.

6. A negative supply shock presents the Fed with a short-run trade-off: it can limit the recession, but only at the cost of ____________________; and it can limit ____________________, but only at the cost of a deeper recession.

7. In response to a supply shock, inflation hawks lean more toward controlling ____________________, at the cost of greater ____________________. Inflation doves lean more toward limiting ____________________, at the cost of higher ____________________.

8. When inflation continues for some time, the public develops ____________________ that the inflation rate in the future will be similar to the inflation rate in the recent past. A continuing, stable rate of inflation gets built into the economy. The built-in rate is usually the rate that has existed for the past few years.

9. In an economy with built-in inflation, the AS curve will shift ____________________ each year, even when output is at full employment and unemployment is at its natural rate. The ____________________ shift of the AS curve will equal the built-in rate of inflation.

10. In the short run, the Fed can bring down the rate of inflation by reducing the rightward shift of the ____________________ curve, but only at the cost of creating a ____________________.

11. To neutralize a positive spending shock when there is built-in inflation, the Fed should ____________________ the interest rate target. This policy can maintain full employment, while keeping the rate of inflation equal to the built-in rate.

12. With built-in inflation, a negative supply shock causes a recession combined with a rise in the ____________________ rate. A ____________________ policy will lean toward reducing inflation at the cost of deepening the recession. A ____________________ policy will lean toward a milder recession, increasing the inflation rate.

13. The Phillips curve illustrates the economy's possible combinations of inflation and ____________________ in the short run, for a given built-in ____________________ rate.

14. In the short run, the Fed can move along the Phillips curve by adjusting the rate at which the ____________________ curve shifts rightward. When the Fed moves the economy downward and rightward along the Phillips curve, the ____________________ rate increases, and the ____________________ rate decreases.

15. In the long run, a decrease in the actual inflation rate leads to a lower built-in inflation rate, and the Phillips curve shifts ____________________.

16. In the short run, there is a tradeoff between inflation and ____________________: The Fed can choose lower ____________________ at the cost of higher inflation, or lower inflation at the cost of higher ____________________. But in the long run, since ____________________ always returns to its natural rate, there is no such tradeoff.

17. In the long run, monetary policy can change the rate of ____________________, but not the rate of ____________________.

18. The long-run Phillips curve is a ____________________ line at the natural rate of unemployment. The Fed can select any point along this line in the long run by using monetary policy to speed or slow the rate at which the ____________________ curve shifts rightward.

19. The Fed has tolerated measured inflation at 3 to 4 percent per year (1) because it knows that the ____________________ rate of inflation is lower; (2) because low rates of inflation may help ____________________ markets adjust more easily, and (3) because there is not much payoff to lowering inflation further.

IMPORTANT CONCEPTS

Write a brief answer below each of the following items.

1. In the table below, assume the economy begins at full employment. Indicate whether the Fed should *increase, decrease,* or make *no change* in the money supply in response to each event. Your answers will depend on the Fed's goal (to prevent any change in *real GDP* in the second column, and to prevent any change in the *price level* in the third column).

Event:	**Change in money supply needed to stabilize real GDP**	**Change in money supply needed to stabilize the price level**
The money demand curve shifts rightward	____________	____________
Investment decreases due to business pessimism	____________	____________
The government cuts taxes	____________	____________
World oil prices increase	____________	____________

2. Suppose that the government cuts taxes and the Fed uses an active monetary policy to prevent any change in real GDP. State what will happen to each of the following by writing *increase*, *decrease* or *no change*.

   a. the money supply ____________

   b. the interest rate ____________

   c. the price level ____________

   d. investment spending ____________

3. Explain what happens to each of the following from one period to the next, in a long-run equilibrium with ongoing inflation.

   a. the AD curve ____________

   b. the AS curve ____________

   c. real GDP ____________

   d. the money supply ____________

   e. the expected rate of inflation ____________

4. Briefly explain how you would illustrate an increase in inflationary expectations using the Phillips curve.

5. What is the key difference between "hawk" and "dove" monetary policies? Do hawks and doves differ in policies after a demand shock, a supply shock, or both? Explain briefly.

6. Suppose the Fed wants to keep real GDP as high as possible without increasing the rate of inflation. In which of the following cases would the Fed want to maintain an unchanged interest rate target? (Write *unchanged target.*) In which cases would it want to change its interest rate target? (Write *raise target* or *lower target.*)

   a. The money demand curve shifts rightward ______________

   b. Government purchases increase ______________

   c. Households increase their desire to save ______________

SKILLS AND TOOLS

For each of the following items, follow the instructions, write the correct answer on the blank, or circle the correct answer.

1. You've been working at the Fed for a while now, and things seem pretty calm. Real GDP is at its full-employment level and the interest rate target is still 8%. For some time, money demand has been given by the equation

$$M^d = 1{,}300 - 100r$$

   where M^d is the quantity of money demanded (in billions of dollars) and r is the interest rate in percentage points. You check the figures from yesterday, and, sure enough, the money supply is right where it needs to be to meet the interest rate target.

a. On the grid provided, draw the money demand curve. Also draw in the money supply curve, assuming the Fed has met its interest rate target of 8 percent. What is the money supply? _______________ billion

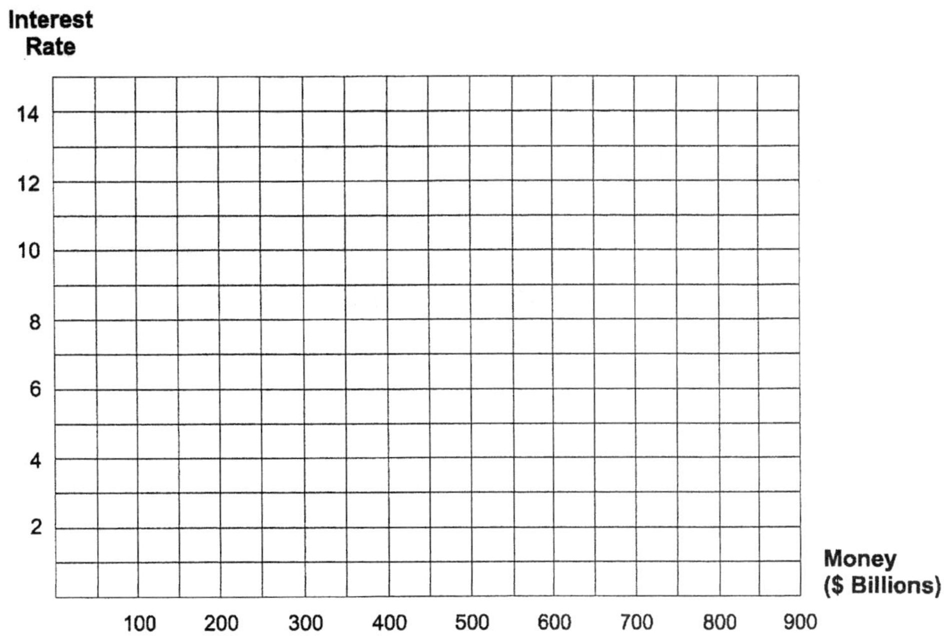

b. At 11:25 a.m. you get a buzz from the boss: New data suggest that money demand has changed to

$$M^d = 1{,}600 - 100r.$$

Draw in this new money demand curve.

c. As 11:30 a.m. draws nearer, you can see all too clearly just what will happen if nothing is done. In the money market, the interest rate will (rise/be unaffected/fall). This will (increase/have no effect on/decrease) interest-sensitive spending, and the aggregate demand (*AD*) curve will then (shift leftward/remain stable/shift rightward). Real GDP will then (rise/fall) and the economy will enter a (boom/period of calm/recession). To keep real GDP at its full employment level, you know you have to stick to your interest rate target. But to keep the interest rate at 8 percent, the money supply will have to be (increased/decreased) to a level of _______________ billion. You illustrate this on your graph, and label it M^S_2.

d. You grab the phone: You've got to get through to the people in New York before 11:30 to tell them what to do. Ring after ring. Ring after ring. Where are they? What's going on up there? Can't they see what's happening? Finally a voice: "Yeah?" You scream into the mouthpiece: ("Sell bonds! Sell bonds!"/"Buy bonds! Buy bonds!"). "We've got to (increase/decrease) the money supply!" They read you loud and clear. "How much? How much?" they want to know. You check your graph and give them the answer: "I want you to (increase/decrease) the money supply by ______________ billion—and I mean now!" you shout. They know, just like you know, that the demand deposit multiplier is 2.5, so they can take it from here. You head back to your desk, confident that, before long, the team in New York will be (buying/selling) bonds in the amount of ______________ billion, the money supply will (increase/decrease) to ______________ billion, and the interest rate will be back on target at 8 percent.

2. Life's been good after the way you handled that money demand thing. Kudos from everyone. Big promotion, too: Now they've got *you* making some of the decisions, and *someone else* making the graphs for *you*. Things are pretty good.

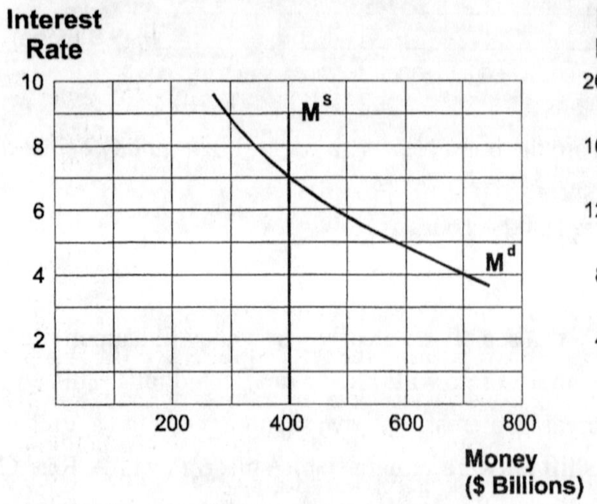

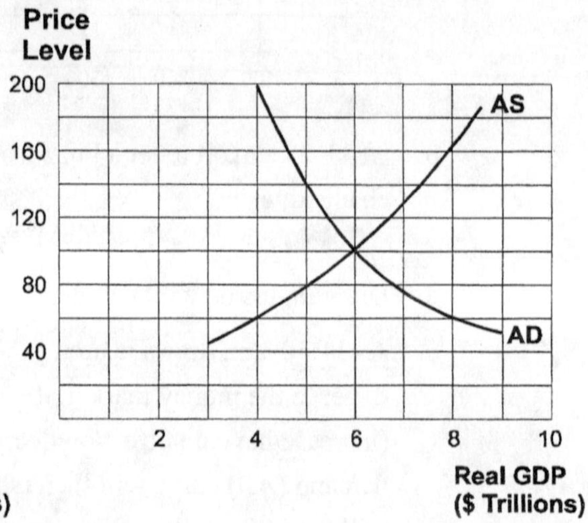

a. Over your (now usual) morning latte, you check the morning's graphs, above: the money supply is at ______________ billion and the equilibrium interest rate is ______________ percent. Since the interest rate target is 7 percent, the interest rate is (a bit too high/right on target/a bit too low). Real GDP is at its full-employment level of ______________ trillion, and the price level is at ______________.

b. You kick back and pick up your copy of *The Wall Street Journal*—and there's the screaming headline: *Investment Spending Plummets as Big Business Gets Bad Case of Jitters!* What does it mean? What does it mean? You know they'll all come running down to ask you any minute now. You reach for *Hall & Lieberman*. Now you remember: an unexpected decline in investment spending is a (positive/negative) spending shock. This will shift aggregate demand (rightward/leftward), causing both the price level and real GDP to (rise/fall). This, in turn, will cause the money demand curve to shift (rightward/leftward).

c. If the Fed does nothing, you've got a pretty good idea that *AD* will shift by $2 trillion at every price level, and money demand will shift by $200 billion at every level of the interest rate. There's no time to wait for your assistant—you've got to plot the new *AD* and money demand curves yourself—so do it now!

d. If these shifts occur, we'd then be looking at short run equilibrium real GDP of _______________ billion which would be (above/below) the full-employment level, and an equilibrium price level of _______________. We'd also be looking at an equilibrium interest rate of _______________ which is (above/below) the target of 7 percent.

e. Once you get a chance to think things over, you see that a passive policy is not the way to go. Besides the short run impact on prices, the interest rate, and real GDP described in part (c), there is also the long run to consider. In the long run, doing nothing means the economy will slide along the (original *AS* curve/new *AD* curve), and output will return to its full employment level, but the price level will (fall further/rise back) to the level of _______________. Of course, the Fed could instead stick to its interest rate target of 7%. To do this, the Fed will have to counter the decrease in investment with a(n) (increase/decrease) in the money supply, pushing the interest rate (up/down) to 7% and, as a result, causing interest-sensitive consumption and investment spending to (rise/fall). This would only shift the *AD* curve (leftward/rightward) from the one graphed in part (c), so this would clearly (be the best policy/*not* be the best policy).

f. The only option you haven't considered would be to change the interest rate target itself. If the Fed did that, it would want to set a target (above/below) its original 7%, and indeed set it even (lower/higher) than the equilibrium in part (c). To do that, the Fed would have to (increase/decrease) the money supply. The resulting (increase/decrease) in the interest rate would cause interest sensitive spending to (increase/decrease) and the economy could be made to (return to full employment GDP and a price level of 100/fall deeper into recession and deflation).

g. Here they come. What are you going to recommend? Should the Fed: (1) follow a passive policy, (2) maintain the interest rate target of 7 percent, or (3) change the target? (1 / 2 / 3).

3. It was Monday, January 23. It was cold in Washington. We were working the night watch out of Price Level. The boss is Alan Greenspan. My partner is Bill Cannon. My name is Phillips.

   For the last few years the unemployment rate had been what everyone calls the natural rate: 4.5 percent—though how it could be "natural" when people were still out of work was beyond me, but that's another story. Right now we were looking at inflation, and inflation had been running pretty high in this town; 14 percent, year after year, and people had just gotten used to it. Everyone thought it just had to be that way. Everyone but me and my partner, that is.

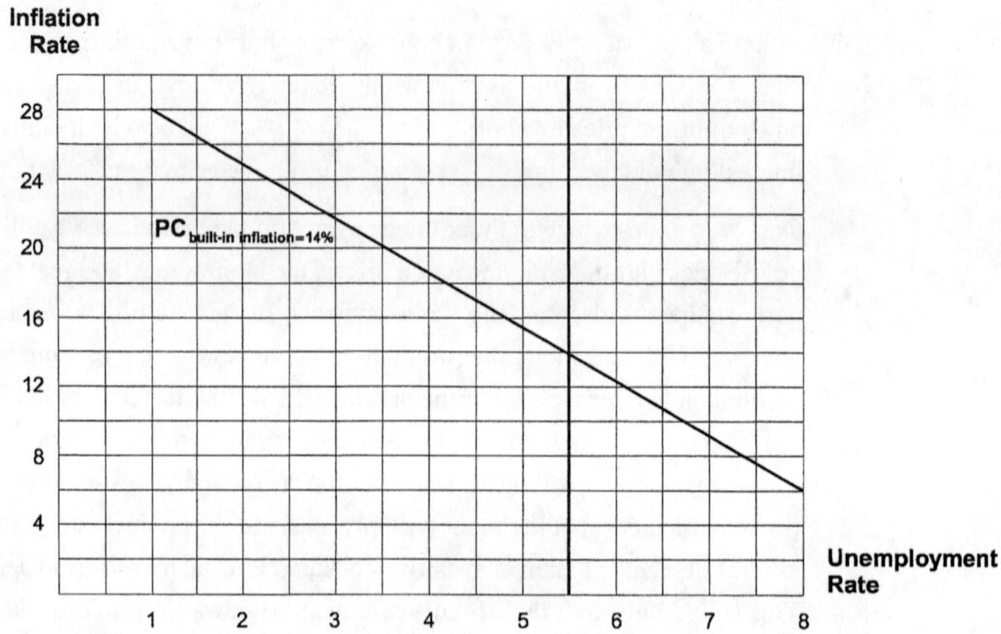

a. "New inflation and unemployment rates are in, Joe."
"Uh-huh."
"Inflation's hit 22%"
"That right?"
"But look at this unemployment rate, Joe."
"I don't need to look at it Bill. I can read the curve. If inflation just hit 22 percent, unemployment must be approximately ______________ percent."

b. "Must have been some kind of a shock, Joe."
"Uh-huh."
"What d'ya think, Joe: Demand shock? Supply shock?"
"With inflation rising and unemployment falling, it's got to have been a (demand/supply) shock now, doesn't it? And a (negative/positive) one at that."

c. "What's gonna happen, Joe?"
"Well, that all depends what the boys upstairs do now, doesn't it? If they hold the actual inflation rate at 22 percent like this for year after year, well, then expectations will change and the built-in rate of inflation will (rise/fall) to _______________ percent, and the *PC* curve is going to shift (upward/downward), now won't it? In the long run, we could then look forward to continuing inflation of 22 percent and an unemployment rate of _______________ percent. On the other hand, they could step right up and counter the shock, and force the inflation rate back down to 14 percent. That way the *PC* curve won't shift."

d. "Is that what you'd do Joe? You'd push inflation back down to 14 percent?"
"Is that what I'd do? No, that's not what I'd do. I'll tell you what I'd do: I'd force inflation all the way down to 8 percent, and I'd do it right now."
"But Joe, if inflation is forced down to 8 percent, in the short run we'll move (down/up) the $PC_{\text{built-in inflation} = 14\%}$ curve and the unemployment rate will (rise/fall) to approximately _______________ percent."
"Yeah. But in the long run, if we can keep the actual inflation rate down to 8 percent, expectations will change and the built-in inflation rate will eventually become _______________ percent, and the *PC* curve will shift (downward/upward) _______________. When it does, we'll be able to have a lower inflation rate of 8 percent and a (lower/higher) unemployment rate of _______________ percent.
"That's pretty tough medicine, Joe."
"Its tough medicine, alright, but inflation's a tough character."
"You really hate inflation, don't you Joe?"
"Hate inflation? You bet I hate inflation. Inflation's a thief, Bill. It comes in the night—every night—and it robs old ladies on fixed pensions of all their purchasing power. That's not my idea of something to like, Bill. Call me old fashioned but that's how I feel."
"Its morning Joe. The day watch just came in. Let's go home."

15-MINUTE PRACTICE TEST

Set a timer, giving yourself just 15 minutes to answer all of the following questions. To see what you *really* know and remember, take the test at least a day *after* you've read the chapter in the text and completed the exercises in this study guide.

Multiple Choice: Circle the letter in front of the single best answer.

1. In recent years, the Fed has
   a. followed a passive monetary policy.
   b. followed an active monetary policy.
   c. been confused and indecisive in its policy-making.
   d. successfully stabilized real GDP, but worsened inflation.
   e. successfully maintained low inflation, but at the cost of many severe recessions.

2. If the Fed wants to prevent any change in real GDP when the money demand curve shifts rightward, it should
   a. pursue an active monetary policy.
   b. maintain its interest rate target.
   c. increase the money supply.
   d. all of the above.
   e. none of the above.

3. When the Fed raises its interest rate target,
   a. the inflation rate usually rises.
   b. real GDP usually rises.
   c. investment spending usually rises.
   d. consumption spending usually rises.
   e. stock and bond prices usually fall.

4. If the Fed pursues a passive monetary policy, a negative supply shock will cause
   a. the price level to fall.
   b. real GDP to rise.
   c. the economy to experience stagflation.
   d. all of the above.
   e. none of the above.

5. When the economy experiences a negative supply shock, and the Fed follows a relatively "dovish" monetary policy, we can expect
   a. relatively greater increases in the price level (or greater increases in the inflation rate).
   b. relatively greater increases in the unemployment rate.
   c. relatively greater decreases in the price level (or greater decreases in the inflation rate).
   d. relatively greater decreases in the unemployment rate.
   e. no change in the price level, in the inflation rate, or the unemployment rate.

6. Fill in the blank: During a negative supply shock, a "hawk" monetary policy will result in a smaller rise in _______________ than would a "dove" monetary policy.
   a. the price level
   b. output
   c. unemployment
   d. all of the above
   e. b and c only

7. A rise in the expected inflation rate causes
   a. the AD curve to shift leftward.
   b. the AS curve to shift downward.
   c. the Phillips curve to shift upward.
   d. a movement rightward along the Phillips curve.
   e. a movement leftward along the Phillips curve.

8. If the Fed begins shifting the AD curve rightward at a faster rate than in the past, the short-run effect is a
   a. movement rightward along the Phillips curve.
   b. movement leftward along the Phillips curve.
   c. downward shift of the Phillips curve.
   d. leftward shift of the AD curve.
   e. downward shift of the AS curve.

9. One harmful consequence of using monetary policy to lower the rate of unemployment below its natural rate is that it causes
   a. a movement rightward along the Phillips curve in the long run.
   b. an upward shift in the Phillips curve in the long run.
   c. a decrease in transfer payments in the short run.
   d. an increase in tax revenue in the short run.
   e. inefficient businesses to survive and prosper since the economy is performing "too well."

10. One reason that the Fed does *not* reduce inflation all the way to zero is that
    a. the Fed does not know how to reduce the inflation rate below one or two percent per year.
    b. Federal law forbids the Fed from reducing the inflation rate to zero.
    c. the Fed fears a "rebound" effect, in which the inflation rate would bounce back up to even higher levels than before the reduction.
    d. the benefits of reducing inflation all the way to zero are too low to justify the costs to society.
    e. the official inflation rate underestimates the true inflation rate, so if the Fed reduced the true rate to zero, the official rate would be negative.

True/False: For each of the following statements, circle T if the statement is true or F if the statement is false.

T F 1. When the unemployment rate falls below the natural rate, real GDP falls below potential output.

T F 2. Under a passive monetary policy, a rightward shift of the money demand curve will cause a leftward shift of the AD curve.

T F 3. Under an active monetary policy designed to stabilize real GDP, a rightward shift of the money demand curve will cause the Fed to raise its interest rate target.

T F 4. To stabilize real GDP, the Fed should respond to a spending shock with a passive monetary policy.

T F 5. When the Fed raises its interest rate target, bond prices tend to fall and stock prices tend to rise.

T F 6. A negative demand shock presents the Fed with a short-run tradeoff: it must choose between higher inflation or higher unemployment.

T F 7. In the long run, the economy's self-correcting mechanism returns the economy back to full employment after a demand shock, but not after a supply shock.

T F 8. In an economy with built in inflation, the AS curve will shift up each year, even when output is at full employment and unemployment is at its natural rate.

CHAPTER 15

FISCAL POLICY: TAXES, SPENDING, AND THE FEDERAL BUDGET

SPEAKING ECONOMICS

Fill in each blank with the appropriate word or phrase from the list provided in the word bank. (For a challenge, fill in as many blanks as you can *without* using the word bank.)

____________________ 1. A tax whose rate increases as income increases.

____________________ 2. The fraction of a given income paid in taxes.

____________________ 3. The fraction of an additional dollar of income paid in taxes.

____________________ 4. The part of the federal budget deficit that varies with real GDP.

____________________ 5. The part of the federal budget deficit that is independent of changes in real GDP.

____________________ 6. Changes in taxes or government spending designed to counteract a boom or recession.

Word Bank

average tax rate	marginal tax rate
countercyclical fiscal policy	progressive tax
cyclical deficit	structural deficit

CHAPTER HIGHLIGHTS

Fill in the blanks with the appropriate words or phrases. If you have difficulty, review the chapter and then try again.

1. When examining budget-related figures over time, it is grossly misleading to use ____________________ figures, since the price level rises over time.

2. Budget-related figures such as government spending or the national debt have meaning only when considered relative to a nation's total ____________________. This is why we should always look at these figures as percentages of ____________________.

3. Viewed as a percentage of ___________________, non-military government purchases have remained low and stable. They have not contributed to growth in total government spending.

4. Viewed as a percentage of ___________________, military purchases have ___________________ dramatically over the past several decades. Like non-military purchases, they have not contributed to any growth in government spending.

5. The decline in ___________________ spending in relation to GDP since the early 1960s has made huge amounts of resources available for other purposes. But because ___________________ spending has little room to fall further, and is likely to rise over the next decade, there can not be any similar freeing up of resources in coming years.

6. In recent decades, _______________ has (have) been the fastest growing part of federal government spending and are currently equal to about 8 percent of GDP.

7. Over the past several decades, and until the early 1990s, federal government spending as a percentage of GDP rose steadily. The main causes were increases in ___________________ payments and increases in ___________________ on the national debt.

8. From 1992 to 2000, federal government spending as a percentage of GDP ___________________ steadily, although it remained a ___________________ percentage than in 1959. The main causes have been the continued sharp ___________________ in military spending, and more modest ___________________ in transfer payments relative to GDP. Over the next decade, total federal spending as a percentage of GDP is unlikely to continue falling, and in fact may rise.

9. Federal revenue has trended ___________________ from around 17 percent of GDP in 1959 to around ___________________ percent in 2001.

10. ___________________—which add to the public's holdings of government bonds—add to the national debt. ___________________—which decrease the public's bond holdings—subtract from the national debt.

11. In a recession, because ___________________ rise(s) and ___________________ fall(s), the federal budget deficit rises. In an expansion, because ___________________ decrease(s) and ___________________ rise(s), the budget deficit falls.

12. Many features of the federal tax and transfer systems act as automatic ___________________. As the economy goes into a recession, these features help to ___________________ the decline in consumption spending, and they also cause the cyclical deficit to rise. As the economy goes into boom, these features help to ___________________ the rise in consumption spending, and they also cause the cyclical deficit to fall.

13. As long as the national debt grows by the same percentage as ________________, the ratios of debt to ________________ and interest payments to ________________ will remain constant. In this case, the government can continue to pay interest on its rising debt without increasing the average tax rate in the economy.

14. The experience of 2001 reinforces the view that the major burden of stabilizing the economy over the short run should be left to the ________________.

IMPORTANT CONCEPTS

Write a brief answer below each of the following items.

1. List the three broad categories of the federal government's spending.

   a.

   b.

   c.

2. Briefly, what is the difference between federal government *purchases* and federal government *spending*?

3. State whether each of the following has experienced an *upward trend*, *downward trend*, or *remained steady* over the past few decades.

   a. transfer payments as a percentage of GDP ____________

   b. total federal government *purchases* as a percentage of GDP ____________

   c. total federal government *spending* as a percentage of GDP ____________

   d. social security tax revenue as a percentage of GDP ____________

   e. total federal tax revenue as a percentage of GDP ____________

4. List three reasons why economists recommend against the use of countercyclical fiscal policy.

   a.

   b.

   c.

SKILLS AND TOOLS

For each of the following items, follow the instructions, write the correct answer in the blank, or circle the correct answer.

1. The table below reports data on the U.S. economy from 1982 to 1999. The figures are in billions of current dollars.

Year	GDP	Military Government Purchases	Non-military Government Purchases	Military Government Purchases as a Percentage of GDP	Non-military Government Purchases as a Percentage of GDP	Total Government Purchases as a Percentage of GDP
1984	$3,932.7	$283.5	$92.8	7.21	2.36	9.57
1985	$4,213.0	$312.4	$101.0	___	___	___
1986	$4,452.9	$332.2	$106.5	7.46	2.39	9.85
1987	$4,742.5	$351.2	$109.3	___	2.30	___
1988	$5,108.3	$355.9	$106.8	6.97	___	9.06
1989	$5,489.1	$363.2	$119.3	6.62	2.17	___
1990	$5,803.2	$374.9	$133.6	___	___	8.76
1991	$5,986.2	$384.5	$142.9	6.42	2.39	8.81
1992	$6,318.9	$378.5	$156.0	___	2.47	___
1993	$6,642.3	$364.9	$162.4	5.49	___	7.94
1994	$7,054.3	$355.1	$165.9	5.03	2.35	___
1995	$7,400.5	$350.6	$170.9	4.74	___	7.05
1996	$7,813.2	$357.0	$174.6	___	2.23	___
1997	$8,318.4	$352.5	$185.6	4.24	2.23	6.47
1998	$8,781.5	$349.1	$190.1	3.98	___	6.14
1999	$9,268.6	$364.5	$199.5	___	2.15	6.09
2000	$9,872.9	$375.4	$214.8	3.80	___	5.98
2001	$10,208.1	$339.0	$216.6	3.32	2.12	___

a. By glancing down the column for non-military government purchases, we can see that, except between 1987 and 1988, this component of government purchases (increased/remained steady/decreased) in nominal terms every single year. In fact, between 1984 and 2001, this component of government spending (more than doubled/kept steady/fell by half). Looking at this, alone, may we conclude that non-military government purchases are a rapidly growing burden on the American economy? (Yes/No). To properly gauge levels and trends in budget-related expenditures, one must always consider (nominal values/absolute real values/the spending as a percent of GDP).

b. Complete the entries in the table. Then, using figures from the table, plot and label military purchases as a percentage of GDP, non-military purchases as a percentage of GDP, and total government purchases as a percentage of GDP on the grid below.

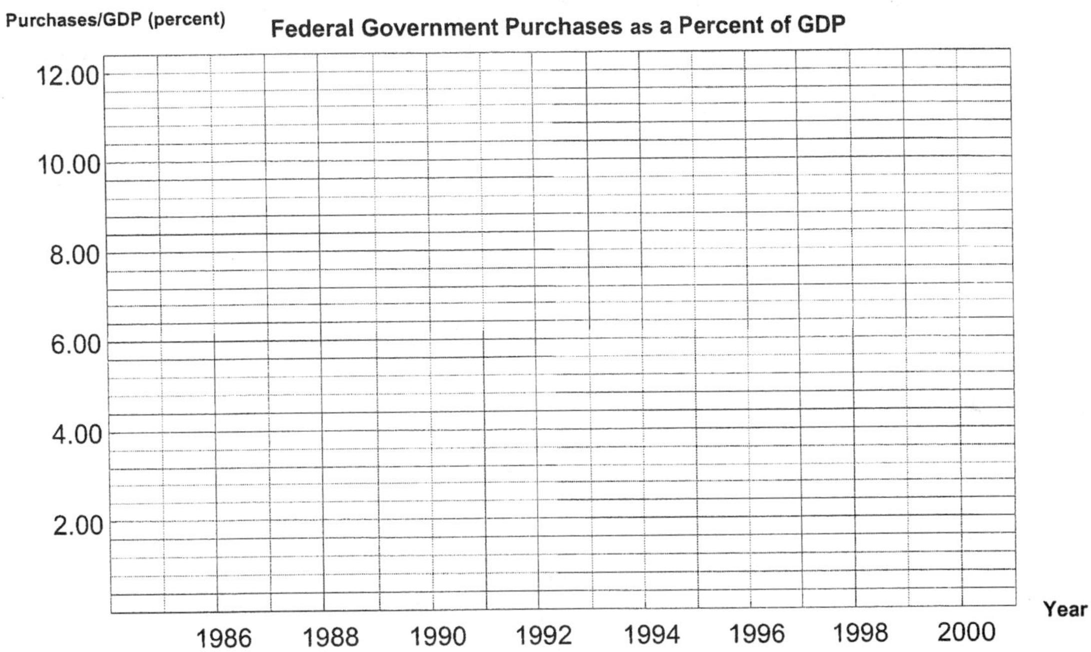

c. Viewed as a percentage of GDP, non-military government purchases (are low and stable/are high and stable/vary wildly). Indeed, between 1984 to 2001, this component of total government spending actually (increased/decreased) as a percentage of GDP, from a level of ______________ percent in 1984 to a level of ______________ percent in 2001.

d. Viewed as a percentage of GDP, military government purchases have steadily decreased since ______________. Over the entire period 1984 to 2001, this component of total government spending reached its peak of ______________ percent of GDP in the year ______________, and fell to its lowest level of ______________ percent in the year ______________.

e. From 1984 to 1986, total government purchases as a percentage of GDP (increased/decreased) from a level of _______________ to a level of _______________. From their peak of _______________ percent in the year _______________, these expenditures as a percentage of GDP (increased/decreased) rather steadily, ending the period in 2001 at a level of _______________ percent of GDP.

2. Remember the economy of Upper Classica? The supply of loanable funds from all sources there is given by the equation

$$F^S = (r\text{-}1)/2,$$

where r is the interest rate measured in percentage points (e.g. seven percent is 7 rather than decimal 0.07). For some time now the government has been spending no more than it collects in taxes, so Upper Classica has enjoyed a period with no deficits or surpluses in the government budget. As a result, total demand for loanable funds in Upper Classica has been stable and given by the equation,

$$F^D = (7\text{-}r)/2,$$

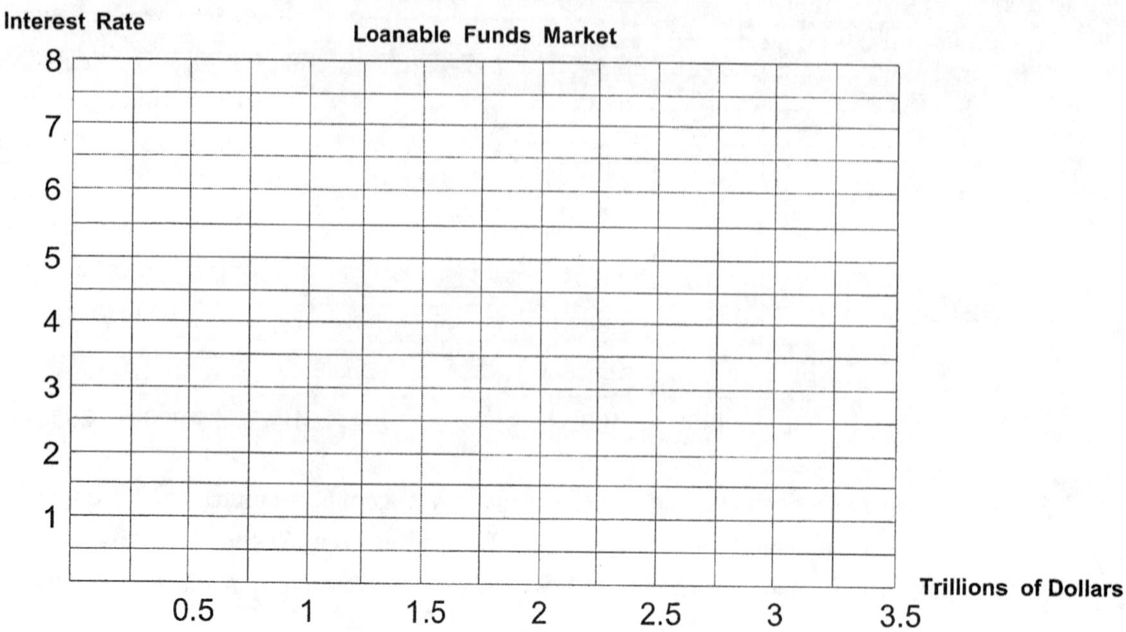

a. Graph the total demand for funds and the total supply of funds in the grid provided.

b. When the government of Upper Classica runs neither a budget deficit nor a budget surplus, the equilibrium interest rate is ______________ percent and the quantity of funds demanded and supplied is ______________ trillion dollars.

It is an election year in Upper Classica and two very attractive candidates have stepped forward, each with a different vision of the country's long run economic future. One candidate favors holding the line on taxes and increasing government spending; the other candidate also favors holding the line on taxes, but wants to reduce government spending, not increase it

c. If the candidate favoring increased government spending were to be elected, and his program enacted, the government of Upper Classica would begin to run budget deficits. If this deficit were to be equal to one (1) trillion dollars per year, then the (demand for/supply of) funds would shift (leftward/rightward) by (less than one trillion/exactly one trillion/more than one trillion) dollars at every level of the interest rate. Draw in that newly shifted curve on the grid above. We can see that this candidate's proposed program of continuing deficits will lead to (a higher/ an unchanged/ a lower) equilibrium interest rate of ______________ percent.

d. If the candidate favoring decreased government spending were to be elected, and her program enacted, the government of Upper Classica would begin to run budget surpluses. If this surplus were to be equal to one-half (0.5) trillion dollars per year, then the (demand for/supply of) funds would shift (leftward/rightward) by (less than one-half trillion/exactly one-half trillion/more than one-half trillion) dollars at every level of the interest rate. Draw in that newly shifted curve on the grid above. We can see that this candidate's proposed program of continuing surpluses will lead to (a higher/ an unchanged/ a lower) equilibrium interest rate of ______________ percent.

3. In the debates last night, the candidates in Upper Classica's election hammered each other over the impact their rival economic plans would have on the average standard of living. The candidate favoring deficits even brought along the graph, below, showing Upper Classica's aggregate production function.

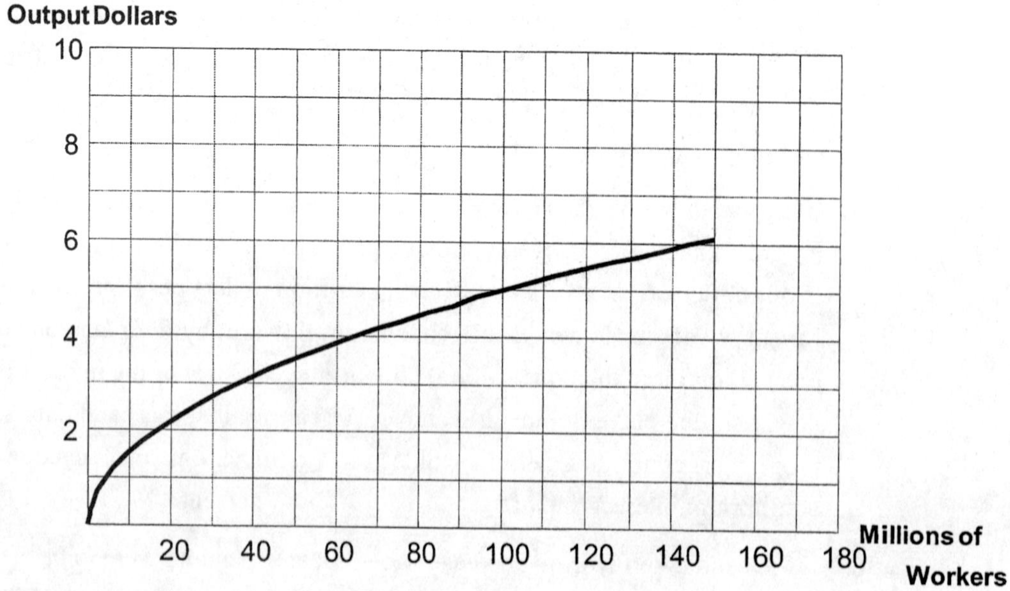

a. Both candidates agreed on how the government's budget affects the aggregate production function, and so average standards of living. Both agreed that by affecting interest rates, the government budget deficit or surplus affects (the money supply/ investment spending) which, in turn, affects the rate of growth of (the stock of bonds/ the stock of capital). Even with no change in economic policy, both agreed that the aggregate production function tends to (shift up/ stay unchanged / shift downward) over time— where they said their policies differed was in how rapidly those shifts would occur.

b. The candidate favoring surpluses argued that her policy, by (increasing /holding constant /decreasing) the (demand for/ supply of) loanable funds, and so forcing the equilibrium interest rate (down/to remain steady/up), would encourage (a greater increase/ no change/ a smaller increase) in investment spending and so tend to shift the aggregate production function (upward/downward) at a (slower/faster) rate. This, of course, would lead to (more rapid/less rapid) improvement in the average standard of living, compared to the status quo.

c. The candidate favoring deficits had to admit that his policy, by (increasing /holding constant /decreasing) the (demand for/ supply of) loanable funds, and so forcing the equilibrium interest rate (down/to remain steady/up), would encourage (a greater increase/ no change/ a smaller increase) in investment spending and so tend to shift the aggregate production function (upward/downward) at a (slower/faster) rate. This, of course, would lead to (more rapid/less rapid) improvement in the average standard of living, compared to the status quo.

4. During the last half hour of their debate, the candidates finally got around to discussing how their rival policies would affect the national debt. No one really cared much about all that until one of the candidates pointed out that continuing deficits in the government budget will cause the national debt to rise. This, in turn, would eventually require the government to reduce spending or increase taxes in order to continue paying the rising interest bill. Just the mere mention of "taxes" seemed to galvanize the audience. The moderator of the debate quickly noted that taxes can affect incentives to work, and asked each candidate to explain how his or her plan would affect the national labor market equilibrium, depicted below.

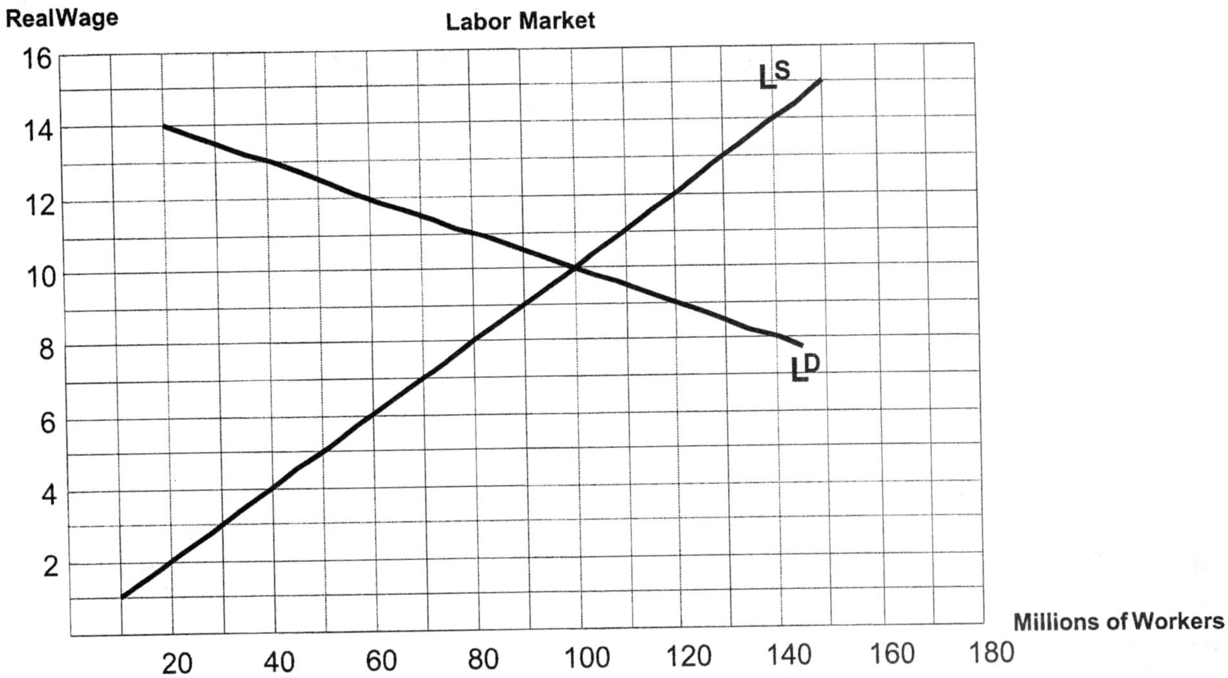

a. The candidate favoring deficits had to answer first. He admitted that the (higher/lower) taxes that might eventually be necessary under his plan would (encourage/discourage) work, and so tend to shift the (demand for/ supply of) labor (rightward/leftward). Since he said he estimated the size of this shift at no more than 30 million workers at each level of the real wage, he confidently predicted that if his plan were enacted the equilibrium real wage would (rise/fall) to _______________ from its current level of 10.

b. To close the debate, the candidate favoring surpluses stepped forward to answer. She declared that the (higher/lower) taxes that might eventually be possible under her plan would (encourage/discourage) work, and so tend to shift the (demand for/ supply of) labor (rightward/leftward). Since she said she estimated the size of this shift at no more than 30 million workers at each level of the real wage, she admitted that if her plan were enacted the equilibrium real wage would (rise/fall) to _______________ from its current level of 10.

15-MINUTE PRACTICE TEST

Set a timer, giving yourself just 15 minutes to answer all of the following questions. To see what you *really* know and remember, take the test at least a day *after* you've read the chapter in the text and completed the exercises in this study guide.

Multiple Choice: Circle the letter in front of the single best answer.

1. When observing how the federal budget has changed over time, it is best to look at how the budget figures have changed
   a. in nominal terms.
   b. in real terms.
   c. as a percentage of GDP.
   d. as a percentage of the national debt.
   e. as a percentage of the budget deficit.

2. Which of the following has declined dramatically in recent decades?
   a. Nominal military spending
   b. Real military spending
   c. Military spending as a percentage of GDP
   d. Real non-military spending
   e. Non-military spending as a percentage of GDP

3. Which of the following has trended upward as a percentage of GDP in recent decades?
   a. Federal transfer payments
   b. Federal government spending
   c. Social security tax revenue
   d. All of the above
   e. None of the above

4. Total federal tax revenue as a percentage of GDP has, in recent decades,
   a. risen dramatically.
   b. fallen dramatically.
   c. remained constant at about 50%.
   d. trended upward slightly, from around 17% to around 20%.
   e. trended upward slightly, from around 2% to around 3%.

5. Which of the following would cause the national debt to rise as a fraction of real GDP?
   a. Any budget deficit greater than zero
   b. Any cyclical budget deficit greater than zero
   c. Any structural budget deficit greater than zero
   d. Only budget deficits greater than about 3% of GDP
   e. Only budget deficits greater than about 10% of real GDP

6. When the federal government runs a budget surplus,
   a. the surplus is equal to the budget deficit.
   b. the national debt decreases..
   c. the government must borrow the surplus in the loanable funds market.
   d. it sells government bonds to the public.
   e. all of the above.

7. In a recession,
   a. tax revenues fall.
   b. transfer payments rise.
   c. the cyclical deficit rises.
   d. all of the above.
   e. none of the above.

8. The structural deficit is the part of the deficit that
   a. rises and falls in recessions and booms.
   b. is due to wasteful, as opposed to useful, government spending.
   c. is due to useful, as opposed to wasteful, government spending.
   d. is due to spending on infrastructure, like roads and bridges.
   e. none of the above.

9. Which of the following acts as an automatic stabilizer in the economy?
   a. Unemployment insurance
   b. Welfare payments
   c. Income taxes
   d. All of the above
   e. None of the above

10. Which of the following is an important explanation for why the budget has gone into surplus in the late 1990s?
    a. Changes in the measurement of GDP.
    b. rapid technological change.
    c. higher inflation.
    d. all of the above.
    e. none of the above.

True/False: For each of the following statements, circle T if the statement is true or F if the statement is false.

T F 1. Viewed as a percentage of GDP, total government purchases have remained steady over the past several decades.

T F 2. Viewed as a percentage of GDP, military spending has trended downward over the past several decades.

T F 3. A federal budget deficit of any size causes the national debt to rise.

T F 4. A federal budget deficit of any size causes the national debt as a percentage of GDP to rise.

T F 5. Economists today believe that countercyclical fiscal policy can be as effective as countercyclical monetary policy in stabilizing the economy.

T F 6. The structural budget deficit is the part of the deficit that is not affected by booms and recessions.

T F 7. In the long run, an increase in transfer payments—with no other fiscal change—can be expected to lead to slower growth in the average standard of living.

T F 8. Both historical experience and economic theory suggest that the United States was on the brink of a "debt disaster" in the 1980s, and that financial collapse was imminent.

CHAPTER 16

EXCHANGE RATES AND MACROECONOMIC POLICY

SPEAKING ECONOMICS

Fill in each blank with the appropriate word or phrase from the list provided in the word bank. (For a challenge, fill in as many blanks as you can *without* using the word bank.)

____________________ 1. The market in which one country's currency is traded for another country's.

____________________ 2. The amount of one country's currency that is traded for one unit of another country's currency.

____________________ 3. A curve indicating the quantity of a specific foreign currency that Americans will want to buy, during a given period, at each different exchange rate.

____________________ 4. A curve indicating the quantity of a specific foreign currency that will be supplied during a given period, at each different exchange rate.

____________________ 5. An exchange rate that is freely determined by the forces of supply and demand.

____________________ 6. An increase in the price of a currency in a floating-rate system.

____________________ 7. A decrease in the price of a currency in a floating-rate system.

____________________ 8. The idea that the exchange rate will adjust in the long run so that the average price of goods in two countries will be roughly the same.

____________________ 9. Simultaneous buying and selling of a foreign currency in order to profit from a difference in exchange rates.

____________________ 10. Arbitrage involving one pair of currencies.

____________________ 11. Arbitrage involving trades among three (or more) currencies.

____________________ 12. A policy of frequent central bank intervention to move the exchange rate.

____________________ 13. A government declared exchange rate maintained by central bank intervention in the foreign exchange market.

____________________________ 14. A change in the exchange rate form a higher fixed rate to a lower fixed rate.

____________________________ 15. A loss of faith that a country can prevent a drop in its exchange rate, leading to a rapid depletion of its foreign currency (e.g. dollar) reserves.

____________________________ 16. Occurs when a decision maker expects to be rescued in the event of an unfavorable outcome, and then changes their behavior so that the unfavorable outcome is more likely.

____________________________ 17. A region whose economies perform better with a single currency than with separate national currencies.

____________________________ 18. The excess of a nation's imports over its exports during a given period.

____________________________ 19. The excess of a nation's exports over its imports during a given period.

____________________________ 20. An inflow of funds equal to a nation's trade deficit.

Word Bank

appreciation
arbitrage
bilateral arbitrage
demand curve for foreign currency
devaluation
depreciation
exchange rate
fixed exchange rate
floating exchange rate
foreign currency crisis
foreign exchange market
managed float
moral hazard
net capital inflow
optimum currency area
purchasing power parity (PPP) theory
supply curve for foreign currency
trade deficit
trade surplus
triangular arbitrage

CHAPTER HIGHLIGHTS

Fill in the blanks with the appropriate words or phrases. If you have difficulty, review the chapter and then try again.

1. The ____________________ is the price of foreign currency in dollars.

2. In our model of the market for pounds, we assume that American households and businesses are the only ____________________ of pounds.

3. In our model of the market for pounds, we assume that British households and firms are the only ____________________ of pounds.

4. When the exchange rate ____________________—that is, when the government does not interfere in the foreign currency market—the equilibrium exchange rate is determined by the intersection of the demand curve and the supply curve.

5. When a floating exchange rate changes, one country's currency will ____________________ (rise in price) and the other country's currency will ____________________ (fall in price).

6. Relative interest rates and expectations of future exchange rates are the dominant forces moving exchange rates in the very ____________________ run.

7. In the ____________________ run, movements in exchange rates are caused largely by economic fluctuations. All else being equal, a country whose GDP rises relatively rapidly will experience a(n) ____________________ of its currency. A country whose GDP falls more rapidly will experience a(n) ____________________ of its currency.

8. According to the purchasing power ____________________ theory, an exchange rate between two countries will adjust in the ____________________ run until the average price of goods is roughly the same in both countries.

9. In the long run, the currency of a country with a higher inflation rate will ____________________ against the currency of a country whose inflation rate is lower.

10. ________________ arbitrage ensures that the exchange rate between any two currencies is the same everywhere in the world.

11. ________________ arbitrage ensures that the price of a foreign currency is the same whether it is purchased directly—in a single foreign exchange market—or indirectly, by buying and selling a third currency.

12. Under a managed float, a country's central bank buys its own currency to prevent a(n) ____________________, and sells its own currency to prevent a(n) ____________________.

13. When a country fixes its exchange rate below the equilibrium value, the result is an excess ____________________ for (of) the country's currency. To maintain the fixed rate, the country's central bank must ____________________ enough of its own currency to eliminate the excess ____________________.

14. When a country fixes its exchange rate above the equilibrium value, the result is an excess ____________________ for (of) the country's currency. To maintain the fixed rate, the country's central bank must ____________________ enough of its own currency to eliminate the excess ____________________.

15. A foreign currency crisis arises when people no longer believe that a country can maintain a fixed exchange rate ____________________ the equilibrium rate. As a consequence, the supply of the currency ____________________, demand for it ____________________, and the country must use up its reserves of dollars and other key currencies even faster in order to maintain the fixed rate.

16. A depreciation of the dollar causes net exports to ____________________—a ____________________ spending shock that ____________________ real GDP in the short run. An appreciation of the dollar causes net exports to ____________________—a ____________________ spending shock that ____________________ real GDP in the short run.

17. Monetary policy has a ____________________ effect when we include the impact on exchange rates and net exports, rather than just the impact on interest-sensitive consumption and investment spending.

18. An increase in the desire of foreigners to invest in the United States contributes to a (an) ____________________ of the dollar. As a result, U.S. exports ____________________ because they are ____________________ expensive for foreigners. Imports ____________________, because they are ____________________ expensive to Americans. The result is a(n) ____________________ in the trade deficit.

19. We can trace the rise in the U.S. trade deficit during the 1980s and 1990s to two important sources: first, relatively high ____________________ in the 1980s; and second, a long held preference for American assets that grew stronger in the 1990s. Each of these contributed to a large capital inflow, a ____________________ value for the dollar, and a trade deficit.

IMPORTANT CONCEPTS

Write a brief answer below each of the following items.

1. In the market where Mexican pesos are exchanged for U.S. dollars, list four changes that would cause the demand curve for pesos to shift *leftward*. (The text discusses five such changes for the case of the British pound.)

   a.

   b.

   c.

   d.

2. List four changes that would cause the supply curve for Mexican pesos to shift *leftward*. (The text discusses five such changes for the case of the British pound.)

   a.

   b.

   c.

   d.

3. Using the supply and demand model of the market where pounds and dollars are traded, state whether each of the following changes would cause the dollar to *appreciate*, *depreciate*, or *remain unchanged* relative to the British pound. In each case, assume that the dollar floats against the pound, and that there are no other changes that affect the exchange rate, other than the one listed.

   a. real GDP in Britain rises ______________

   b. the interest rate in the United States rises ______________

   c. the interest rate in Britain falls ______________

   d. Americans develop a taste for British tea ______________

   e. Americans and Brits expect the pound to depreciate in the near future ______________

   f. the price level in Britain rises ______________

4. Suppose the dollar floats against the Japanese yen, and the Fed increases the U.S. money supply. State whether each of the following variables would *increase*, *decrease*, or *remain unchanged.*

   a. real GDP in the United States ______________

   b. the interest rate in the United States ______________

   c. the exchange rate (dollars per yen) ______________

   d. United States net exports to Japan ______________

5. Suppose a country fixes its exchange rate with the dollar *above* the equilibrium exchange rate. Therefore, it must buy its own currency in the foreign exchange market to maintain the fixed rate. State whether the country would have to buy more, less, or the same amount of its own currency after each change listed below.

   a. real GDP in the country increases ______________

   b. the interest rate in the country increases ______________

   c. people suddenly gain confidence in the country's ability to maintain the fixed rate

      ____

   d. citizens of the country develop an increased taste for foreign goods ______________

SKILLS AND TOOLS

For each of the following items, follow the instructions, write the correct answer in the blank, or circle the correct answer.

1. A currency table is a convenient and very common way to display exchange rate information. The table below was obtained one day in April, 2002, from *Yahoo!* at the URL http://quote.yahoo.com/m3?u

   Notice that currencies are arranged in rows and columns. Looking across each row, you obtain the price of the column-currency in units of the row-currency: Looking down any column, you obtain the price of the column-currency in units of the row-currency.

Currency Last Trade	U.S. $ N/A	¥en 11:40am	Euro 11:39am	Can $ 11:36am	U.K. £ 11:40am	Aust $ 11:38am	SFranc 11:40am
U.S. $		0.007505		0.6256		0.5345	
¥en	133.2		117.4	83.35		71.22	80.24
Euro €	1.135	0.008519	1	0.7101	1.637	0.6067	0.6835
Can $			1.408		2.305		0.9626
U.K. £	0.6935	0.005205	0.611	0.4339		0.3707	0.4176
Aust $			1.648	1.17	2.698		1.127
SFranc	1.661	0.01246		1.039	2.394	0.8876	1

   a. Fill in the blanks.

   b. If a Canadian resident were planning to buy a French bond costing € 200,000, at the exchange rates prevailing on this day in April, she would have to spend _______________ Canadian dollars.

   c. If an American resident were planning to buy a French bond costing € 200,000, at the exchange rates prevailing on this day in April, he would have to spend _______________ U.S. dollars.

   d. If a Japanese resident were planning to buy British real estate costing UK £1,000,000, at the exchange rates prevailing on this day in April she would have to spend _______________ Japanese Yen.

   e. If an American resident were planning to buy a British automobile costing £20,000, at the exchange rates prevailing on this day in April, he would have to spend _______________ U.S. dollars.

f. If a German resident were planning to buy Swiss fertilizer costing SFranc 50,000, at the exchange rates prevailing on this day in April, he would have to spend _______________ Euros.

2. Suppose that the United States and Europe trade only with one another. The American demand for European euros is given by

$$D^{€} = 14 - 10e.$$

The European supply of euros is

$$S^{€} = 7.5e.$$

Here, $D^{€}$ is quantity of euros demanded, $S^{€}$ is quantity of euros supplied, both in hundreds of millions per day. The variable *e* in both equations is the exchange rate, giving the dollar price of a unit of European currency.

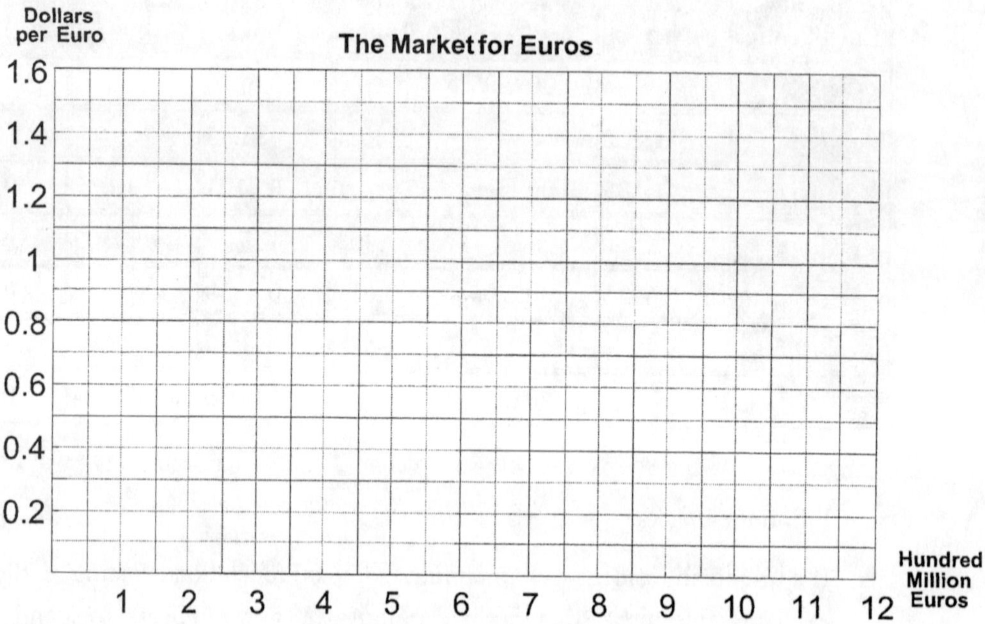

a. Plot the demand and supply curves for European euros. Label them $D^{€}_1$ and $S^{€}_1$.

b. At an exchange rate of $1, American buyers of European goods and assets will want to buy _______________ hundred million European euros on the foreign exchange market. At that same price, European buyers of American goods and assets will want to sell _______________ hundred million European euros. At an exchange rate of $1 the quantity of euros demanded will (exceed/equal/be exceeded by) the quantity of euros supplied. As a result, the European euro will tend to (appreciate/remain unchanged/depreciate) and the U.S. dollar will tend to (appreciate/remain unchanged/depreciate). The foreign exchange market is in equilibrium when the exchange rate is _______________.

c. Suppose the United States experiences a sharp recession. This will cause (American demand for European euros/European supply of euros) to shift (leftward/rightward). If the amount of this shift is €3.5 hundred million at every level of the exchange rate, what is the new equilibrium exchange rate? _______________ Illustrate by drawing in the new supply or demand curve, whichever is appropriate.

d. Following the shift in part (c), and after much national soul-searching, European consumers discover that they really do love American movies after all. This change in tastes toward American products will cause (American demand for European euros/European supply of euros) to shift (leftward/rightward). If the amount of this shift is €1.75 hundred million at every level of the exchange rate, what is the new equilibrium exchange rate? _______________ Illustrate by drawing in the new supply or demand curve, whichever is appropriate.

3. Imagine you are hard at work as a currency trader in New York City. You study your computer screen and notice the following data from the most recent trades:

Time: 11:43 a.m. Eastern Standard Time

Place: New York Inter-Bank market

Items:

Price of pound sterling in dollar-pound market:	$1.80
Price of European euro in dollar-euro market :	$0.90
Price of pound sterling in euro-pound market:	€1.60

Your heart starts pounding.

a. You notice that the direct price of one pound to Americans is _______________. At the same time, the indirect price of one pound to Americans is _______________.

No time to lose ... You've got authority to spend up to $90,000 if you see an opportunity, and you do. You start punching up the orders:

b. First, you place an order to buy (euros/pounds) in the (dollar-euro/dollar-pound) market, spending all your $90,000. This gets you _______________ in (pounds/euros).

c. You place another order to sell everything you just acquired in (b) to obtain (euros/pounds/dollars) in the (euro-pound/dollar-euro/dollar-pound) market. This gets you _______________ in (pounds/dollars/euros).

d. You place your last order to sell everything you just acquired in (c) to obtain (euros/pounds/dollars) in the (euro-pound/dollar-euro/dollar-pound) market. This gets you _______________ in (pounds/dollars/euros).

e. Comparing the $90,000 you spent in (b) with what you just acquired in (d), you realize you just earned your firm _______________ dollars of arbitrage profit in a few seconds. Not bad. Of course, as you watch the data on your screen start to change, it is clear other people have now caught on to the situation, too. As many other traders start placing orders just like yours, you expect to see that the price of the euro in the dollar-euro market (rise/fall), while the price of the pound in the euro-pound market will (rise/fall), and the price of the pound in the pound-dollar market will (rise/fall).

4. Suppose once again that the United States and Europe are the only two countries that trade with one another. Given current economic conditions in each country, American demand for European euros is again given by

$$D^{€} = 14 - 10e,$$

but European supply of euros is

$$S^{€} = 1.75 + 7.5e.$$

As before, $D^{€}$ is quantity of euros demanded, $S^{€}$ is quantity of euros supplied, both in hundreds of millions per day. The variable e in both equations is the exchange rate, giving the dollar price of a unit of European currency.

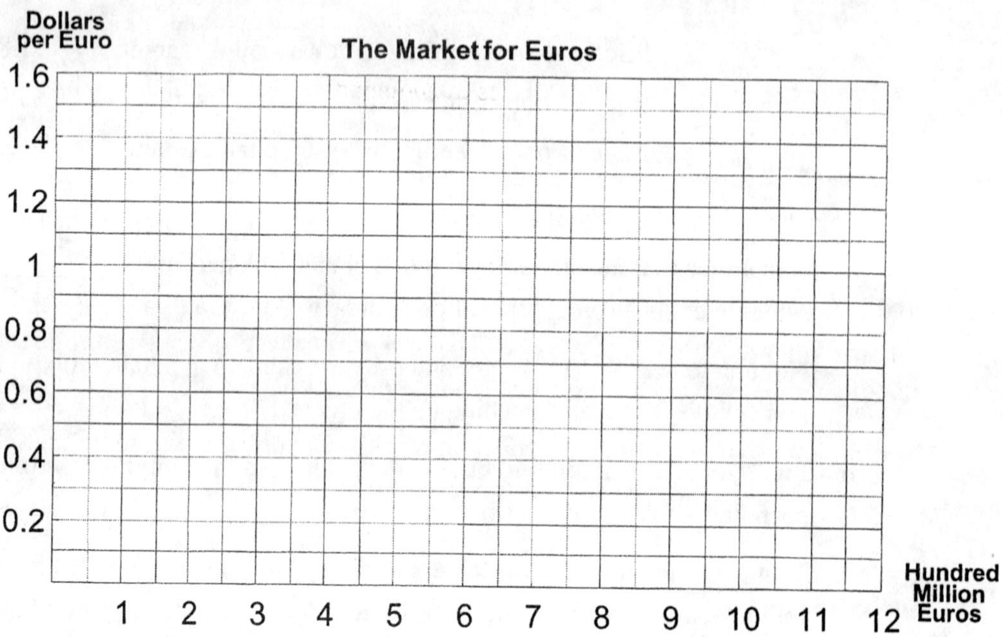

a. Solve the demand and supply equations to determine the equilibrium exchange rate and quantity of euros traded. The equilibrium exchange rate is _______________ dollars per euro. Plot these demand and supply curves for European euros. Label them $D^{€}_{1}$ and $S^{€}_{1}$.

b. Suppose that equilibrium real GDP in the United States is above its full-employment level. American policy-makers have considered their options, and decided to use monetary policy to bring equilibrium real GDP to its full-employment level. To do that, the Fed will have to (increase/decrease) the money supply. This will (increase/decrease) the interest rate and so (increase/decrease) interest-sensitive spending. Equilibrium real GDP will then (increase/decrease) to its full-employment level through the usual multiplier process. If, in a closed economy, the money supply would have to change by $50 billion to achieve this policy goal, in an open economy we know that the required change in the money supply will be (greater/smaller) than $50 billion. Because of its impact on the exchange rate, monetary policy is (less/more) effective in an open economy than it is in a closed economy.

c. If the Fed pursues the policy described in (b), there will be an impact on the foreign exchange market. The U.S. interest rate will (fall/rise), and this will make European assets (more/less) attractive to American buyers compared to American assets. As American buyers (increase/decrease) their purchases of European assets, the (demand for/supply of) European euros will shift (leftward/rightward). This effect, alone, will tend to make the euro (appreciate/depreciate) and to make the dollar (appreciate/depreciate). Suppose the amount of this shift is € 1.5 hundred million at every exchange rate. Plot the resulting demand or supply curve and label it appropriately.

d. In addition, as the Fed pursues the policy described in (b) and the U.S. interest rate (falls/rises) as described in (c), this will make American assets (more/less) attractive to European buyers compared to European assets. As European buyers (increase/decrease) their purchases of American assets, the (demand for/supply of) European euros will shift (leftward/rightward). This effect, alone, will tend to make the euro (appreciate/depreciate) and to make the dollar (appreciate/depreciate). Suppose the amount of this shift is € 2 hundred million at every exchange rate. Plot the resulting demand or supply curve and label it appropriately.

e. Together, the effects described in (c) and (d) cause the euro to (appreciate/depreciate) and the dollar to (appreciate/depreciate). From the graph, we can see that, in the end, the exchange rate (increased/decreased) from _______________ dollars per euro in part (a) to _______________ dollars per euro in part (d).

15-MINUTE PRACTICE TEST

Set a timer, giving yourself just 15 minutes to answer all of the following questions. To see what you *really* know and remember, take the test at least a day *after* you've read the chapter in the text and completed the exercises in this study guide.

Multiple Choice: Circle the letter in front of the single best answer.

1. In the yen-dollar market, which of the following would shift the demand curve for Japanese yen rightward?
   a. An increase in real GDP in Japan
   b. An increase in the U.S. interest rate
   c. An increase in the Japanese price level
   d. All of the above
   e. None of the above

2. In the yen-dollar market, which of the following would shift the supply curve for Japanese yen rightward?
   a. An increase in real GDP in Japan
   b. An increase in the Japanese price level
   c. An increase in the U.S. interest rate
   d. All of the above
   e. None of the above

3. In the very short run (e.g., day to day), the most important influence on exchange rates is changes in
   a. relative inflation rates.
   b. the business cycle.
   c. relative interest rates.
   d. purchasing power parity.
   e. tastes for foreign goods.

4. Bilateral arbitrage assures us that
   a. similar goods will cost the same in different countries.
   b. inflation rates will tend to be similar among countries that trade with each other.
   c. a rise in a country's interest rate will cause its currency to appreciate.
   d. the exchange rate between any two currencies will be the same regardless of the country in which foreign currency is bought.
   e. the price of foreign currency will be the same whether the foreign currency is purchased directly or indirectly (i.e., through a third currency).

5. "You should go to Portugal, man. Everything there is, like, dirt cheap." If this statement is true, it is an apparent violation of
   a. comparative advantage.
   b. bilateral arbitrage.
   c. triangular arbitrage.
   d. the law of demand.
   e. purchasing power parity.

6. Under a managed float, a government will
   a. never intervene in the foreign exchange market.
   b. occasionally intervene in the foreign exchange market.
   c. fix the exchange rate against the currency of its trading partner.
   d. restrict the flow of capital into and out of the country.
   e. set up two different exchange rates: one for exports and another for imports.

7. If a country fixes its exchange rate below the equilibrium value, so its currency is artificially cheap to foreigners, it must
   a. buy its own currency in the foreign exchange market.
   b. sell its own currency in the foreign exchange market.
   c. sell other countries' currencies in the foreign exchange market.
   d. get permission from the United States and other powerful economies.
   e. raise its interest rates higher than they would be under a floating rate.

8. With floating exchange rates, an increase in government purchases causes GDP to rise by less when we take foreign trade into account, because the rise in G causes a
   a. fall in the interest rate.
   b. depreciation of the domestic currency.
   c. rise in net exports.
   d. all of the above.
   e. none of the above.

9. According to what you have learned in the chapter, which of the following would worsen a foreign currency crisis?
   a. The country in crisis raises its interest rate.
   b. The country in crisis discovers and announces previously unknown reserves of foreign currency.
   c. Residents of the country in crisis develop an increased taste for foreign goods.
   d. Residents of other countries develop an increased taste for the goods of the country in crisis.
   e. All of the above.

10. Under floating exchange rates, which of the following would cause U.S. net exports to decrease?
    a. A decrease in the U.S. money supply.
    b. An appreciation of the dollar.
    c. A depreciation of the currency of one of our major trading partners/
    d. All of the above
    e. None of the above

True/False: For each of the following statements, circle T if the statement is true or F if the statement is false.

T F 1. "Hot money" explains how exchange rates are determined in the long run.

T F 2. If exchange rates float, an increase in the U.S. interest rate will cause the U.S. dollar to appreciate against the currencies of its trading partners.

T F 3. An increase in U.S. GDP will cause the supply curve for British pounds to shift rightward.

T F 4. Bilateral arbitrage works to make the exchange rate between any two currencies the same, no matter in which country the currency is purchased.

T F 5. Under a managed float, a country's central bank sometimes buys its own currency to prevent it from depreciating, and sells its own currency to prevent it from appreciating.

T F 6. With floating exchange rates, an increase in the U.S. money supply will cause the U.S. dollar to depreciate and net exports to increase.

T F 7. If a country fixes its currency against the dollar, and currently the fixed exchange rate is the same as the equilibrium exchange rate, then a sudden decrease in that country's interest rate would require it to begin buying its own currency in the foreign exchange market.

T F 8. If a country has a trade deficit, it must also have a net capital inflow.

FINAL EXAM IN MACROECONOMICS

This exam is meant to test your understanding of *all* of macroeconomics, rather than just the material in individual chapters. To distinguish between memorization and understanding, many of these problems require you to *apply* the theory in a new way.

Answers and explanations are provided at the end. Keep in mind that (1) your own instructor may emphasize different material—including lecture material that may differ from the book; (2) your instructor may have asked the class to skip certain sections of the book (these questions will look entirely unfamiliar to you); and (3) your instructor's exam may or may not include multiple choice questions. So—although this exam will give you a chance for self-assessment—it may *not* be representative of the exam your instructor will give.

Give yourself 1¼ hours to do the exam. Answer all questions you can answer easily first, then go back to the more difficult ones.

1. Economists divide resources into the following three categories:

   a. labor, raw materials and land.
   b. labor, capital and raw materials.
   c. labor, physical capital and human capital.
   d. labor, capital and land.
   e. human capital, physical capital, and land.

2. Which of the following would be considered a *macroeconomic* problem?

   a. The danger of bankruptcy of a very large corporation.
   b. Inflation in the Philippines.
   c. The price that doctors charge for medical care.
   d. Technological change in the production of milk.
   e. Layoffs in the steel industry.

3. Which of the following is a positive economic statement?

   a. If Congress votes for a tax cut, the inflation rate will rise next year.
   b. If the price of milk rises, the price of breakfast cereal will fall.
   c. If the population continues growing at its current rate, and teachers' wages don't rise, we will have a shortage of teachers by the year 2020.
   d. All of the above.
   e. None of the above.

4. If Jim doesn't study another 3 hours for his econ exam, he will get a B+ instead of an A in the course. But in order to study for the exam, he will have to leave work (where he is paid by the hour) two hours early, and he will also miss the performance of a friend who is playing guitar for an hour at a local club. For Jim, the opportunity cost of studying enough to get an A rather than a B+ in his econ course is

   a. the wages he would lose by leaving work early.
   b. the wages he would lose by leaving work early *and also* the opportunity to see his friend perform.
   c. the wages he would lose by leaving work early *and also* any losses he would suffer from getting a B+ rather than an A in the course.
   d.. the wages he would lose by leaving work early *and also* any losses he would suffer from getting a B+ rather than an A in the course.
   e. the wages he would lose at his job *and also* the opportunity to see his friend perform and also any gains he would enjoy from getting an A rather than a B+ in the course.

5. If an economy is operating on its production possibilities frontier between military and civilian goods, then

   a. it is producing the maximum possible quantity of military goods, and cannot produce any more.
   b. it is producing the maximum possible quantity of civilian goods, and cannot produce any more.
   c. both a. and b.
   d. it can only produce more of either good if there is a recession and the recession is ended.
   e. it cannot produce any more of military goods without at the same time producing less of civilian goods.

6. Which of the following is the best example of the law of demand? (Assume there are no other changes other than those in each statement.)

   a. When the price of automobiles rises, the price of auto tires decreases.
   b. When the price of automobiles rises, the price of auto tires increases.
   c. When the price of automobiles rises, people by fewer autos.
   d. When the price of automobiles rises, people by fewer tires.
   e. When income rises, people buy more automobiles *and* more tires.

7. Which of the following would cause the supply curve for apples to shift rightward?

   a. A change in tastes makes people want more apples, driving up the price, and leading apple farms to harvest more carefully in order to sell more apples.
   b. A rise in income makes people want more apples, driving up the price, and leading apple farms to harvest more carefully in order to sell more apples. A rise in population increases results in greater demand for apples, driving up the price, and leading apple farms to harvest more carefully in order to sell more apples.
   c. All of the above.
   d. None of the above.

8. Which of the following events, with no other changes, would always increase the equilibrium quantity of gasoline purchased, but would have an ambiguous effect on the equilibrium price of gasoline (that is, we can't say for certain whether the price would rise or fall)?

   a. Automobiles become cheaper.
   b. Income rises.
   c. Income rises and there is a decrease in the cost of transporting gasoline from refineries to gas stations.
   d. Income rises and there is an increase in the cost of transporting gasoline from refineries to gas stations.
   e. Income falls and automobiles become cheaper.

9. During the great depression of the 1930s, the unemployment rate

   a. could not be measured at all, since there was no Department of Labor.
   b. reached about the same level as it did during the recession of 1990-91.
   c. reached about 25 percent—higher than it has ever been since.
   d. reached about 50 percent—and it reached that level only once in the decades following, and then only for a single year.
   e. reached almost 90 percent, as jobs disappeared throughout the economy.

10. Economists have identified our three most important macroeconomic goals as

    a. rapid economic growth, falling prices, and high employment.
    b. rapid economic growth, a trade surplus, and high employment.
    c. a high saving rate, stable prices, and high employment.
    d. national security, stable prices and high employment.
    e. rapid economic growth, stable prices and high employment.

11. Which of the following would be included in U.S. GDP?

    a. The value of the groceries you buy at the store.
    b. The value of an automobile purchased by Hertz to be rented out later to customers.
    c. Steel that was produced but not sold during the year.
    d. All of the above.
    e. None of the above.

12. Which of the following would be considered "government purchases" when measuring GDP?

    a. The salary of a city police officer.
    b. U.S. government social security payments to retired workers.
    c. The groceries that a U.S. postal worker buys at the store.
    d. All of the above.
    e. None of the above.

13. Suppose that, in a given year, consumption spending is $5 trillion, exports are $3.2 trillion, imports are $4 trillion, government transfer payments to households are $2 trillion, business spending on plant and equipment is $1 trillion, new housing construction is $0.5 trillion, government purchases of goods and services are $3 trillion, taxes are $3.5 trillion, and inventories of unsold goods during the year decline from $4 trillion to $3.3 trillion. Then using the expenditure approach, GDP during the year is

    a. $6 trillion.
    b. $8 trillion.
    c. $10 trillion.
    d. $11.2 trillion.
    e. $12 trillion

14. Suppose that, in a given year, a country's GDP using the expenditure approach is $5 trillion. Then, during that year, the total income earned by the owners of the country's resources (or factors of production) will be

    a. $5 trillion.
    b. $5 trillion minus total payments made for intermediate goods.
    c. $5 trillion minus total taxes paid by households and businesses.
    d. $5 trillion minus both payments for intermediate goods and taxes paid by households and businesses.
    e. $5 trillion *minus* the sum of total rent, total profit and total interest.

15. In order to build each of its DVD player, a firm buys $100 of components, pays out $200 in salaries, and sells each player to the public for $600, earning $300 in profit. The total contribution of each DVD player to GDP is

    a. $100.
    b. $300.
    c. $500.
    d. $600.
    e. $1,200.

16. Suppose that, during the year, nominal GDP grows by 6 percent, real GDP grows by 2 percent, and the population grows by 2 percent. Then, during the year, the standard of living (using the typical definition of that term)

    a. rises by 10 percent.
    b. rises by 8 percent.
    c. rises by 6 percent.
    d. rises by 4 percent.
    e. doesn't rise at all.

17. Which of the following problems probably causes GDP to *underestimate* total production?

    a. GDP's treatment of non-market activity.
    b. GDP's treatment of most quality improvements.
    c. GDP's treatment of the underground economy.
    d. All of the above.
    e. None of the above.

18. Suppose the price of the typical consumer's market basket rises from $150 to $160 during a year. Then, according to the CPI, the inflation rate for the year would be

    a. 6.25 percent.
    b. 6.66 percent.
    c. 7.00 percent.
    d. 10 percent.
    e. none of the above.

19. In the United States, currency is

    a. fully-backed paper money.
    b. commodity money.
    c. fiat money.
    d. all of the above.
    e. none of the above.

20. The prices of which of the following are tracked by the CPI?

    a. fresh milk bought in the store.
    b. computers purchased by businesses.
    c. building materials purchased by the government.
    d. all of the above.
    e. none of the above.

21. Over some period of time, which of the following combinations is impossible?

    a. a rising price level and an increasing inflation rate.
    b. a rising price level and a decreasing inflation rate.
    c. a rising price level and a stable inflation rate.
    d. an unchanging price level and a rising inflation rate.
    e. an unchanging price level and a zero inflation rate.

22. Suppose the wage rate is $10 per hour at the beginning of the year, and $15 per hour at the beginning of the *next* year. Suppose, too, that during this period, the price level rises from 2.0 to 2.2. Then, over the year, the *real* wage rises by

    a. 0 percent.
    b. 20 percent.
    c. 30 percent.
    d. 36 percent.
    e. 50 percent.

23. Suppose a worker's nominal wage rises by 3 percent per year for three years. At the same time, the price level rises by 5 percent per year for three years. Then, at the end of the three years, the real wage will have

    a. increased by 2 percent.
    b. decreased by 2 percent.
    c. decreased by 5.5 percent.
    d. decreased by 6.1 percent.
    e. decreased by 15 percent.

24. Suppose you lend a friend $500 for a year, and at the end of the year she pays you back $550. Meanwhile, there was 2 percent inflation during the year. Then the real interest rate you received on your loan was approximately

    a. 48 percent.
    b. 10 percent.
    c. 8 percent.
    d. 5 percent.
    e. -2 percent.

25. Which of the following is a *critical assumption* of the classical model?

    a. markets clear.
    b. there is only one kind of labor.
    c. the government budget is balanced.
    d. all of the above.
    e. none of the above.

26. In the classical model, equilibrium in which of the following markets assures that Say's Law holds?

    a. the labor market.
    b. the market for loanable funds.
    c. the market for consumers goods and services.
    d. the market for net exports.
    e. the market for human capital.

27. In the classical model, suppose the labor market clears at a wage of $40 per hour. Then, if the hourly wage were stuck at $50 for some time, there would be

    a. an excess demand for labor.
    b. an excess supply of labor.
    c. full employment, but at a higher than necessary wage.
    d. a downward shift of the production function.
    e. an upward shift of the production function.

28. In the classical/long-run model, which of the following would cause real GDP to increase?

    a. an increase in transfer payments to the poor and the retired.
    b. an increase in consumption spending.
    c. an increase in the government defense budget.
    d. an increase in the capital stock.
    e. all of the above.

29. In the classical model, a rise in the interest rate will cause

    a. a decrease in saving.
    b. a decrease in the government's demand for loanable funds.
    c. an increase in business demand for loanable funds.
    d. all of the above.
    e. none of the above.

30. In the classical model, an increase in the desire to work among the population would cause

a. an increase in total output.
b. an upward shift in the production function.
c. a rise in the interest rate.
d. all of the above.
e. none of the above.

31. In the classical model, if the government is running a budget deficit and raises taxes to decrease the deficit,

a. output will rise.
b. the interest rate will fall.
c. saving will rise.
d. all of the above.
e. none of the above.

32. In the classical model, if the government is running a budget surplus, then equilibrium in the loanable funds market ensures us that the surplus is equal to

a. saving.
b. planned investment.
c. planned investment minus saving.
d. saving minus planned investment.
e. saving plus taxes.

33. In the long run, an increase in labor supply will

a. increase employment and increase the wage rate.
b. increase output and decrease the wage rate.
c. cause the production function to shift downward.
d. cause the production function to shift upward.
e. lead to an excess supply of labor and unemployment.

34. A less-developed country with a population of 50 million has a GDP of $50 billion. 80 percent of the population is over the age of 16, and 50 percent of those over 16 are working. Labor productivity in this country would be equal to

a. $2,500
b. $2,000
c. $1,250
d. $250
e. $43

35. In the long run, which of the following would tend to *decrease* a nation's labor productivity, all else remaining the same?

a. An increase in labor supply.
b. An upward shift of the production function.
c. An increase in the capital stock.
d. All of the above.
e. None of the above.

36. Which of the following policies would increase output or the growth rate of output in the long run *even if* labor supply is completely inelastic (the labor supply curve is vertical)?

    a. A subsidy to business firms for hiring.
    b. A decrease in the tax on income that is saved.
    c. An increase in government spending on transfer payments.
    d. An increase in consumption spending.
    e. A repeal of the investment tax credit.

37. Which of the following can explain why the U.S. economy goes into recessions so often?

    a. Leftward shifts of the labor supply curve.
    b. Leftward shifts of the labor demand curve.
    c. Rightward shifts of the labor demand curve.
    d. None of the above.
    e. All of the above.

38. At each level of employment, the labor supply curve tells us

    a. the opportunity cost to the last worker of taking a job.
    b. the opportunity cost to some firm from hiring another worker.
    c. the marginal benefit to some firm from hiring another worker.
    d. the additional taxes the government would collect if another worker is hired.
    e. the productivity of labor.

Questions 39 – 43 refer to an economy in the short run in which the following holds (all figures in $ billions): planned investment is 4,000; government purchases are 1,000; net taxes are 300, exports are 400, autonomous consumption is 400, imports are 500, and the marginal propensity to consume is 0.9.

39. In this economy, the government is running a budget

    a. surplus of $300 billion.
    b. surplus of $730 billion.
    c. deficit of $700 billion.
    d. deficit of $1,000 billion.
    e. deficit of $1,300 billion.

40. In this economy, net exports are equal to

    a. $900 billion.
    b. $500 billion.
    c. $400 billion.
    d. $100 billion.
    e. -$100 billion.

41. In this economy, equilibrium GDP is equal to

    a. $49,270 billion.
    b. $49,300 billion.
    c. $50,270 billion.
    d. $50,300 billion.
    e. $51,300 billion.

42. In this economy, if government purchases were to rise by $1,000 billion, GDP would rise by

a. $0.
b. $700 billion.
c. $1,000 billion.
d. $3,000 billion.
e. $10,000 billion.

43. In this economy, if taxes were to rise by $1,000 billion, real GDP would

a. rise by more than $1,000 billion.
b. rise, but by less than $1,000 billion.
c. fall by more than $1,000 billion.
d. fall, but by less than $1,000 billion.
e. remain unchanged in the short run.

44. Which of the following will shift up the economy's aggregate expenditure line in the short run?

a. an increase in income.
b. an increase in taxes.
c. an increase in the desire of the public to save.
d. an increase in net exports.
e. all of the above.

45. If in the short run, GDP is greater than equilibrium GDP, then

a. there is excess unemployment in the economy.
b. inventories are rising.
c. inventories are falling.
d. total investment is negative.
e. planned investment is growing.

46. Which of the following is *not* included in the money supply?

a. paper bills that people carry in their wallets.
b. coins that people carry in their pockets.
c. funds that people hold in their checking accounts.
d. travelers checks that people hold in their wallets.
e. shares of corporate stock that could be easily sold.

47. The members of the Federal Reserve Board of Governors are

a. appointed for life.
b. elected every four years.
c. chosen by the president without the need for any Congressional approval.
d. by law former state governors.
e. none of the above.

48. If the Federal Reserve purchases $10,000 in government bonds from a bond dealer, and the bond dealer deposits the proceeds into a checking account at First National Bank, then in First National's balance sheet, we will see

    a. an increase in liabilities only.
    b. an increase in assets only.
    c. an increase in liabilities and a decrease in assets.
    d. a decrease in liabilities and an increase in assets.
    e. none of the above.

49. If the required reserve ratio os 0.25 and a bank has $500 million in demand deposits, $400 million in bonds, and $100 million in property and buildings, then to meet its reserve requirements, it must hold reserves equal to

    a. $500 million.
    b. $250 million.
    c. $225 million.
    d. 150 million.
    e. $125 million.

50. If the Fed buys $100 million in government bonds, and the required reserve ratio is 0.25, then—making the typical simplifying assumptions—we can expect total demand deposits to grow by

    a. $25 million.
    b. $100 million.
    c. $250 million.
    d. $400 million.
    e. $500 million.

51. The U.S. has not suffered from a banking panic since the great depression primarily because

    a. we are a much wealthier country today.
    b. the media works to calm people down, helping to prevent panic.
    c. there is FDIC protection of bank deposits.
    d. Congress stands ready to use appropriate fiscal policy to help stabilize the economy.
    e. international trade is a much more important part of our economy today than during the great depression.

52. Which of the following will shift the money demand curve rightward?

    a. A drop in the interest rate.
    b. A rise in GDP.
    c. A drop in employment.
    d. All of the above.
    e. None of the above.

53. If the Fed purchases government bonds,

    a. the interest rate will fall.
    b. the money supply curve will shift rightward.
    c. investment spending will increase.
    d. all of the above.
    e. none of the above.

54. If the interest rate is *above* the equilibrium interest rate, then we know there is

    a. an excess supply of money.
    b. an excess supply of bonds.
    c. an excess supply of both money and bonds.
    d. an excess demand for both money and bonds.
    e. an excess demand for money, but no excess demand or supply for bonds.

55. When the Fed conducts an open market operation by selling government bonds, the result will be

    a. an increase in the interest rate.
    b. an increase in real GDP.
    c. an increase in the money supply.
    d. all of the above.
    e. none of the above.

56. Which of the following will shift the economy's aggregate demand curve leftward?

    a. an increase in taxes.
    b. an increase in the money supply.
    c. an increase in the price level.
    d. all of the above.
    e. none of the above.

57. Which of the following will move us rightward and upward along an unchanged aggregate supply curve?

    a. An increase in firms' average markup over costs.
    b. An increase in oil prices.
    c. An increase in real GDP.
    d. All of the above.
    e. None of the above.

58. When the economy is hit with a negative demand shock,

    a. the aggregate supply curve shifts leftward and the price level rises.
    b. the aggregate demand curve shifts leftward and the price level rises.
    c. the aggregate demand curve shift rightward and the price level rises.
    d. the aggregate demand curve shifts rightward and the price level falls.
    e. none of the above.

59. Which of the following does *not* occur as the economy self-corrects from an equilibrium GDP greater than full-employment GDP?

    a. the price level rises.
    b. output falls.
    c. employment falls.
    d. the money supply falls.
    e. the unemployment rate rises.

60. If the Fed wants to pursue an *active* monetary policy to prevent a recession when there is a rise in the price of oil, then the Fed

    a. should increase the money supply.
    b. should shift the AD curve rightward.
    c. will have to accept higher inflation in the short run.
    d. all of the above.
    e. none of the above.

61. If we observe that the price level is falling at the same time that output is falling, which of the following could be the cause?

    a. a negative demand shock.
    b. a positive demand shock.
    c. a negative or adverse supply shock.
    d. a positive supply shock.
    e. any of the above could be the cause.

62. Most economists believe that, to stabilize the economy from quarter to quarter, the dominant policy should be

    a. fiscal policy.
    b. exchange rate policy.
    c. monetary policy.
    d. oil price policy.
    e. tax policy.

63. Which of the following, with no other changes, would cause the U.S. dollar to depreciate against the Euro?

    a. A decrease in U.S. income.
    b. A rise in the U.S. money supply.
    c. An increase in income in Europe.
    d. All of the above.
    e. None of the above.

64. Suppose the Polish Zloty is at its equilibrium floating exchange rate with the U.S. dollar, and then the Polish government decides to fix the exchange rate at its current value. If the interest rate in the U.S. rises, the result will be

    a. an immediate appreciation of the Zloty against the dollar.
    b. an immediate appreciation of the dollar against the Zloty.
    c. an excess demand for the Zloty.
    d. an excess supply of the Zloty.
    e. an excess supply of dollars.

65. Suppose that, over many years, the annual inflation rate in the U.S. is 5 percent, in Britain it is 8 percent, and in continental Europe it is 10 percent. Then, over the long run, we would expect

    a. the dollar to depreciate against the British pound.
    b. the dollar to depreciate against the Euro.
    c. the British pound to depreciate against the Euro.
    d. all of the above.
    e. none of the above.

ANSWERS TO QUESTIONS

ANSWERS FOR CHAPTER 1

Speaking Economics

1. economics
2. scarcity
3. resources
4. labor
5. capital
6. human capital
7. land
8. microeconomics
9. macroeconomics
10. positive economics
11. normative economics
12. model
13. simplifying assumption
14. critical assumption

Chapter Highlights

1. scarcity
2. resources
3. land; labor; capital
4. micro
5. macro
6. positive
7. normative
8. abstract
9. conclusions
10. critical

Important Concepts

1. a. microeconomic; positive
   b. macroeconomic; positive
   c. microeconomic; positive
   d. microeconomic; normative
   e. macroeconomic; positive
   f. microeconomic; normative
   g. macroeconomic; normative

2. a. labor
   b. capital
   c. capital
   d. land
   e. labor
   f. capital
   g. labor
   h. capital

3. False: The right amount of detail depends on the purpose for which the model will be used. In general, a model should have as few details as possible to accomplish its purpose.

4. False: The two types of assumptions are "simplifying assumptions" and "critical assumptions."

Skills and Tools

1. a.

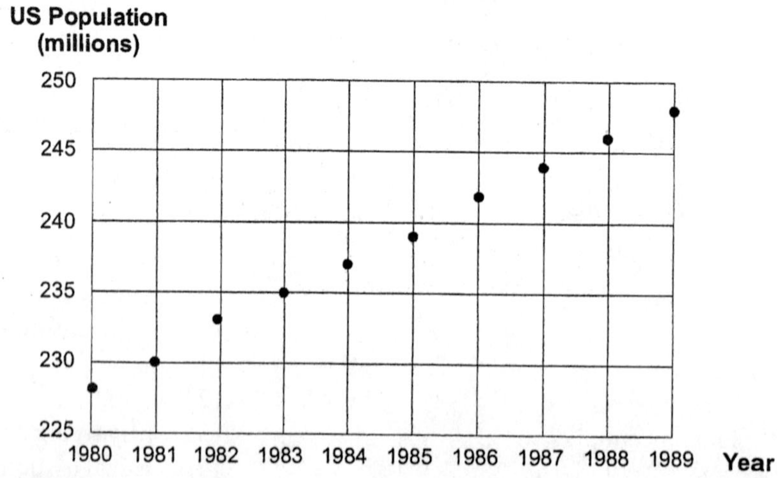

b. (iv)

c.

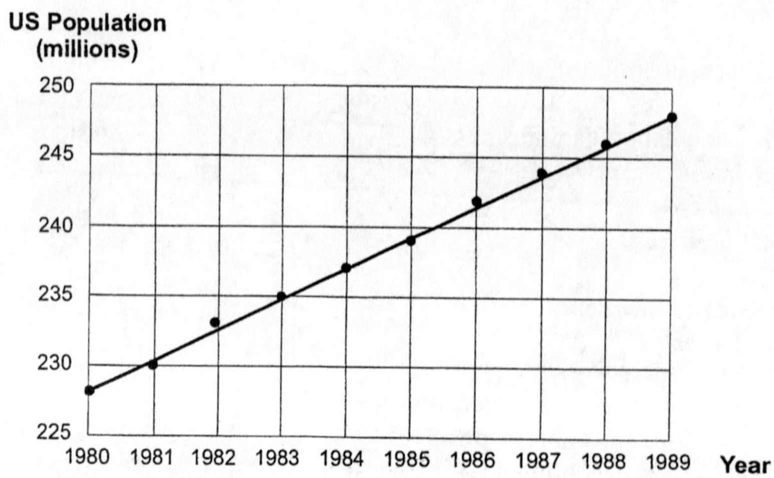

d. Population increased by approximately 2.24 million per year. Your answer can differ from this by a bit because it will depend on how you drew your line with the ruler. To get your answer, though, calculate how much population increased along the vertical axis (the rise) as you move from any one year to the next year along the horizontal axis (the run) on the line you drew.

2. a. 30 to 60; 90 to 120; positive
   b. 0 to 30; 60 to 90; negative
   c. Maximum value of Y = 1,000 is achieved at X = 60; Minimum value of Y = 200 is achieved at X = 90.

3.

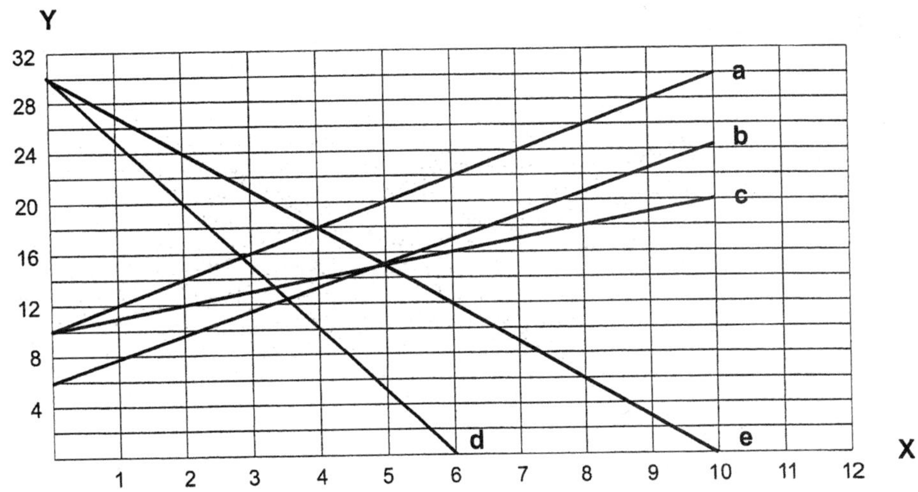

a. 10; 2; increases; constant
b. 5; 2; increases; constant
c. 10; 1; increases; constant
d. 30; –5; decreases; constant
e. 30; –3; decreases; constant

10-Minute Practice Test

Multiple Choice

1. c
2. e
3. d
4. b
4. b
5. c
6. b

True/False

1. F
2. F
3. F
4. T
5. F

ANSWERS FOR CHAPTER 2

Speaking Economics

1. opportunity cost
2. production possibilities frontier (PPF)
3. law of increasing opportunity cost.
4. productive inefficiency
5. specialization
6. exchange
7. absolute advantage
8. comparative advantage
9. resource allocation
10. traditional economy
11. command economy; centrally planned economy
12. market economy
13. market
14. price
15. communism
16. socialism
17. capitalism
18. economic system

Chapter Highlights

1. opportunity cost
2. opportunity cost; resources
3. increasing; greater
4. inefficient
5. specialization; exchange; specialization; exchange
6. absolute advantage
7. comparative advantage
8. comparative advantage
9. command
10. market

Important Concepts

1. False; if the individual had not gone to college, he/she would only have had *one* of the full-time jobs, not all three of them. To determine the foregone income, we would use the job that *would* have been chosen if the person did not go to college. If, for example, the person would have chosen to be a truck driver, then the opportunity cost of a year in college would be the direct money cost of college plus $45,000 in foregone income.

2. The law of increasing opportunity cost.

3. In any order
   (a) productive inefficiency
   (b) recession.

4. In any order
   (a) The development of expertise from specializing in a single task
   (b) the reduction in unproductive time to switch among different tasks
   (c) gains from comparative advantage.

5. Yes, this is consistent with comparative advantage. College professors have a comparative advantage in other activities, such as writing research papers and teaching. The opportunity cost of locating library materials is higher for them than for their students.

6. In any order
   (a) tradition
   (b) command
   (c) the market

7. In any order
   (a) communism
   (b) socialism
   (c) capitalism

8. In any order
   a. market capitalism – resource allocation by the market; private resource ownership
   b. centrally planned capitalism – resource allocation by command; private resource ownership
   c. centrally planned socialism – resource allocation by command; state resource ownership
   d. market socialism – resource allocation by the market; state resource ownership

Skills and Tools

1. a.

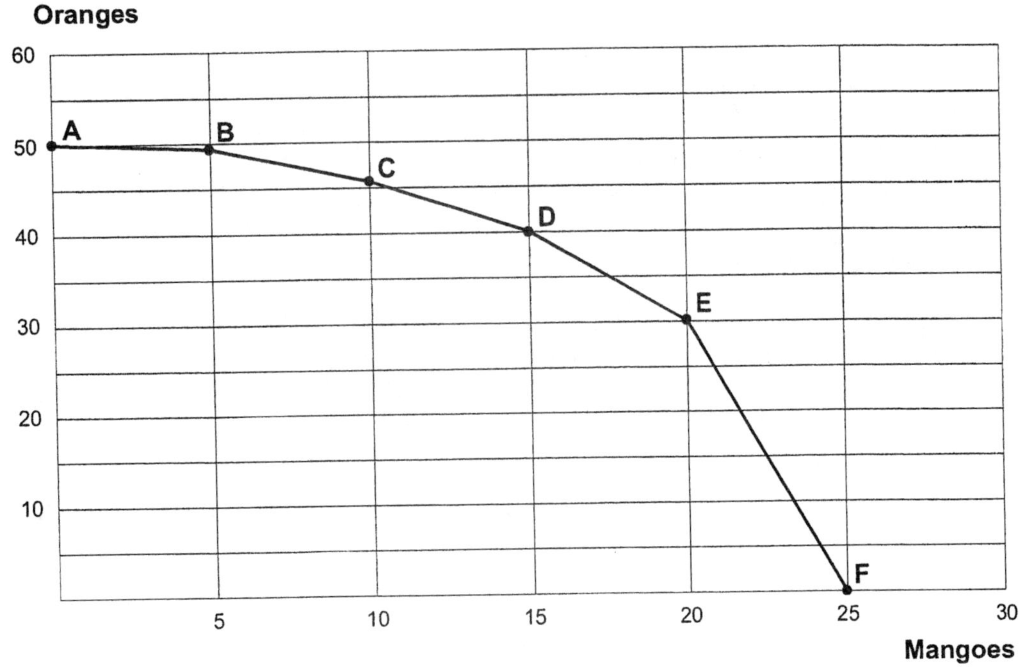

   b. 1; 5; 5; 1
   5; 3; 3
   5; 6; 5; 10; 5; 30
   increasing

   c. 5; 30; 30; 5
   10; 5; 5
   6; 5; 3; 5
   increasing

2. a. are not; zero; zero; no
   b. cannot; improve; acquire more

3. Constant; 50; Y; 50; Y; 50; Y; constant

4. Increases; less than; greater than

5. a. sweaters; fish
   b. 2; 1/3; fish; sweaters

15-Minute Practice Test

Multiple Choice

1. c
2. d
3. a
4. b
5. b
6. e
7. d
8. c
9. a
10. e

True/False

1.	F	5.	F
2.	F	6.	T
3.	T	7.	F
4.	T	8.	F

ANSWERS FOR CHAPTER 3

Speaking Economics

1. aggregation
2. imperfectly competitive market
3. perfectly competitive market
4. individual's quantity demanded
5. market quantity demanded
6. law of demand
7. demand schedule
8. demand curve
9. change in quantity demanded
10. change in demand
11. income
12. wealth
13. normal good
14. inferior good
15. substitute
16. complement
17. technology
18. firm's quantity supplied
19. market quantity supplied
20. law of supply
21. supply schedule
22. supply curve
23. change in quantity supplied
24. change in supply
25. alternate good
26. equilibrium
27. excess demand
28. excess supply

Chapter Highlights

1. market
2. buyers, sellers (either order)
3. imperfectly competitive
4. competitive (or perfectly competitive); price (or market price)
5. competitive (or perfectly competitive)
6. demanded; price
7. market quantity demanded; price
8. law; fall
9. demand curve; price
10. downward
11. quantity demanded
12. shift; change in demand
13. income, wealth (either order); income, wealth (either order); right
14. increase; right
15. decrease; left
16. technology; inputs; outputs
17. prices; price
18. supplied; price
19. market quantity supplied
20. increase
21. price; price
22. upward
23. quantity supplied
24. shift; change in supply
25. decrease; left
26. rises; falls; left
27. increase; right
28. right
29. decrease; left
30. equilibrium
31. equilibrium; equilibrium
32. left
33. right
34. market; market; market
35. goals; constraints; goals; constraints
36. equilibrium; equilibrium; equilibrium
37. equilibrium

Important Concepts

1. Income (decrease, since it's a normal good); wealth (decrease, since it's a normal good); price of a substitute (decrease); price of a complement (increase); population (decrease); expectations (e.g., an expectation that the price will *fall* in the future); tastes (a change in tastes *away* from the good).

2. Prices of inputs (decrease); profitability of alternate good (decrease); technology (e.g., a cost-saving technological advance); productive capacity (increase, e.g. from an increase in the number of firms); expected future price of the good (decrease).

3. In a perfectly competitive market, there are so many small buyers and sellers that *no one of them can influence the market price*. Each buyer and seller takes the market price as given. In an imperfectly competitive market, at least some buyers or sellers have the ability to influence the price of the product.

4. False. Income is what you earn over a *period* of time. Your wealth is the total value of what you own, minus what you owe, at a given *moment* in time.

5. False. A "change in demand" refers only to a shift in the demand curve. The phrase, "change in quantity demanded" is used for a movement along the demand curve.

Skills and Tools

1. a.

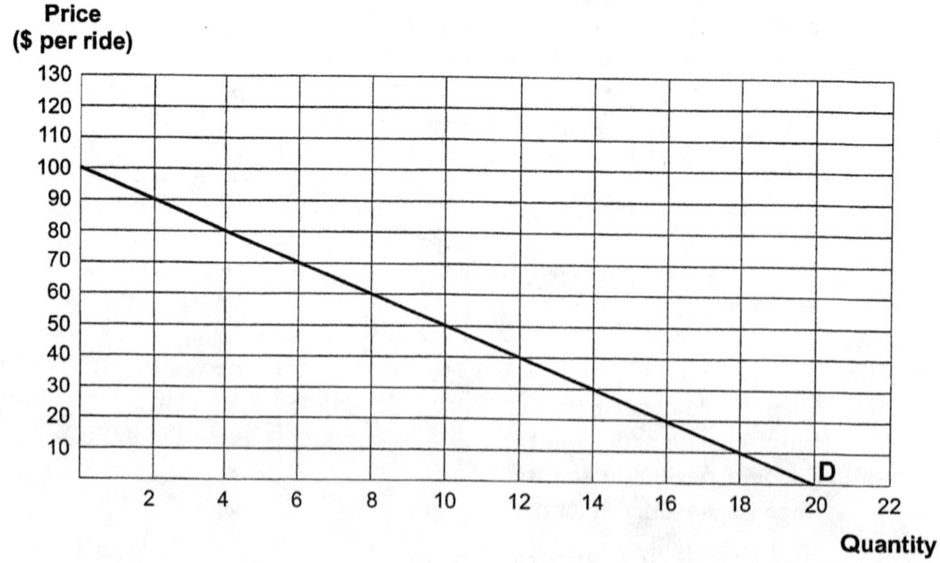

b. 10; fall; 2; rise; 18

2. a.

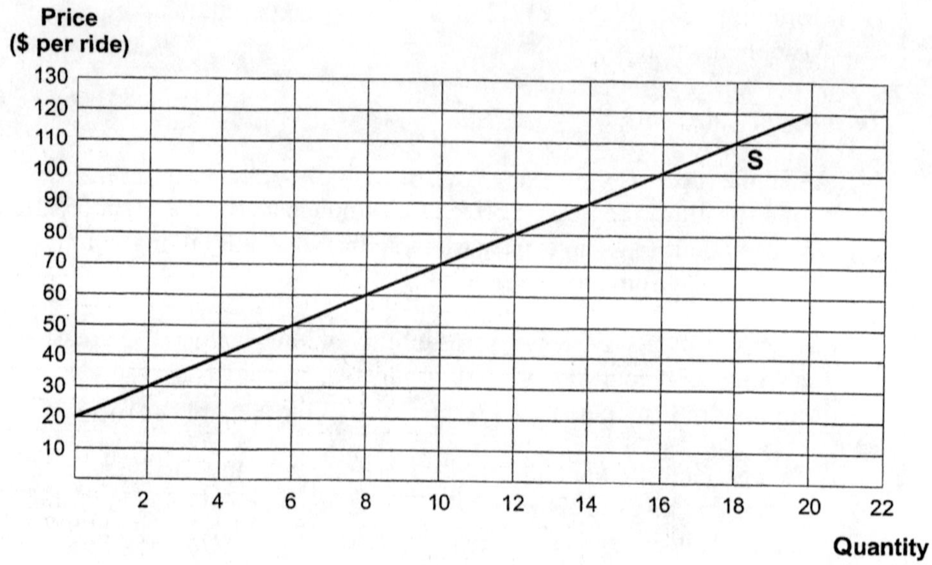

b. 6; rise; 14; fall; 2

3.

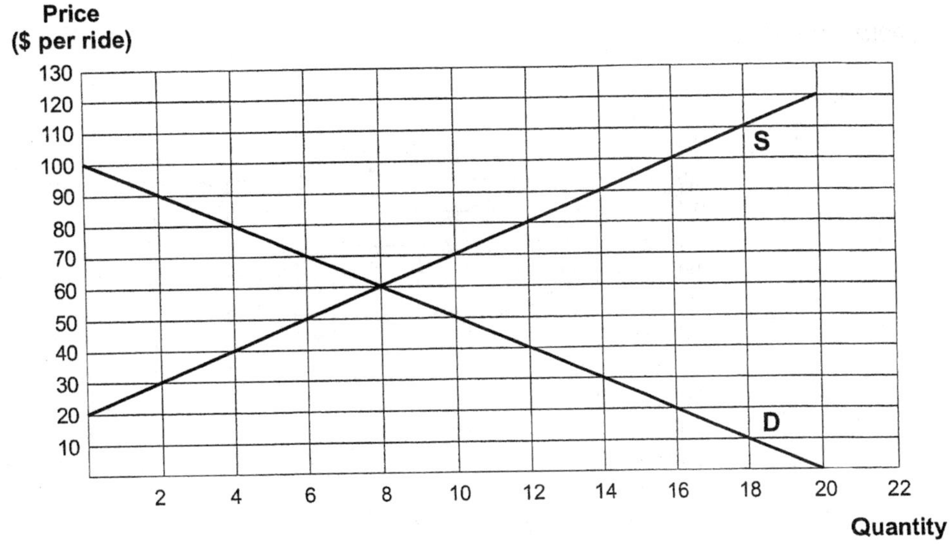

a. 60; 8
b. supply; 8; fall sellers; sell
c. demand; 8; rise; buyers; buy

4. a. $120
b. increase; rightward
c.

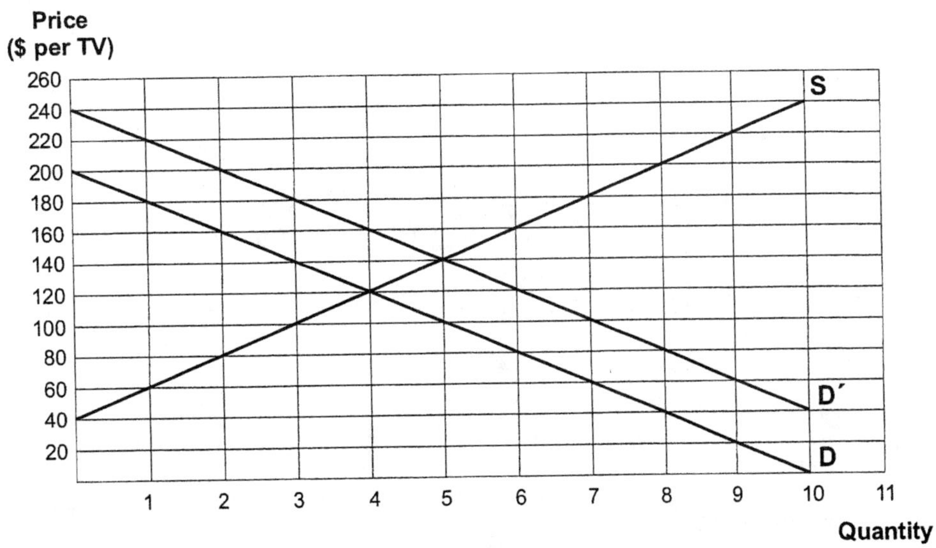

d. Equilibrium price is now $140, where D′ intersects S
e. decrease; leftward

f.

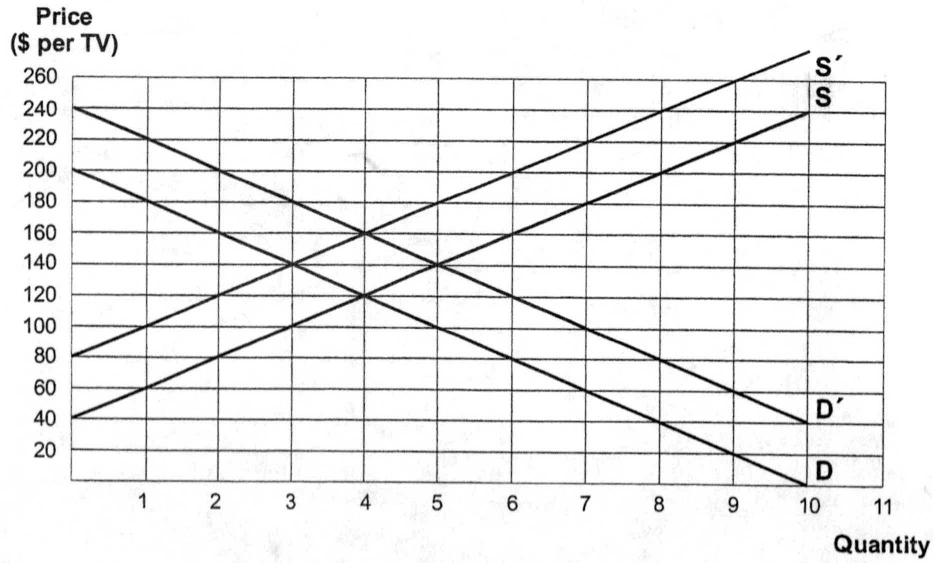

g. Equilibrium price is now $160, where S′ intersects D′

5. a.

P	Q^D	Q^S
$450	20	80
400	30	70
350	40	60
300	50	50
250	60	40
200	70	30
150	80	20[3]

b. supplied; demanded; excess supply; 40; fall; $300

c. demanded; supplied; excess demand; 60; rise; $300

6.

P	Q^D	Q^S
$270	2	20
210	6	15
90	14	5
30	18	0

7. P_e = \$150; Yes; 10; Yes

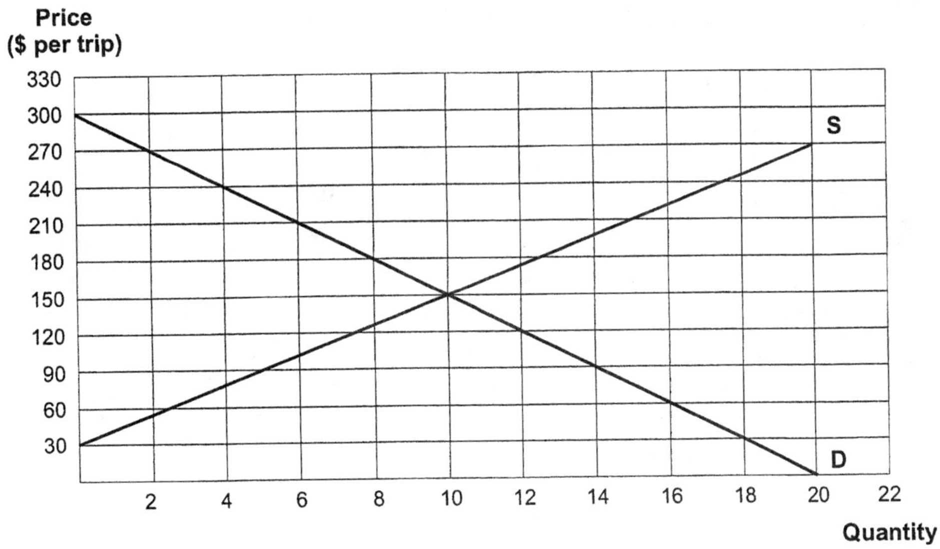

8. a. \$1,600; 300
   b. 350; 100; excess demand; 250
   c. 250; 500; excess supply; 250

15-Minute Practice Test

Multiple Choice

1. e
2. b
3. d
4. a
5. d
6. b
7. b
8. c
9. b
10. c

True/False

1. F
2. F
3. T
4. F
5. T
6. F
7. F
8. T

ANSWERS FOR CHAPTER 4

Speaking Economics

1. business cycles
2. expansion
3. peak
4. recession
5. trough
6. depression
7. aggregation

Chapter Highlights

1. stable prices (or low inflation)
2. real gross domestic product (or real GDP)
3. unemployment rate
4. expansion; peak; recession; trough
5. aggregation

Important Concepts

1. (in any order):
   rapid economic growth,
   high employment
   stable prices (or low inflation)

2. An expansion is a period of rising output; a peak occurs when output reaches its highest point during an expansion.

3. Disagreement can be positive (about how the economy works) or normative (about what we should do about the economy, based on our differing values).

10-Minute Practice Test

Multiple Choice

1. e
2. d
3. b
4. c
5. d
6. c
7. b
8. c

True/False

1. F
2. F
3. T
4. F
5. F

ANSWERS FOR CHAPTER 5

Speaking Economics

1. gross domestic product (GDP)
2. intermediate good
3. final good
4. flow variable
5. stock variable
6. expenditure approach
7. consumption
8. capital stock
9. private investment
10. net investment
11. government purchases
12. transfer payments
13. net exports
14. value added
15. value added approach
16. factor payments
17. factor payments approach
18. nominal variable
19. real variable
20. nonmarket production
21. frictional unemployment
22. seasonal unemployment
23. structural unemployment
24. cyclical unemployment
25. full employment
26. potential output
27. labor force
28. unemployment rate
29. involuntary part-time workers
30. discouraged workers

Chapter Highlights

1. gross domestic product; final; the nation's borders
2. intermediate; final; intermediate; final
3. flow
4. expenditure
5. households
6. plant, equipment (either order): home; inventories (or inventory stocks)
7. (either order): private; government
8. Transfer; transfers (or transfer payments); purchases
9. net; imports
10. intermediate goods
11. firms
12. factor
13. firms; profit; households
14. income (or factor payments)
15. nominal; real
16. nominal; current; purchasing
17. Short; short
18. cyclical; (any order): seasonal, frictional, structural
19. consume

Important Concepts

1. GDP is the total value of all final goods and services produced for the marketplace during a given year, within the nation's borders.

2. (any order): expenditure approach; factor payments approach; value added approach

3. a. yes; G
   b. no; nothing produced
   c. no; nothing produced
   d. yes; C
   e. no; nothing produced
   f. yes; I
   g. yes; NX
   h. yes; I

4. a. flow
   b. flow
   c. stock
   d. stock
   e. stock
   f. flow
   g. flow
   h. flow

5. (any order): seasonal; frictional; structural; cyclical

Skills and Tools

1. a. $5,490
   b. $1,221
   c. $1,476
   d. $106
   e. $8,293
   f. Wear and tear on factory equipment, Existing homes which were destroyed, Depreciation of government assets, Transfer payments

2. a. (See table.)

	Firm	Cost of Intermediate Goods	Revenue	Value Added
Cars	Rubber Company	$0.00	$0.75	$0.75
	Tire Company	$0.75	$1.50	$0.75
	Steel Company	$0.00	$2.00	$2.00
	Car Manufacturer	$3.50	$4.00	$0.50
	Car Dealer	$4.00	$4.50	$0.50
Food	Farmer	$0.00	$0.75	$0.75
	Supermarket	$0.75	$1.00	$0.25

   b. $5.50

3. a. $930
   b. $315
   c. $150
   d. $1,605
   e. $3,000
   f. $350 of the total revenue of Summertime Farming comes from the sale of intermediate goods to Savory Sandwiches. This $350 is not included when calculating GDP using the expenditure approach, because it is already included in spending on the final goods produced by Savory Farms. Other than the this $350, the rest of the total revenue represents sales of final goods, so GDP is $1,400 - $350 + $1,950 = $3,000, just as we found using the factor payments approach in e. above.

4. a. 212 million; 148.5 million; 4.7%
   b. remain unchanged; 148.5 million
   c. remain unchanged; remain unchanged
   d. decrease; decrease; 3.4%
   e. decrease; decrease; 2.7%
   f. decrease; 0%
   g. increase; increase; 6.0%

15-Minute Practice Test

Multiple Choice

1. d
2. d
3. b
4. c
5. b
6. e
7. e
8. a
9. d
10. e

True/False

1. F
2. F
3. T
4. T
5. F
6. T
7. F
8. F

ANSWERS FOR CHAPTER 6

Speaking Economics

1. unit of value
2. means of payment
3. Federal Reserve System
4. fiat money
5. price level
6. index
7. Consumer Price Index (CPI)
8. inflation rate
9. deflation
10. indexation
11. nominal variable
12. real variable
13. GDP price index
14. nominal interest rate
15. real interest rate

Chapter Highlights

1. nominal; nominal; 100
2. GDP; consumer
3. average
4. purchasing power
5. the rate of inflation
6. anticipated (or expected)
7. inaccurate; higher; lower
8. resources
9. more rapidly; more slowly; over-
10. over
11. over
12. over
13. increase

Important Concepts

1. Commodity money has some value in itself, because it has an important non-money use. Fiat money has no intrinsic value; it is money because the government declares that it is money.

2. (either order): redistributive cost; resource cost.

3. (three of the following four, in any order): substitution bias—leads to *over*estimate; new technologies—leads to *over*estimate; quality changes—leads to *over*estimate; growth in discounting—leads to *over*estimate.

Skills and Tools

1. a. (See table.)

	Avg. Temperature (Degrees F)	Temperature Index (May = 100)
January	33	47.1
February	30	42.9
March	42	60.0
April	56	80.0
May	70	100.0
June	78	111.4
July	84	120.0
August	88	125.7
September	79	112.9
October	75	107.1
November	63	90.0
December	45	64.3

   b. increased; 100; 111.4; 11.4%; higher
   c. 90.0; 10%; lower
   d. February; October; April

2. a. (See graph.)

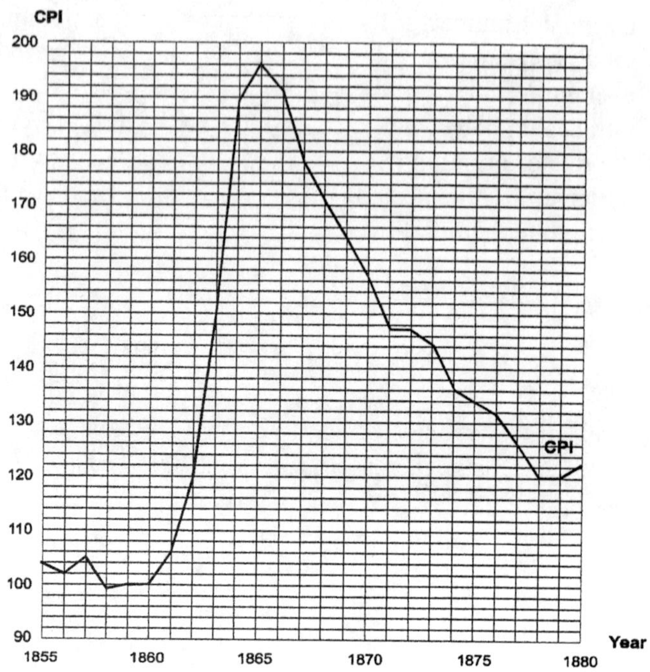

b. increased; 100; 196; 96%; higher; decreased; 23%; higher
c. (See table.)

Year	CPI	Inflation Rate	Year	CPI	Inflation Rate
1860	100		1865	196	
		6.0%			–2.6%
1861	106		1866	191	
		14.2%			–6.8%
1862	121		1867	178	
		24.8%			–3.9%
1863	151		1868	171	
		25.2 %			–4.1%
1864	189		1869	164	
		3.7%			–4.3%
1865	196		1870	157	

d. inflation; inflation; 3.7%; 1864; 1865; 25.2%; 1863; 1864
e. deflation; deflation; 1866; 1867

3. a. increased every year; increased every year
b. (See graph.)

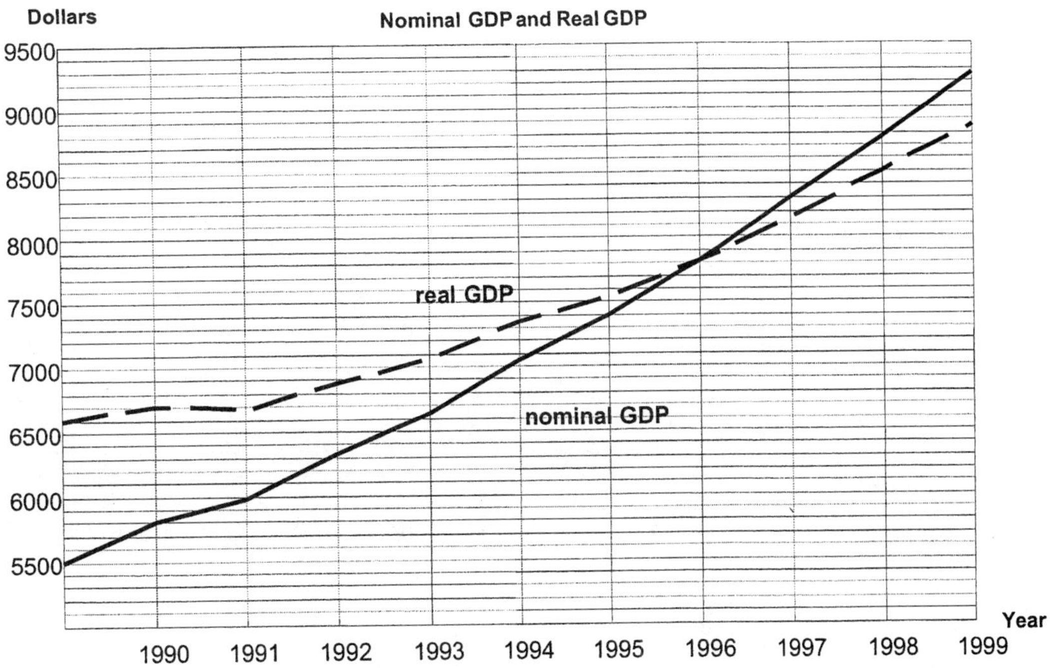

c. did not; decreased; 6,707.9; 6,676.4; increased; 5,803.2; 5,986.2; increased; 86.5; 89.7; decreased; increased; increased; greater; increased

4. a. (See table.)

Year	Prime Bank Interest Rate (Nominal)	Inflation Rate	Prime Bank Interest (Real)
1991	8.5%	3.1%	5.4%
1992	6.3%	2.9%	3.4%
1993	6.0%	2.7%	3.3%
1994	7.1%	2.7%	4.4%
1995	8.8%	2.5%	6.3%
1996	8.3%	3.3%	5.0%
1997	8.4%	1.7%	6.7%
1998	8.4%	1.6%	6.8%
1999	8.0%	2.7%	5.3%
2000	9.2%	3.4%	5.8%
2001	6.9%	1.6%	5.3%

b. (See graph.)

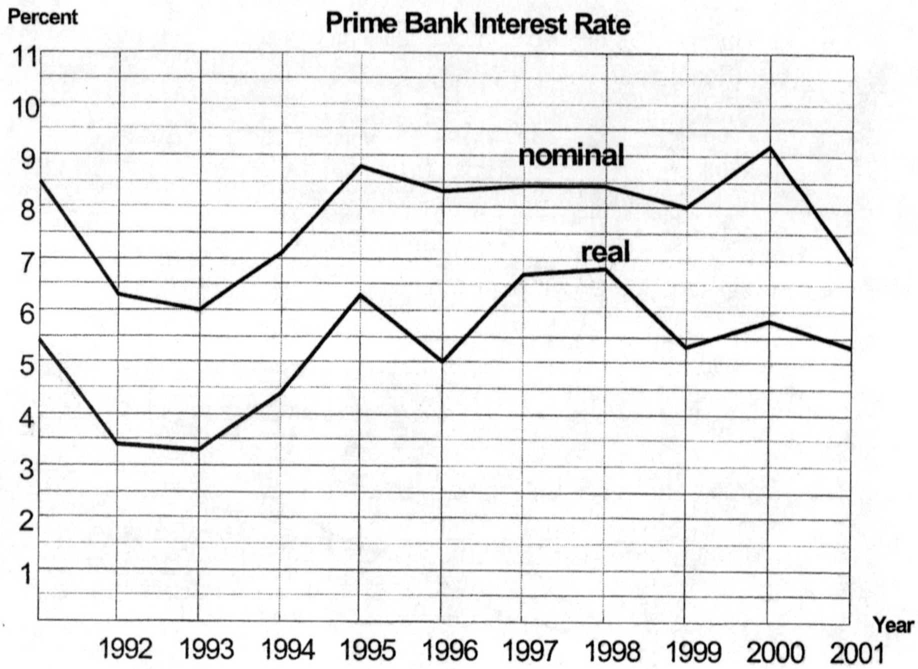

15-Minute Practice Test

Multiple Choice

1. b
2. e
3. c
4. b
5. d
6. d
7. a
8. d
9. c
10. b

True/False

1. F
2. F
3. F
4. T
5. T
6. T
7. F
8. F

ANSWERS FOR CHAPTER 7

Speaking Economics

1. classical model
2. market clearing
3. labor supply curve
4. labor demand curve
5. aggregate production function
6. circular flow
7. Say's law
8. net taxes
9. (household) saving
10. leakages
11. injections
12. planned investment spending
13. loanable funds market
14. budget deficit
15. budget surplus
16. national debt
17. supply of funds curve
18. investment demand curve
19. government demand for funds curve
20. total demand for funds curve
21. fiscal policy
22. crowding out
23. complete crowding out

Chapter Highlights

1. classical
2. markets clear
3. resources
4. upward; increases; rise
5. increases; rise; downward
6. classical
7. labor; technology
8. potential (or full-employment)
9. output
10. Say
11. injections; net taxes; government
12. deficit; G – T; surplus; T - G
13. State; local; deficit; deficit; surplus; surplus
14. interest rate
15. falls; downward
16. interest rate
17. rises; remains unchanged; rises
18. loanable funds
19. government; net taxes; output
20. decrease; increase
21. classical; private
22. loanable funds; businesses purchases

Important Concepts

1. Markets clear. This means that the price adjusts in every market until quantity supplied and quantity demanded are equal.

2. The labor market; the aggregate production function

3. The loanable funds market

4. Leakages (either order): saving; net taxes. Injections (either order): investment spending; government purchases.

5. a. no change
   b. no change
   c. increase
   d. increase
   e. decrease

Skills and Tools

1. a. (See graph.)

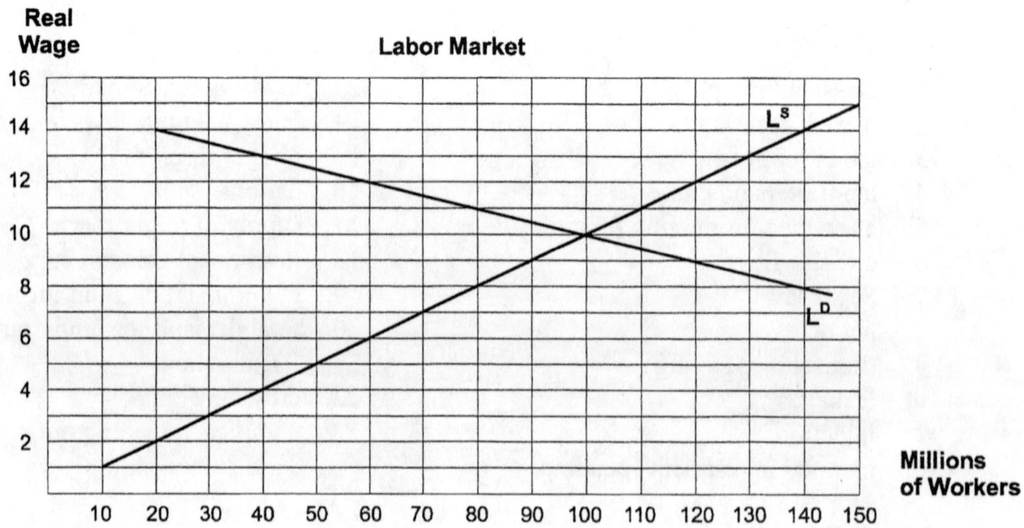

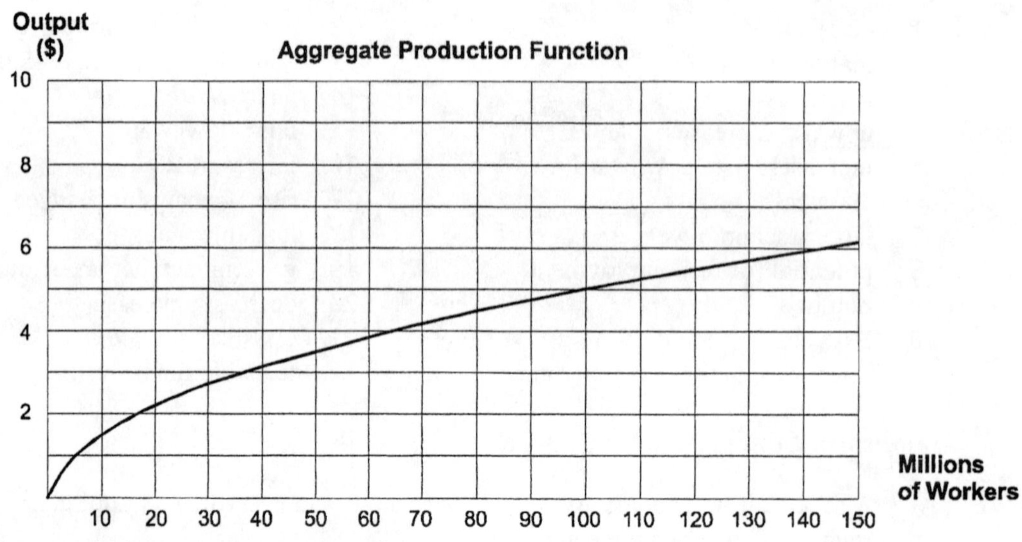

   b. 60; 120; excess supply; fall below
   c. 140; 80; excess demand; rise above
   d. 100; 100; equilibrium; remain at
   e. (See the graph.)
   f. $5 trillion

2. a. (See graph.)

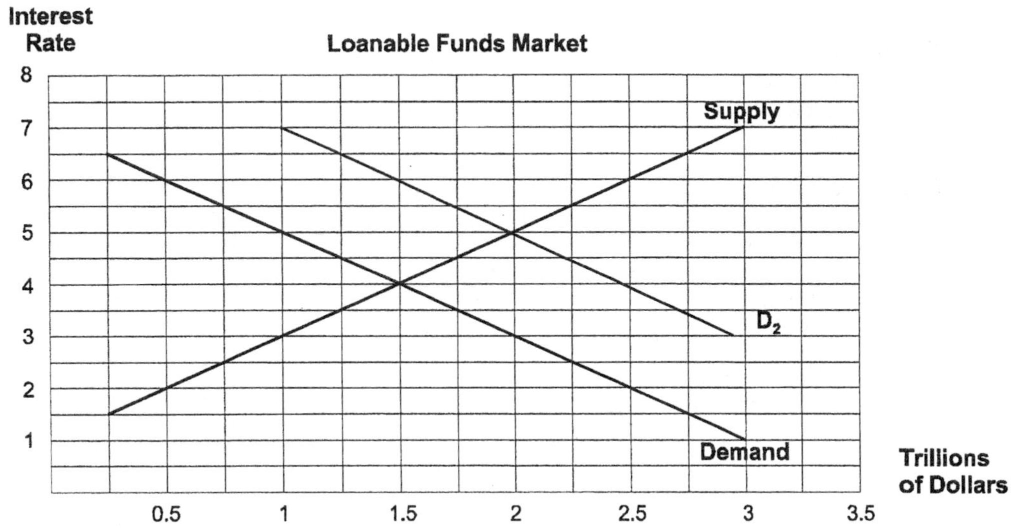

b. rises; demand; negative; decreases
c. deficit; .5, G – T = .5; deficit; demand; borrow; .5
d. add; Total Demand = 3.0 – (1/2)*r* + .5 = 3.5 – (1/2)*r* (See graph.)
e. excess supply; fall below; excess demand rise above; 4%
f. 1.5; deficit; .5; 1.0; 1.5; 1.5
g.

Flows in the Economy of Upper Classica (Trillions of Dollars)

Total Output			5.0
Total Income			5.0
Consumption Spending	(C)		2.5
Investment Spending	(I)		1.0
Government Spending	(G)		1.5
Net Tax Revenue	(T)	1.0	
Household Saving	(S)	1.5	

h. equal; S + T; 2.5; I + G; 2.5; does

3. a. demand curve; rightward; $1; demand (See following graph.)
   b. rise, 5; increase; increase; decrease; decrease
   c. increase; increase; 0.5; decrease; 0.5; decreases; 0.5; decrease; the same amount; did

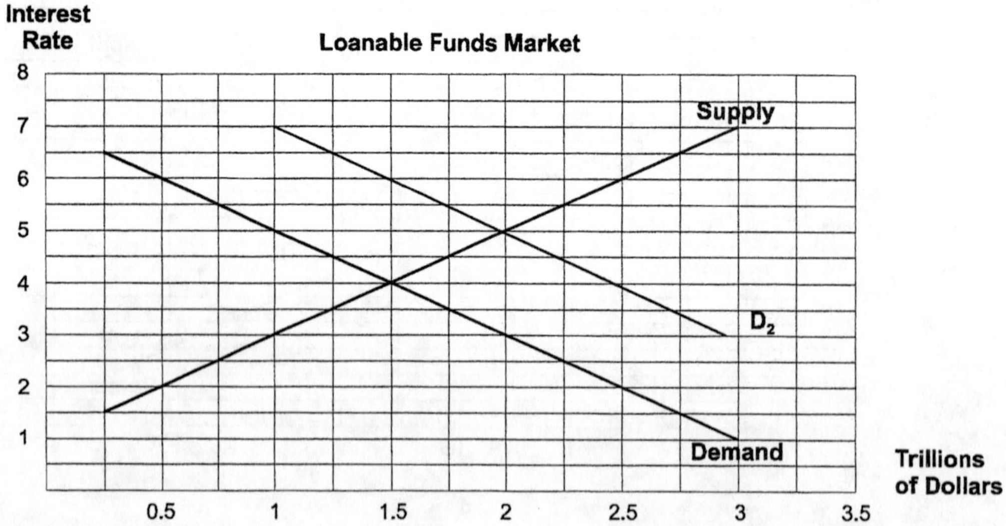

15-Minute Practice Test

Multiple Choice

1. a
2. e
3. b
4. c
5. a
6. b
7. b
8. b
9. b
10. e

True/False

1. F
2. F
3. F
4. T
5. T
6. T
7. F
8. T

ANSWERS FOR CHAPTER 8

Speaking Economics

1. average standard of living
2. productivity (or labor productivity)
3. capital per worker
4. corporate profits tax
5. investment tax credit
6. capital gains tax
7. consumption tax
8. human capital
9. technological change
10. patent protection

Chapter Highlights

1. long; short
2. the population; rise; the population; fall
3. rightward; rightward
4. supply
5. demand
6. decrease; decrease
7. employment; employment
8. taxes; rightward
9. saving
10. growing; reduce; increase
11. investment
12. human; upward
13. human
14. R&D; R&D
15. tradeoffs
16. tradeoffs; costs
17. cuts
18. consumption (or consumer)
19. increase; increase
20. growth; growth
21. population
22. (either order): consumption, capital; consumption; capital

Important Concepts

1. a. labor market diagram; labor supply curve shifts rightward
   b. labor market diagram; labor supply curve shifts rightward
   c. labor market diagram; labor supply curve shifts rightward
   d. labor market diagram; labor demand curve shifts rightward
   e. loanable funds market diagram; investment demand curve, and therefore the total demand for funds curve, shifts rightward
   f. loanable funds market diagram; supply of funds curve (household saving) shifts rightward. (Note: as a result of the increase in investment, the capital stock will grow more rapidly, so the aggregate production function will shift up more rapidly as well.)
   g. loanable funds market diagram; budget deficit, and therefore the total demand for funds curve, shifts leftward. (Note: as a result of the drop in the interest rate, investment will increase, the capital stock will grow more rapidly, and the aggregate production function will shift up more rapidly as well.)
   h. loanable funds market diagram; the supply of funds curve, shifts rightward.
   i. aggregate production function diagram; aggregate production function shifts upward

2. (three of the following four, in any order): budgetary costs; consumption costs; opportunity costs of workers' time; sacrifice of other social goals

3. (in any order): very low output per capital; high population growth rates; poor infrastructure

Skills and Tools

1. a.; b.; and c (See graph.)

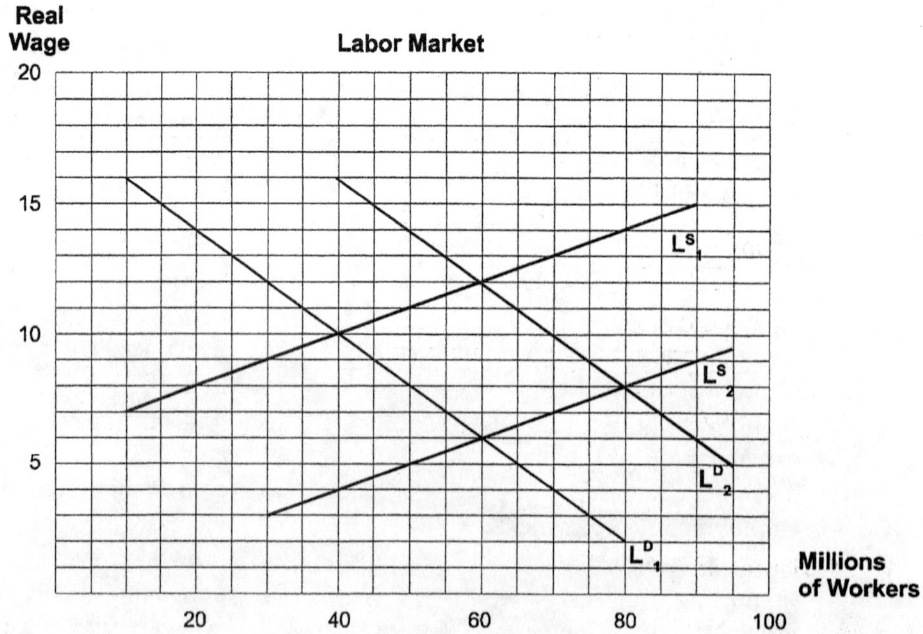

d. 10; 40; 16; ($16 trillion / 40 million, or $400,000)
e. right; (See graph labeled $L^D{}_2$.)
f. 12; 60; 21; ($21 trillion / 60 million, or $350,000); increased; increased; increased; decreased
g. right (See graph labeled $L^S{}_2$.)
h. 8; 80; 24; ($24 trillion / 80 million, or $300,000); decreased; increased; increased; decreased
i. decreased; $10; $8; increased; 40 million; 80 million; increased; $16 trillion; $24 trillion; decreased; ($16 trillion / 40 million, or $400,000); ($24 trillion / 80 million, or $300,000); decrease; decrease

2. a. $10; 40 million; $16 trillion; ($16 trillion / 40 million, or $400,000)
b. (See following graph.)
c. be unaffected; be unaffected; rise; rise; $10; 40 million; $20 trillion dollars; ($20 trillion / 40 million, or $500,000)
d. increase; decrease; increase; increase; decrease
e. $400,000; $12; 60 million; $6; 60 million; ($24 trillion / 60 million, or $400,000)

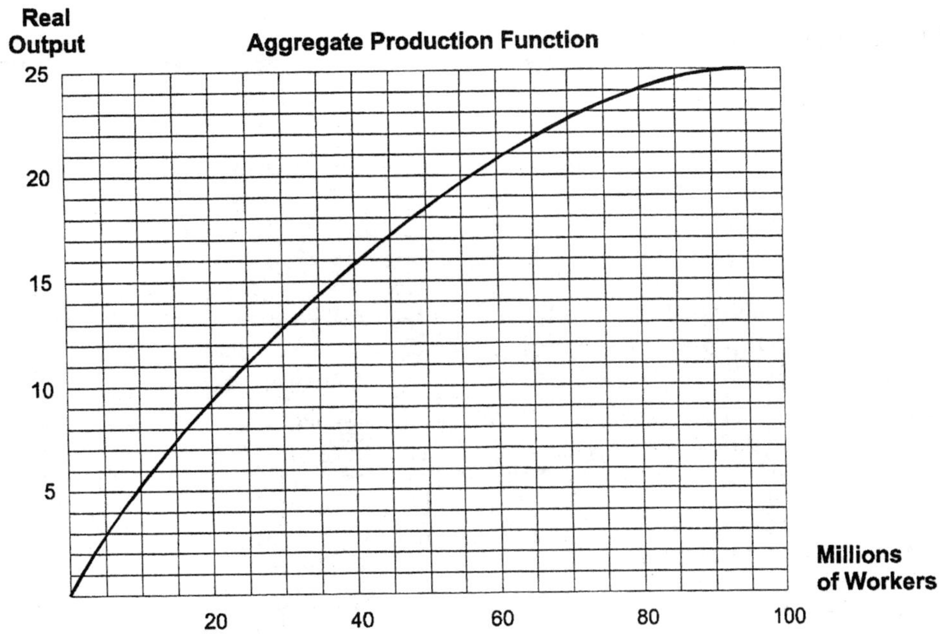

15-Minute Practice Test

Multiple Choice

1. b
2. c
3. b
4. d
5. d
6. b
7. c
8. d
9. e
10. a

True/False

1. F
2. T
3. F
4. F
5. T
6. F
7. F
8. F

ANSWERS FOR CHAPTER 9

Speaking Economics

1. boom
2. disequilibrium
3. spending shock

Chapter Highlights

1. (either order): labor demand, labor supply; (either order): labor demand, labor supply
2. short; clears; clears; short
3. opportunity cost
4. wage rate
5. equlibrium
6. greater
7. increase; greater;
8. decrease; less;
9. above;
10. normal
11. below;
12. normal

Important Concepts

1. (either order): Sudden shifts in labor supply are unlikely to occur; even if they occurred, they could not accurately explain the facts of recessions, in which employment drops in spite of workers' desire to work.
2. In a recession, the benefit to the firm is greater than the opportunity cost to the worker. In a boom, the opportunity cost to the worker is greater than the benefit to the firm.
3. The difference between the opportunity cost to the worker and the benefit to the firm imply that mutual gains are possible by increasing or decreasing employment.

Skills and Tools

1. a. (See the following graph.) $12; 120
   b. disequilibrium; below; in a recession
   c. 8; 16; exceeds; are; increase; rise above
   d. decrease; increase; 120; 12; 12; 12; would not; equilibrium; long run equilibrium

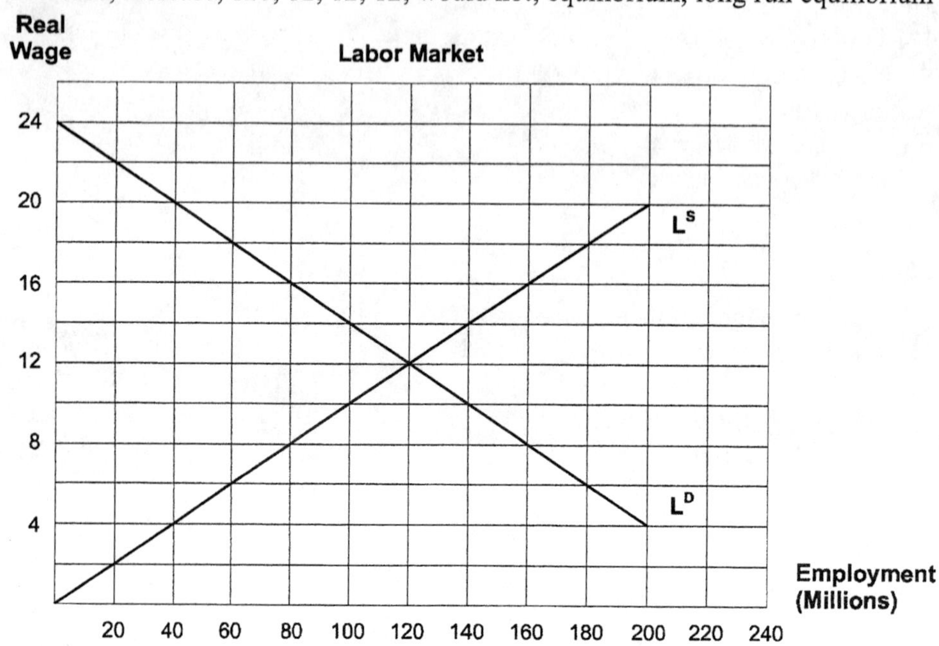

2. a. $12; 120
   b. disequilibrium; above; in a boom
   c. risen; 12; 16; 16; 8; is exceeded by; let some workers go; decrease; fall below
   d. 120; 12; 12; 12; equilibrium; long run equilibrium

10-Minute Practice Test

Multiple Choice

1. c
2. e
3. a
4. b
5. b
6. c

True/False

1. T
2. F
3. F
4. T
5. T

ANSWERS FOR CHAPTER 10

Speaking Economics

1. short-run macro model
2. disposable income
3. consumption function
4. autonomous consumption
5. marginal propensity to consume (MPC)
6. consumption-income line
7. aggregate expenditure (AE)
8. equilibrium GDP
9. expenditure multiplier
10. automatic stabilizers

Chapter Highlights

1. (either order): consumption, income; (either order): income, consumption; (either order): consumption, income
2. consumption; disposable; disposable
3. zero; one
4. marginal propensity to consume (or MPC); marginal propensity to consume (or MPC)
5. income; anything else besides income
6. plant; new home; Inventory
7. investment; government; outside of
8. businesses; foreign; final; C $+I^p$+G+NX
9. MPC
10. fall; equilibrium
11. rise; equilibrium
12. (either order): output or GDP, agg. exp.
13. GDP or output; aggregate expenditure
14. 45-degree
15. 45-degree; inventories; reduce
16. 45-degree; inventories; increase
17. Equilibrium; 45-degree
18. spending; spending
19. spending; spending
20. equilibrium GDP
21. 1/(1 – MPC)
22. rise; fall
23. multiplier; multiplier
24. autonomous; net exports; aggregate expenditure; expenditure
25. stabilizer; reduces; more
26. zero; full-employment; zero
27. recession; bel0ow

Important Concepts

1. (any order)
consumption spending (C)
investment spending (I)
government purchases (G)
net exports (NX)

2. a. C = a + bDI, where *b* is the MPC
b. 1/(1 – MPC)
c. –MPC/(1 – MPC)

3. (any order)
a decrease in autonomous consumption (a)
a decrease in investment spending (I)
a decrease in government purchases (G)
a decrease in net exports (NX)
an increase in net taxes (T).

4. Yes, equilibrium GDP would increase, but by exactly $100 billion. With an MPC of zero, the expenditure multiplier has a value of 1/(1 – 0) = 1, so the $100 billion increase in G would be multiplied by 1 to get the rise in equilibrium GDP.

Skills and Tools

1. a. (See table.)

Income or GDP ($ Billions)	Tax Collections ($ Billions)	Disposable Income ($ Billions)	Consumption Spending ($ Billions)
3,000	1,000	2,000	2,500
3,500	1,000	2,500	2,750
4,000	1,000	3,000	3,000
4,500	1,000	3,500	3,250
5,000	1,000	4,000	3,500
5,500	1,000	4,500	3,750
6,000	1,000	5,000	4,000
6,500	1,000	5,500	4,250
7,000	1,000	6,000	4,500
7,500	1,000	6,500	4,750

b. (See graph.)

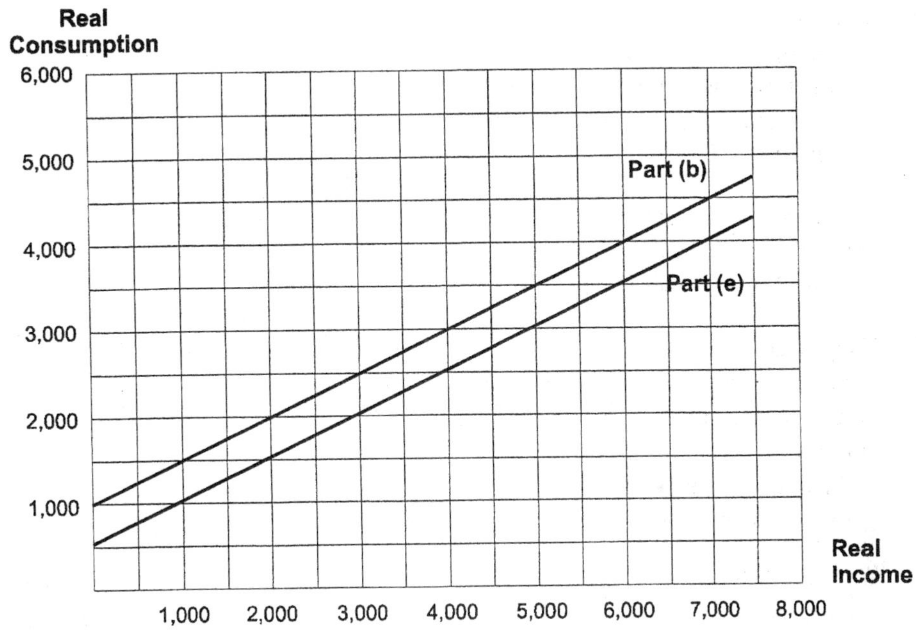

c. 0.5
d. decrease; $1,000; 0.5; decrease; $500; downward; $500
e. 0.5
f. decrease; increase; increase

2. a. (See table.)

Income or GDP ($ Billions)	Consumption Spending ($ Billions)	Investment Spending ($ Billions)	Government Purchases ($ Billions)	Aggregate Expenditure ($ Billions)
3,000	2,500	800	450	3,750
3,500	2,750	800	450	4,000
4,000	3,000	800	450	4,250
4,500	3,250	800	450	4,500
5,000	3,500	800	450	4,750
5,500	3,750	800	450	5,000
6,000	4,000	800	450	5,250
6,500	4,250	800	450	5,500
7,000	4,500	800	450	5,750
7,500	4,750	800	450	6,000

b. $C + I^p + G + NX$; rise; fall; equals

c. (See graph.)

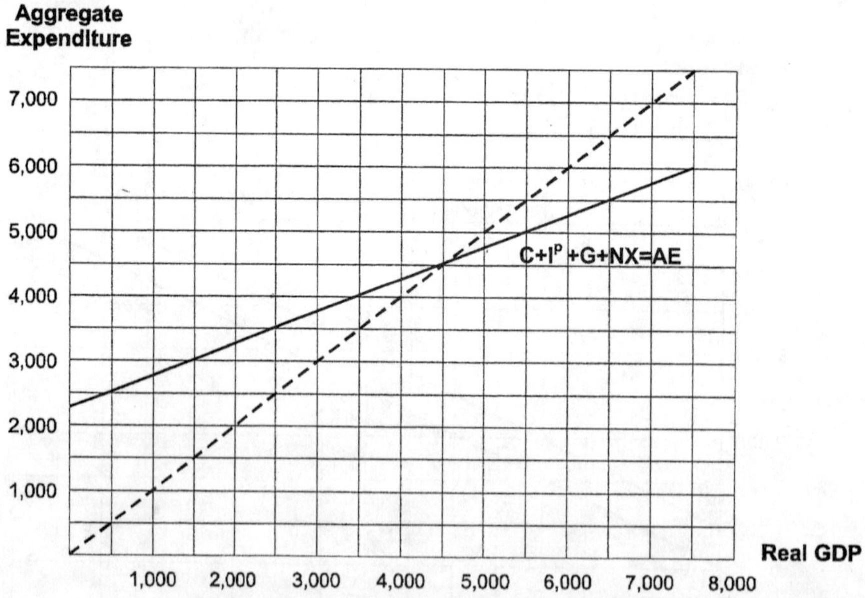

d. is not; \$3,500; greater than; less output than; –1,000; increase their output; rise
e. is; \$4,500; equal to; as much output as; 0; keep their output constant; remain constant
f. is not; \$5,500; less than; more output than; 1,000; decrease their output; fall
g. below; too low; unemployment; increase; increase; rise to

3. a. 1/3
 b. 3/2 or 1.5
 c. \$300 billion
 d. decrease; \$100 billion; decrease; \$100 billion
 e. downward; 100; (See graph.)

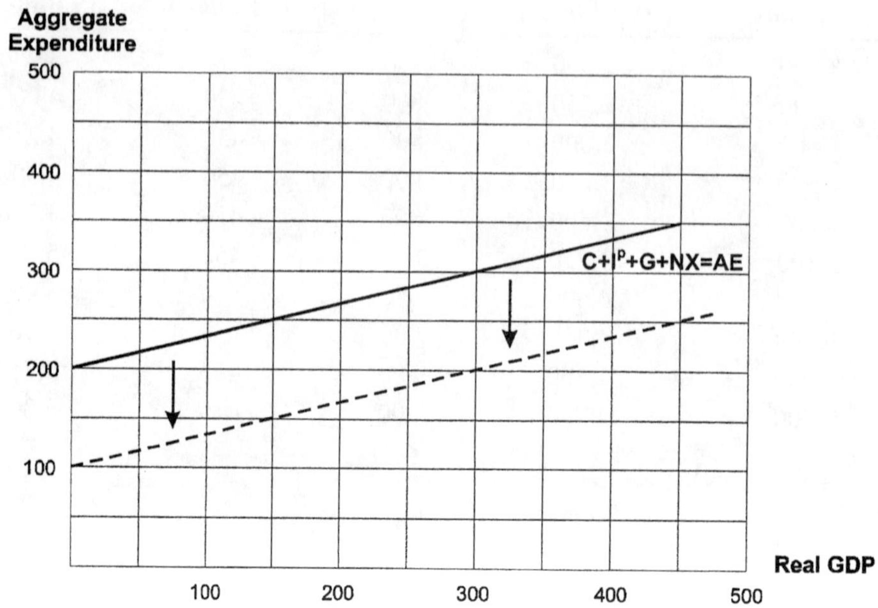

4. a. (See table.)

Country	MPC	Multiplier	Change in Equilibrium GDP due to: $\Delta I^P = +200$	$\Delta G = -100$	$\Delta a = +400$	$\Delta NX = -150$
1	0.40	1.67	333.33	-166.67	666.67	-250
2	0.50	2.00	400	–200	800	-300
3	0.60	2.50	500	–250	1,000	-375
4	0.75	4.00	800	-400	1,600	-600
5	0.80	5.00	1,000	–500	2,000	-750
6	0.90	10.00	2,000	-1,000	4,000	-1,500

b. increase; $100; 4; $400
c. decrease; $40; 5; $200

5. a. disposable income; subtracting; T; Y
b. C = 70 + 0.5Y
c. AE = 200 + 0.5Y
d. $400 billion
e. 0.5
f. 2
g. $430 billion

6. a. 0.5
b. 2
c. –1
d. $10,000 billion
e. decrease; 2,000; increase; 1,000

15-Minute Practice Test

Multiple Choice

1. b
2. d
3. e
4. d
5. e
6. c
7. e
8. e
9. c
10. d

True/False

1. T
2. F
3. T
4. F
5. F
6. T
7. T
8. T

ANSWERS FOR CHAPTER 11

Speaking Economics

1. liquidity
2. cash in the hands of the public
3. demand deposits
4. M1
5. M2
6. financial intermediary
7. balance sheet
8. bond
9. loan
10. reserves
11. required reserves
12. required reserve ratio
13. net worth
14. central bank
15. Federal Open Market Committee
16. discount rate
17. open market operations
18. excess reserves
19. demand deposit multiplier
20. run on the bank
21. banking panic

Chapter Highlights

1. cash; cash
2. cash; demand; checking account; travelers; cash; demand
3. owns; owes
4. reserves
5. government; open market operations
6. reserves
7. 1/RRR
8. required
9. secrecy
10. FDIC (or Federal Deposit Insurance Corporation)

Important Concepts

1. (any order): cash in the hands of the public; demand deposits; other checking account deposits; travelers checks

2. a. yes, assets
   b. yes, assets
   c. yes, assets
   d. no
   e. yes, liabilities
   f. yes, assets
   g. yes, liabilities

3. The FOMC includes all seven members of the board of governors, but it *also* includes five of the twelve Federal Reserve Bank Presidents on a rotating basis.

4. a. Nominates members of the Board of Governors, who serve on the FOMC
   b. Approves President's nominations for Board of Governors
   c. Help elect boards who select each of the 12 Federal Reserve Bank Presidents, who, in turn, rotate as members of the FOMC.

Skills and Tools

1. a. $1,103
   b. $2,948
   c. Public's credit limit on all credit cards; Public's stock market holdings

2. a. (See balance sheet.)

First Bank of Minnewaska

Assets		**Liabilities and Net Worth**	
Property and building	$21 million	Demand deposit liabilities	$150 million
Government bonds	$55 million	Net worth	$21 million
Loans to corporations	$20 million		
Loans to private citizens	$45 million		
Cash in vault	$12 million		
In account with the Fed	$18 million		
Total Assets	$171 million	Total Liabilities plus Net Worth	$171 million

   b. $21 million
   c. $30 million; required; 0.2

3. a. increased; $5,000; excess reserves; 4,000; can make new loans; 4,000; increase; $4,000
   b. (See balance sheet.)

Changes in First Bank of Minnewaska's Balance Sheet

Action	**Changes in Assets**	**Changes in Liabilities**
Fed buys $5,000 bond from Sabre-Tooth Trading, which deposits $5,000 check from Fed deposits into its checking account:	+$5,000 in reserves	+$5,000 in demand deposits
First Bank lends out excess reserves in amount of $4,000 dollars:	–$4,000 in reserves +$4,000 in loans	
The total effect on First Bank from beginning to end:	+$1,000 in reserves +$4,000 in loans	+$5,000 in demand deposits

   c. increased; 4,000; excess reserves; $3,200; can make new loans; $3,200; increase; $3,200

d. (See balance sheet.)

Changes in *Bank Too!'s* Balance Sheet

Action	Changes in Assets	Changes in Liabilities
Cindy deposits $4,000 Loan check into her checking account:	+$4,000 in reserves	+$4,000 in demand deposits
Bank Too! lends out excess reserves in amount of $3,200 dollars:	+$3,200 in reserves +$3,200 in loans	
The total effect on *Bank Too!* from beginning to end:	+$800 in reserves +$3,200 in loans	+$4,000 in demand deposits

e. (See table.)

Round	Change in Demand Deposits at This Bank	Change in Demand Deposits at All Banks
First Bank of Minnewaska	$5,000	$5,000
Bank Too!	$4,000	$9,000
Bank 3	$3,200	$12,200
Bank 4	$2,560	$14,760
Bank 5	$2,048	$16,808
Bank 6	$1,638	$18,446
Bank 7	$1,311	$19,757
Bank 8	$1,049	$20,806
...		
All Other Banks	$4,194	$25,000

f. makes new loans; creates; increase; 5

4. a. decreased; 2,000; deficient reserves; 1,600; must call in loans; $1,600; decrease; $1,600

b. (See balance sheet.)

Changes in First Bank of Minnewaska's Balance Sheet

Action	Changes in Assets	Changes in Liabilities
Fed sells $2,000 bond to SabreTooth, which pays with $2,000 check drawn on its checking account at First Bank.	–$2,000 in reserves	–$2,000 in demand deposits
First Bank calls in loans in amount of $1,600 dollars:	+$1,600 in reserves –$1,600 in loans	
The total effect on First Bank from beginning to end:	–$400 in reserves –$1,600 in loans	–$2,000 in demand deposits

c. (See table.)

Round	Change in Demand Deposits at This Bank	Change in Demand Deposits at All Banks
First Bank of Minnewaska	–$2,000	–$2,000
Bank 2	–$1,600	–$3,600
Bank 3	–$1,280	–$4,880
Bank 4	–$1,024	–$5,904
Bank 5	–$819	–$6,723
Bank 6	–$655	–$7,379
Bank 7	–$524	–$7,903
Bank 8	–$419	–$8,322
...		
All Other Banks	–$1,678	–$10,000

d. call in loans; extinguishes; decrease; 5

5. a. (See table)

Country	*RRR*	Demand Deposit Multiplier	*Change in Money Supply due to Open Market:* Sale of $200	Purchase of $100	Sale of $400
1	0.1	10.0	–2,000	1,000	–4,000
2	0.2	5.0	–1,000	500	–2,000
3	0.4	2.5	–500	250	–1,000
4	0.5	2.0	–400	200	–800
5	0.8	1.25	–250	125	–500
6	1.0	1.0	–200	100	–400

b. increase; 1,000; purchases; decrease; decrease; buy; $200
c. decrease; 1,000; sales; increase; increase; sell; 500

15-Minute Practice Test

Multiple Choice

1. a
2. a
3. e
4. c
5. a
6. b
7. d
8. e
9. c
10. d

True/False

1. T
2. F
3. F
4. T
5. T
6. F
7. F
8. F

ANSWERS FOR CHAPTER 12

Speaking Economics

1. wealth constraint
2. money demand curve
3. money supply curve
4. excess supply of money
5. excess demand for bonds
6. federal funds rate

Chapter Highlights

1. wealth
2. interest
3. means of payment; interest; interest; means of payment
4. wealth; money
5. the interest rate; the interest rate
6. supply; right; supply; left
7. Equilibrium
8. demand
9. falls; rises
10. buying; falls; selling; rises
11. falls; durables; rises
12. upward; downward
13. interest rate
14. rise; investment
15. interest rate; interest rate
16. interest rate; interest rate
17. loanable funds; money
18. fall; rightward; rise

Important Concepts

1. money and bonds

2. a. money demand shifts leftward; b. money supply shifts leftward; c. money supply shifts rightward; d. money demand shifts rightward; e. money demand shifts leftward (because people expect the interest rate to fall and bond prices to rise); f. money demand shifts rightward (because income rises)

3. Monetary policy would be completely ineffective, since the channel through which it works—causing changes in the interest rate and then changes in consumption and investment spending—would be cut off.

4. a. decrease; b. increase; c. decrease; d. decrease; e. decrease (both because income goes down and because the interest rate rises); f. decreases (because the interest rate rises)

Skills and Tools

1. a. (See graph.)
   b. (See graph.)
   c. less than; excess supply; 250; excess demand; 250; buy more; rise; fall
   d. greater than; excess demand; 150; excess supply; $150; sell more; fall; rise
   e. 7; equal to; equilibrium; equal to

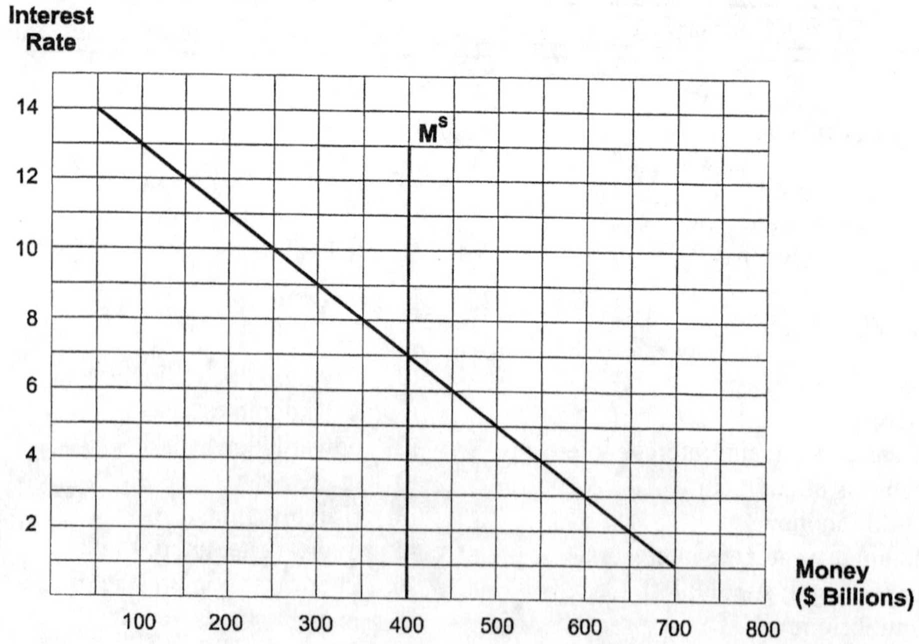

2. a. 8%
   b. increase; \$200; 450; buy; 2; buy; \$100
   c. (See graph.)
   d. decrease; \$100; \$150; sell; 2; sell; \$50
   e. (See graph.)

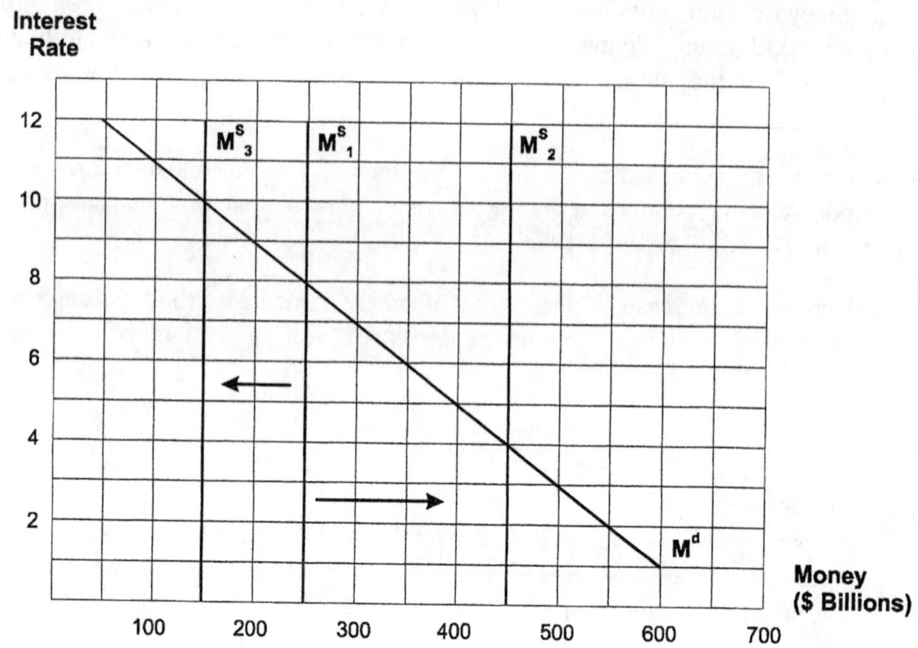

3. a. leftward; rise; 9; increase; decrease; consumption and planned investment; downward; decrease; a multiple of; decrease; demand; fall
   b. (See graph.)
   c. (See graph.)

Panel A

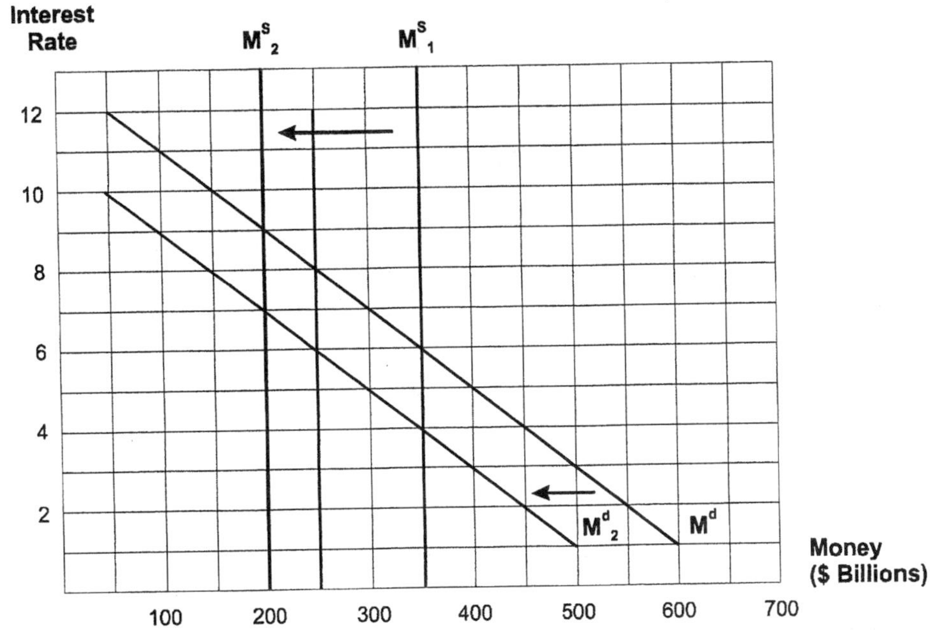

Panel B

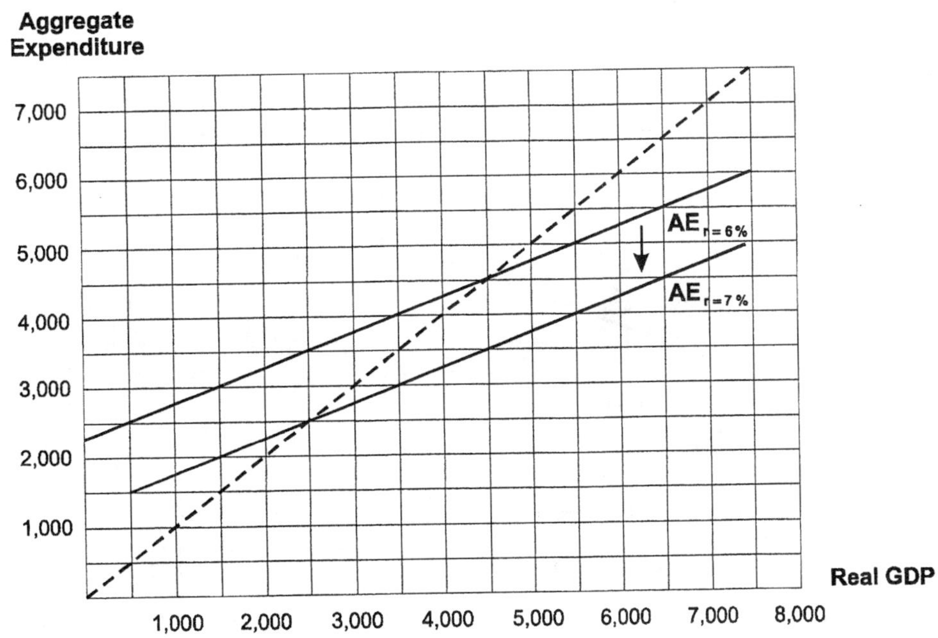

   d. fall; \$25

4. a. upward; \$75; \$150; \$300; (See graph.)
   b. increase; demand; demand; rightward; rise; decrease; downward
   c. (See graph.)

Panel C

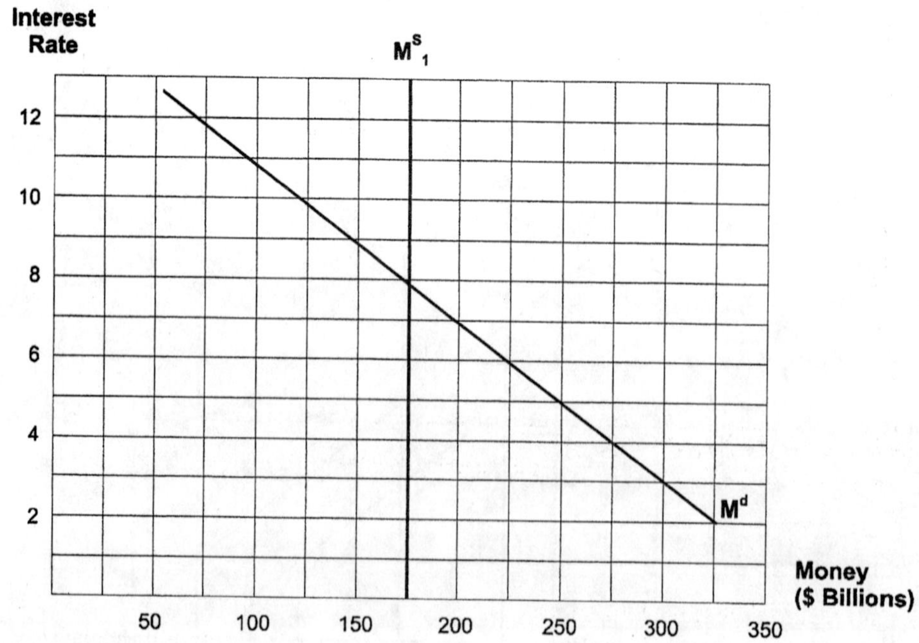

Panel D

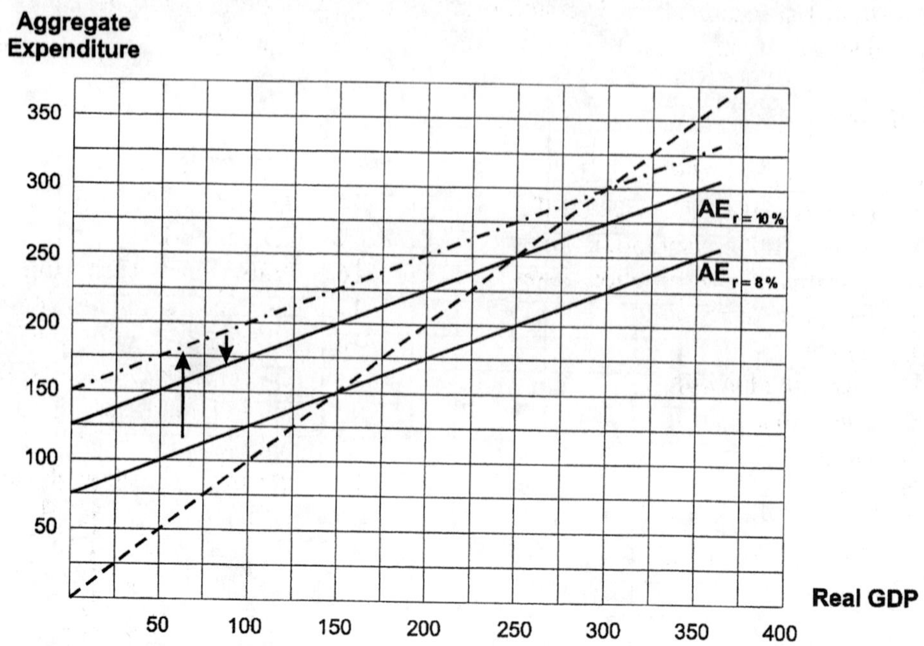

d. rise; crowded out; \$25; \$150; \$300; \$150; \$250; will still cause GDP to rise but by a smaller multiple of any given change in spending

15-Minute Practice Test

Multiple Choice

1. c
2. b
3. e
4. d
5. d
6. d
7. b
8. d
9. a
10. e

True/False

1. F
2. F
3. F
4. T
5. T
6. T
7. F
8. F

ANSWERS FOR CHAPTER 13

Speaking Economics

1. aggregate demand (AD) curve
2. aggregate supply (AS) curve
3. short-run macroeconomic equilibrium
4. demand shock
5. supply shock
6. self-correcting mechanism
7. long-run aggregate supply curve
8. stagflation

Chapter Highlights

1. decrease; price level
2. the price level; the price level
3. investment; consumption; taxes
4. investment; consumption; taxes
5. increase; decrease
6. unit costs
7. markup; markeup
8. rises; falls
9. wage
10. wage
11. rise; rise; fall; fall
12. price level; output
13. real GDP (or output); real GDP (or output)
14. demand shock; supply shock
15. AD; less; AD
16. rightward; rise; leftward; fall
17. rise; upward; fall; downward
18. full-employment (or potential)
19. self-correcting; rise; rise; decrease; fall; fall; increase
20. long
21. upward; increasing; downward; decreasing
22. supply

Important Concepts

1. a. increases
   b. decreases
   c. remains the same
   d. decreases
   e. decreases
   f. increases
   g. remains the same

2. a. increases
   b. increases
   c. remains the same
   d. increases
   e. increases
   f. remains the same

3. a. AD shifts rightward
   b. AD shifts leftward
   c. AD shifts rightward
   d. AD shifts rightward
   e. AS shifts upward
   f. AS shifts upward
   g. AS shifts downward

4.

	Event		
Short run effect on:	**the money supply decreases**	**government purchases decrease**	**world oil prices decrease**
the price level	decrease	decrease	decrease
output	decrease	decrease	increase
average nominal wage	no change	no change	no change

5.

	Event		
Long run effect on:	**the money supply decreases**	**government purchases decrease**	**world oil prices decrease**
the price level	decrease	decrease	no change
output	no change	no change	no change
average nominal wage	decrease	decrease	increase

Skills and Tools

1.

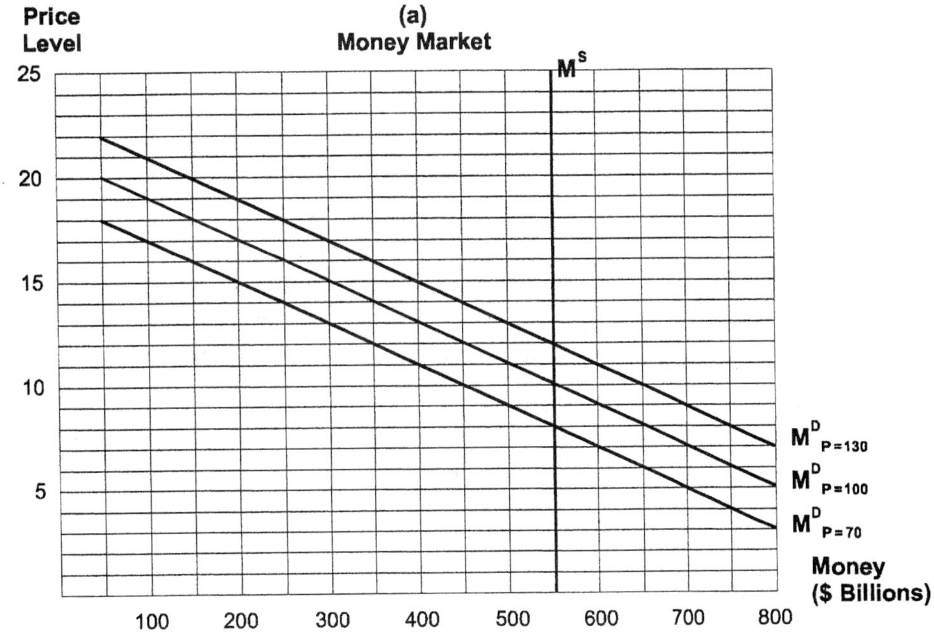

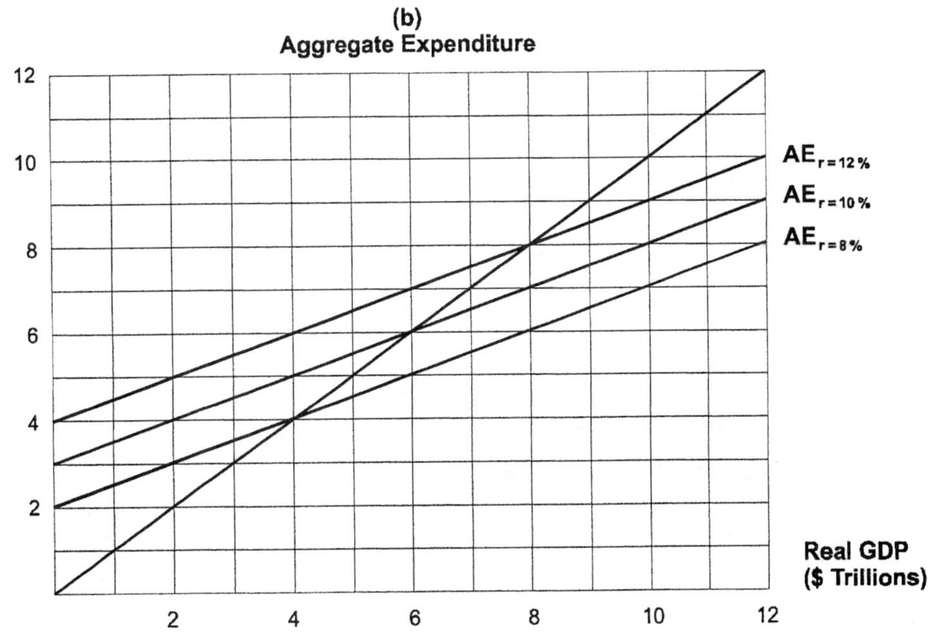

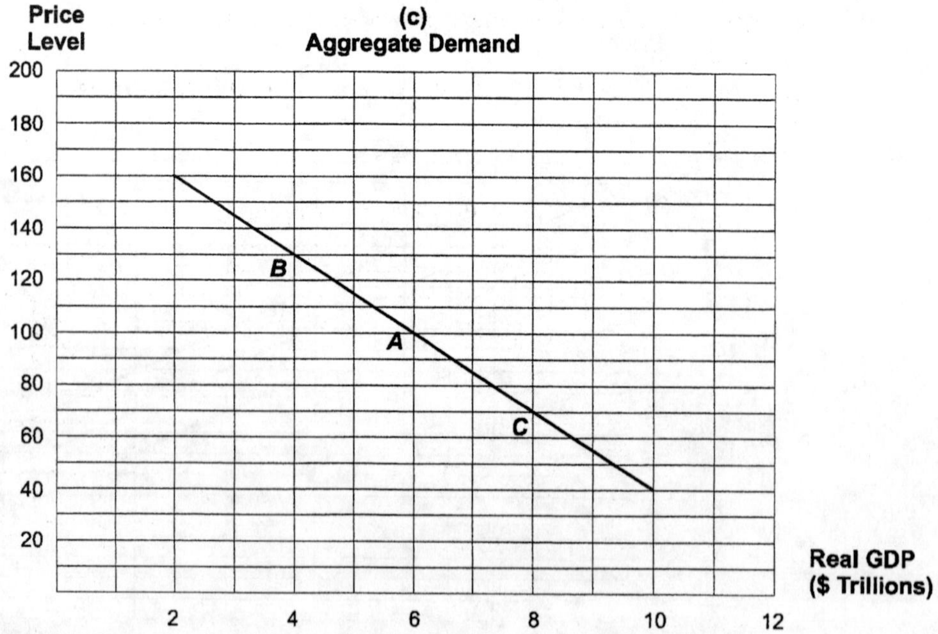

a. (See graph.); 10%.
b. (See graph.)
c. $6 trillion; (See graph.)
d. rightward; money demand curve
e. (See graph.); increase; 12
f. fall; downward
g. (See graph.); decrease; $4
h. decreases; $6; $4; (See graph.)
i. leftward; money demand curve
j. (See graph.); decrease; 8
k. rise; upward
l. (See graph.); increase; $8
m. increases; $6; $8; (See graph.)
n. (See graph.)

2. a. (See graph.)
   b. greater; increases; increase; increase; rise; raise; increase
   c. (See graph.)
   d. smaller; decreases; decrease; decrease; fall; lower; decrease
   e. (See graph.)
   f. (See graph.)

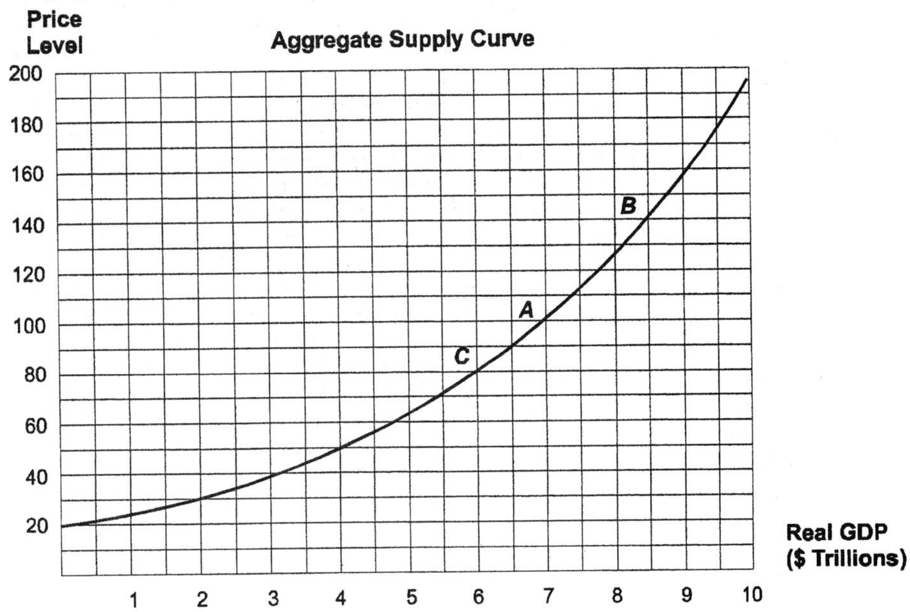

3. a. (See graph.)
   b. Yes; 100; $6 trillion
   c. increase; decrease; decrease; leftward
   d. (See graph.)
   e. decreases; decrease; decrease; decrease; fall; increase; decrease; less
   f. $4; 80
   g. below; high; down; downward; 60; $6 trillion
   h. (See graph.)

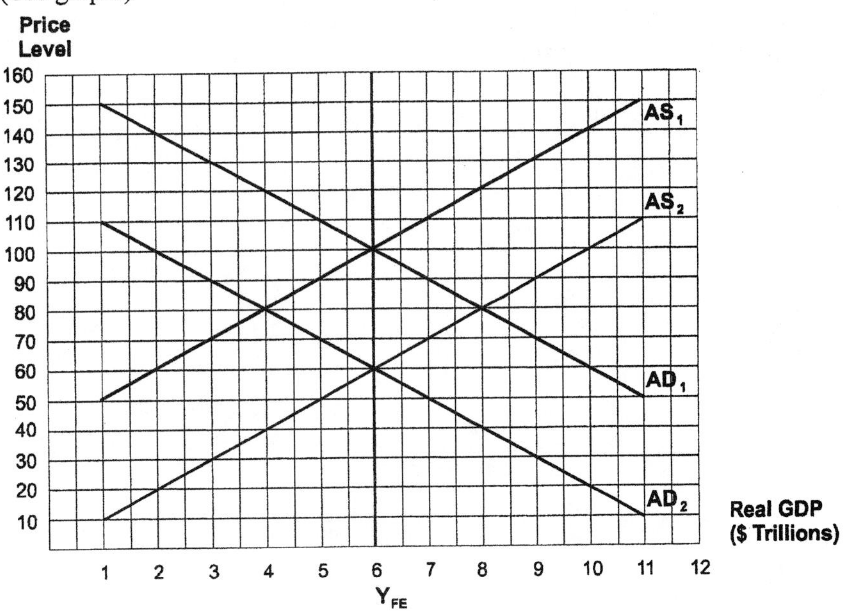

4. a. decrease; downward
   b. (See graph.); 90; $7 trillion
   c. above; low; up; upward; 100; $6 trillion
   d. (See graph.)

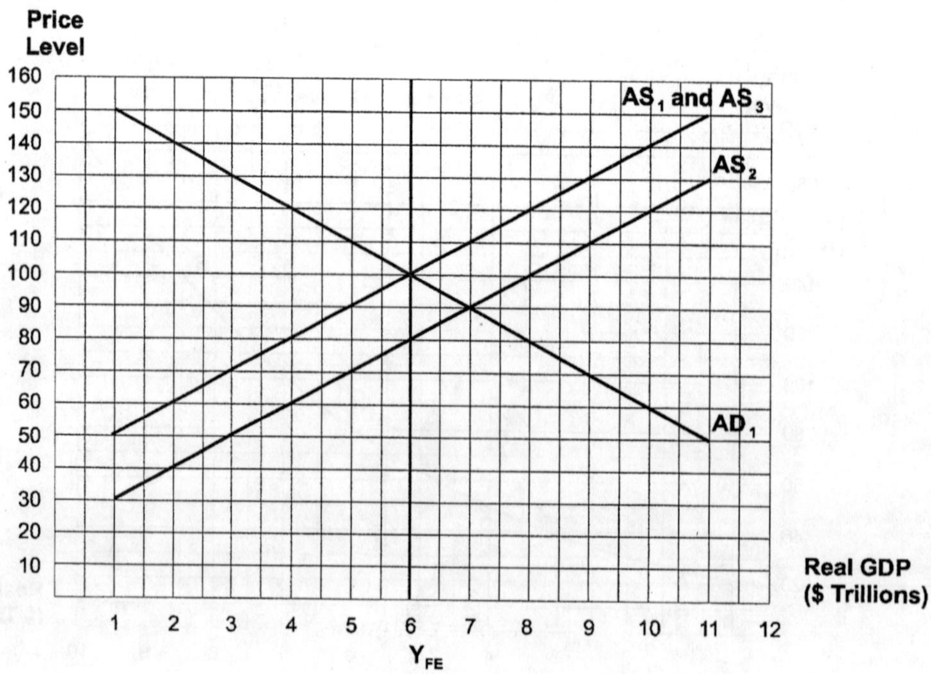

15-Minute Practice Test

Multiple Choice

1. d
2. d
3. d
4. a
5. c
6. b
7. b
8. d
9. e
10. d

True/False

1. F
2. T
3. T
4. T
5. F
6. F
7. F
8. T

ANSWERS FOR CHAPTER 14

Speaking Economics

1. natural rate of unemployment
2. passive monetary policy
3. active monetary policy
4. interest rate target
5. Phillips curve
6. long-run Phillips curve

Chapter Highlights

1. greater; smaller
2. money supply; price
3. price; increase; decrease
4. fall; rise
5. raise; fall; lower; rise
6. more (or higher) inflation; inflation
7. inflation; unemployment; unemployment; inflation
8. expectations
9. upward; upward
10. AD; recession
11. raise
12. inflation; hawk; dove
13. unemployment; inflation
14. AD; unemployment; inflaiton
15. downward
16. unemployment; unemployment; unemployment; unemployment
17. inflation; unemployment
18. vertical; AD
19. true; labor

Important Concepts

1.

Event:	Change in money supply needed to stabilize real GDP	Change in money supply needed to stabilize the price level
The money demand curve shifts rightward	increase	increase
Investment decreases due to business pessimism	increase	increase
The government cuts taxes	decrease	decrease
World oil prices increase	increase	decrease

2. a. decrease
   b. increase
   c. no change
   d. decrease

3. a. shifts rightward
   b. shifts upward
   c. doesn't change
   d. increases
   e. doesn't change

4. An increase in inflationary expectations causes the actual inflation rate to be higher at any given rate of unemployment. This is illustrated by an *upward shift* in the Phillips curve.

5. A hawk policy tries to limit any rise in the inflation rate; a dove policy tries to limit any rise in the unemployment rate. Hawks and doves agree on what to do after a demand shock: neutralize the shock by shifting the AD curve back where it was. This will prevent any change in both unemployment or inflation. But hawks and doves do disagree about what to do after a supply shock, because any policy that limits the rise in inflation means higher unemployment, and any policy that limits the rise in unemployment means higher inflation.

6. a. unchanged target
   b. raise target
   c. lower target (because consumption spending will decrease, which is a negative demand shock)

Skills and Tools

1. a. (See graph.); $500
   b. (See graph.)

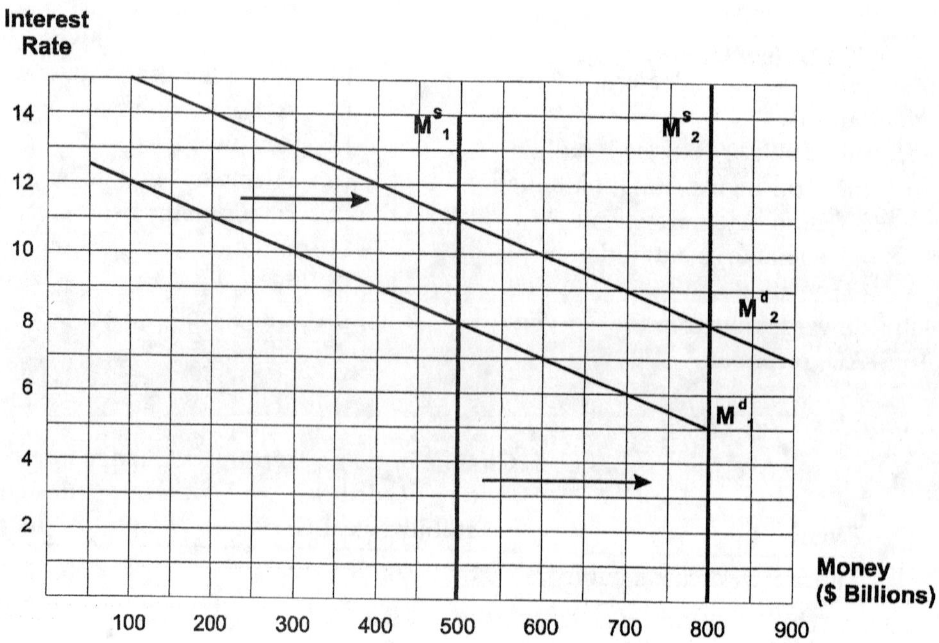

   c. rise; decrease; shift leftward; fall; recession; increased; $800; (See graph.)
   d. Buy bonds! Buy bonds!; increase; increase; $300; buying; $120; increase; $800

2. a. $400; 7; right on target; $6; 100
   b. negative; leftward; fall; leftward
   c. (See graph.)

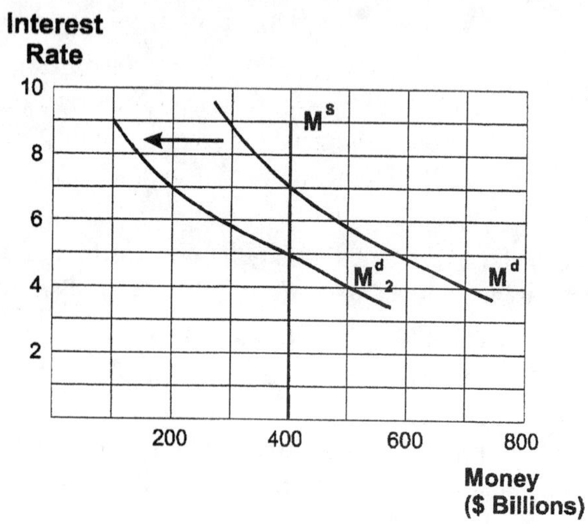

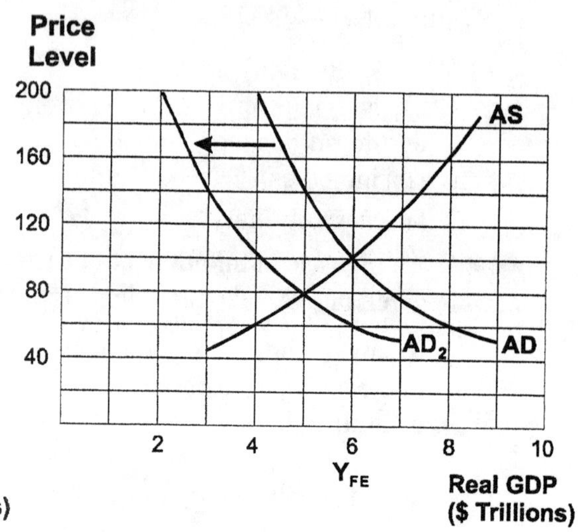

d. $5; below; 80; 5%; below
e. new AD curve; fall further; 60; decrease; up; fall; leftward; *not* be the best policy
f. below; lower; increase; decrease; increase; return to full-employment GDP with a price level of 100
g. 3

3. a. 3
   b. demand; positive
   c. rise; 22; upward; 5.5
   d. down; rise; 7.5; 8; downward; lower; 5.5

15-Minute Practice Test

Multiple Choice

1. b
2. d
3. e
4. c
5. a
6. a
7. c
8. b
9. b
10. d

True/False

1. F
2. T
3. F
4. F
5. F
6. F
7. F
8. T

ANSWERS FOR CHAPTER 15

Speaking Economics

1. progressive tax
2. average tax rate
3. marginal tax rate
4. cyclical deficit
5. structural deficit
6. countercyclical fiscal policy

Chapter Highlights

1. nominal
2. income (or GDP); income (or GDP)
3. GDP
4. GDP; declined
5. military; military
6. Transfer payments
7. transfer; interest
8. fell; higher; decreases; decreases
9. upward; 20
10. Deficits; Surpluses
11. transfer payments; tax revenue; transfer payments; tax revenue;
12. stabilizers; reduce; reduce
13. (nominal) GDP; (nominal) GDP (nominal) GDP
14. Federal Reserve

Important Concepts

1. (any order): government purchases; transfer payments; interest on the national debt

2. Federal government purchases are spending on goods and services only; federal government spending includes *all* outlays: purchases, transfer payments and interest on the national debt.

3. a. upward trend
   b. downward trend
   c. upward trend
   d. upward trend
   e. upward trend

4. (any order): timing problems; irreversibility; the Fed's reaction

Skills and Tools

1.

Year	GDP	Military Government Purchases	Non-military Government Purchases	Military Government Purchases as a Percentage of GDP	Non-military Government Purchases as a Percentage of GDP	Total Government Purchases as a Percentage of GDP
1984	$3,932.7	$283.5	$92.8	7.21	2.36	9.57
1985	$4,213.0	$312.4	$101.0	7.42	2.40	9.81
1986	$4,452.9	$332.2	$106.5	7.46	2.39	9.85
1987	$4,742.5	$351.2	$109.3	7.41	2.30	9.71
1988	$5,108.3	$355.9	$106.8	6.97	2.09	9.06
1989	$5,489.1	$363.2	$119.3	6.62	2.17	8.79
1990	$5,803.2	$374.9	$133.6	6.46	2.30	8.76
1991	$5,986.2	$384.5	$142.9	6.42	2.39	8.81
1992	$6,318.9	$378.5	$156.0	5.99	2.47	8.46
1993	$6,642.3	$364.9	$162.4	5.49	2.44	7.94
1994	$7,054.3	$355.1	$165.9	5.03	2.35	7.39
1995	$7,400.5	$350.6	$170.9	4.74	2.31	7.05
1996	$7,813.2	$357.0	$174.6	4.57	2.23	6.80
1997	$8,300.8	$352.5	$185.3	4.25	2.23	6.48
1998	$8,759.9	$348.6	$190.1	3.98	2.17	6.15
1999	$9,256.1	$364.5	$206.1	3.94	2.23	6.16
2000	$9,872.9	$375.4	$214.8	3.80	2.18	5.98
2001	$10,208.1	$339.0	$216.6	3.32	2.12	5.44

a. increased; more than doubled; No; the spending as a percentage of GDP
b. (See table and graph.)
c. are low and stable; decreased; 2.36; 2.12
d. 1986; 7.46; 1986; 3.32; 2001
e. increased; 9.57; 9.85; 9.85; 1986; decreased; 5.44

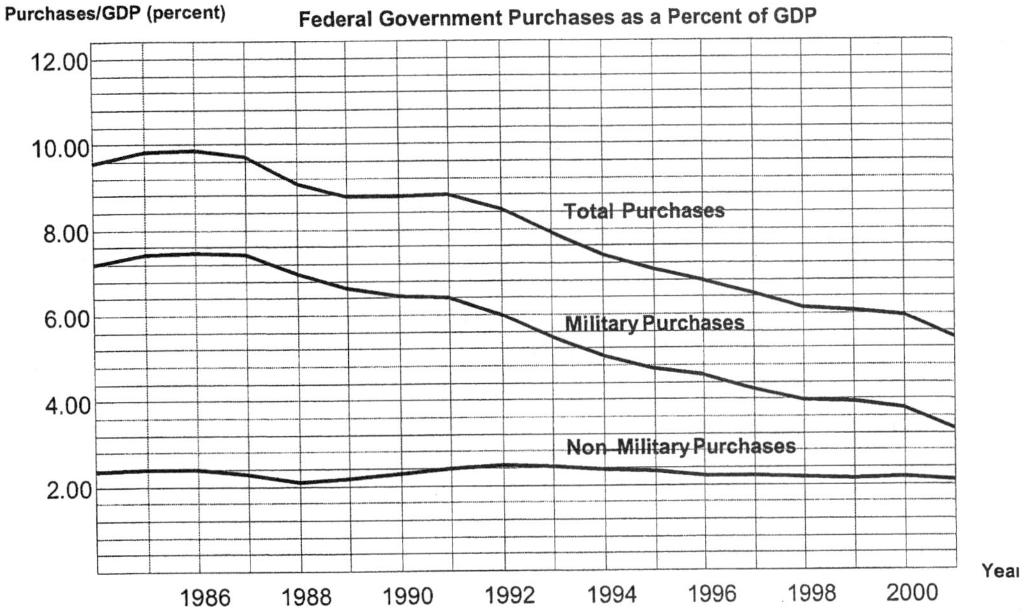

2. a. (See graph)
   b. 4; 1.5
   c. demand for; rightward; exactly one trillion; a higher; 5.
   d. demand for; leftward; exactly one-half trillion; a lower; 3.5

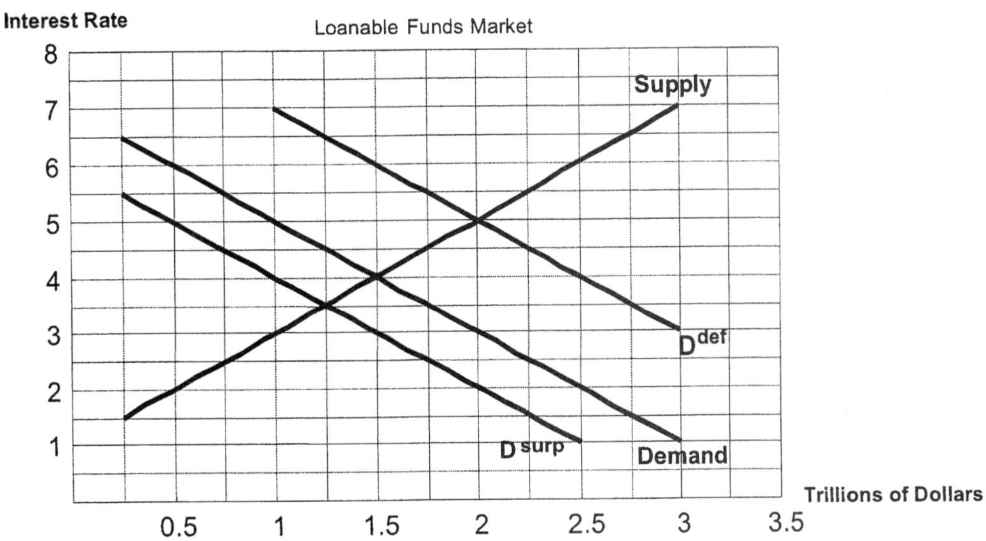

3. a. investment spending; the stock of capital; shift up
   b. decreasing; demand for; down; a greater increase; upward; faster; more rapid.
   c. increasing; demand for; up; a smaller increase; upward; slower; less rapid.

4. (See graph)
   a. higher; discourage; supply of; leftward; rise;
   b. lower; encourage; supply of; rightward; 9.

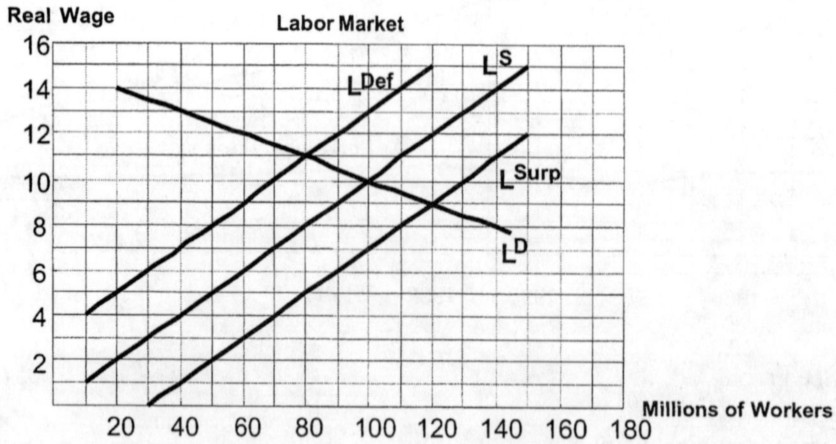

15-Minute Practice Test

Multiple Choice

1. c
2. c
3. d
4. d
5. d
6. b
7. d
8. e
9. d
10. b

True/False

1. F
2. T
3. T
4. F
5. F
6. T
7. T
8. F

ANSWERS FOR CHAPTER 16

Speaking Economics

1. foreign exchange market
2. exchange rate
3. demand curve for foreign currency
4. supply curve for foreign currency
5. floating exchange rate
6. appreciation
7. depreciation
8. purchasing power parity (PPP) theory
9. arbitrage
10. bilateral arbitrage
11. triangular arbitrage
12. managed float
13. fixed exchange rate
14. devaluation
15. foreign currency crisis
16. moral hazard
17. optimum currency area
18. trade deficit
19. trade surplus
20. net capital inflow

Chapter Highlights

1. exchange rate
2. buyers (or demanders)
3. sellers (or suppliers)
4. floats
5. appreciate; depreciate
6. short
7. 7. short; depreciation; appreciation
8. parity; long
9. depreciate
10. bilateral
11. triangular
12. depreciation; appreciation
13. demand; sell; demand;
14. supply; buy; supply
15. above; increases; decreases
16. rise; positive; increases; fall; negative; decreases
17. stronger (or greater)
18. appreciation; decrease; more; increase; less
19. interest rates; higher

Important Concepts

1. (four of the following five, in any order): a decrease in U.S. GDP; a fall in the U.S. price level relative to the Mexican price level; a shift in U.S. tastes away from Mexican goods; a rise in the U.S. interest rate relative to the Mexican interest rate; and an expected depreciation of the peso relative to the dollar (or, equivalently, an expected appreciation of the dollar relative to the peso)

2. (four of the following five, in any order): a drop in Mexico's GDP; a rise in the U.S. price level relative to the Mexican price level; a shift in Mexican tastes away from U.S. goods; a drop in the U.S. interest rate relative to the Mexican interest rate; and an expected depreciation of the dollar relative to the peso (or, equivalently, an expected appreciation of the peso relative to the dollar)

3. a. dollar appreciates
   b. dollar appreciates
   c. dollar appreciates
   d. dollar depreciates
   e. dollar appreciates
   f. dollar appreciates

4. a. increase
   b. decrease
   c. increase (yen appreciates and dollar depreciates)
   d. increase

5. a. buy *more* of its own currency.
   b. buy *less* of its own currency.
   c. buy *less* of its own currency.
   d. buy *more* of its own currecy.

Skills and Tools

1. a. (See table.)

Currency Last Trade	U.S. $ N/A	¥en 11:40am	Euro 11:39am	Can $ 11:36am	U.K. £ 11:40am	Aust $ 11:38am	SFranc 11:40am
U.S. $	1	0.007505	0.881	0.6256	1.442	0.5345	0.6022
¥en	133.2	1	117.4	83.35	192.1	71.22	80.24
Euro €	1.135	0.008519	1	0.7101	1.637	0.6067	0.6835
Can $	1.598	0.012	1.408	1	2.305	0.8544	0.9626
U.K. £	0.6935	0.005205	0.611	0.4339	1	0.3707	0.4176
Aust $	1.871	0.01404	1.648	1.17	2.698	1	1.127
SFranc	1.661	0.01246	1.463	1.039	2.394	0.8876	1

   b. 281,600
   c. 176,200
   d. 192,100,000
   e. 28,840
   f. 34,175

2. a. (See graph.)

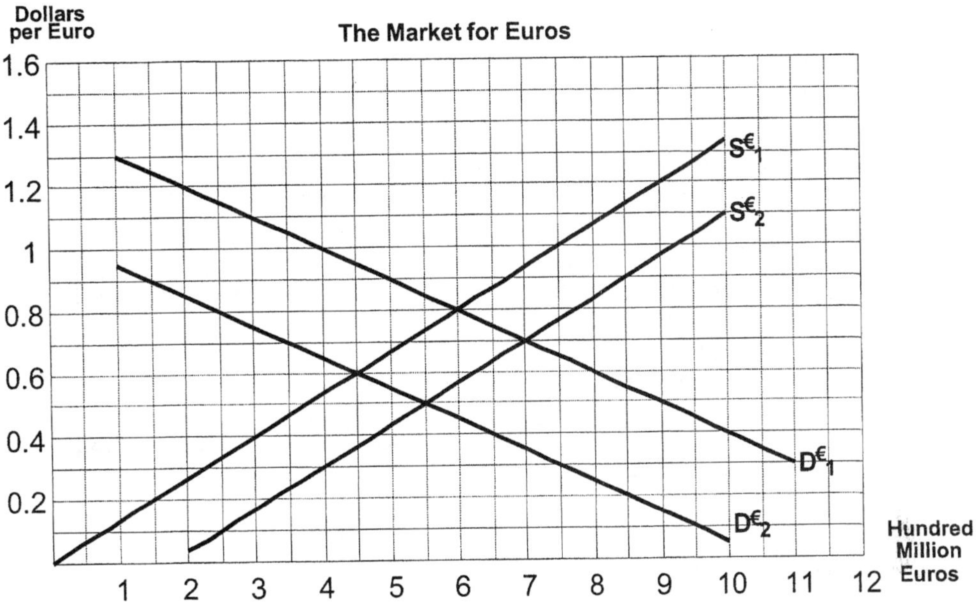

b. 4; 7.5; be exceeded by; depreciate; appreciate; $0.80
c. American demand for European euros; leftward; $0.60; (See graph.)
d. European supply of euros; rightward; $0.50; (See graph.)

3. a. $1.80; $1.44
b. euros; dollar-euro; 100,000; euros
c. pounds; euro-pound; 62,500; pounds
d. dollars; dollar-pound; 112,500; dollars
e. $22,500; rise; fall; fall

4. a. 0.7; (See graph.)
   b. decrease; increase; decrease; decrease; smaller; more
   c. rise; less; decrease; demand for; leftward; depreciate; appreciate; (See graph.)
   d. rises; more; increase; supply of; rightward; depreciate; appreciate; (See graph.)
   e. depreciate; appreciate; decreased; 0.7; 0.50

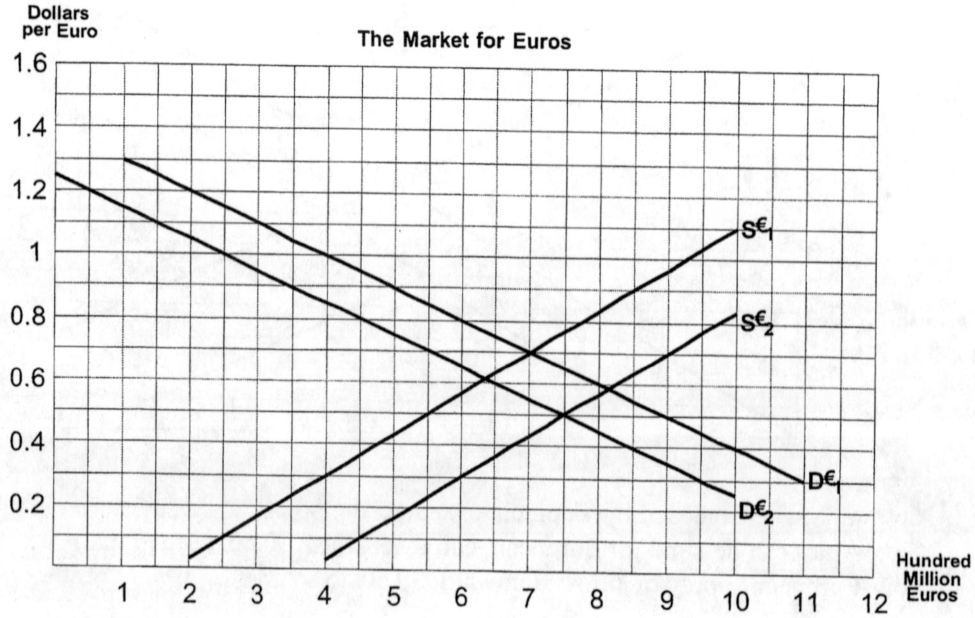

15-Minute Practice Test

Multiple Choice

1. e
2. d
3. c
4. d
5. e
6. b
7. b
8. e
9. c
10. d

True/False

1. F
2. T
3. F
4. T
5. T
6. T
7. T
8. T

ANSWERS TO

FINAL EXAM IN MACROECONOMICS

1. d. is correct. Remember that "land" includes the natural resources that are found under and on the land itself. Also remember that "raw materials" used by businesses are themselves made from resources (for example, lumber is a raw material used by the paper industry, but it is made from land, labor and capital (the trees are natural resources and are included in "land," and labor and capital are used to cut down trees to make lumber).

2. b. is correct. All of the other choices are microeconomic problems, because they deal with specific markets, industries or firms, rather than an entire economy.

3. d. is correct. a., b., and c are all statements about how the economy or a part of it works, whether they are accurate or not. A normative statement would state what we *should* do, based on both positive economic analysis and our values.

4. b. is correct. The opportunity cost of any choice or decision is what is given up to make that decision. In this case, Jim would be giving up *both* the wages *and* the performance in order to study the additional three hours. c., d., and e. are incorrect because the losses or gains from receiving an A or a B+ are not things that are given up by studying, so they not part of the opportunity cost of that choice.

5. e. is correct. Being on the PPF means that producing more of one thing requires the sacrifice of something else. Note that d. is incorrect because if the economy were in recession, then by definition it would not be on its PPF.

6. c. is correct. The law of demand states the negative relationship between the price of a good and the quantity demanded *of the same good.* Also, it does not involve changes in income (choice e.).

7. e. (none of the above) is correct. This may seem like a tricky question, but it is actually central to an understanding of supply and demand. In all three choices a., b., and c., a rise in price induces producers to sell more apples. In each case, we move *along* the supply curve for apples, but there is no shift of the supply curve. A shift in supply occurs only when sellers want to sell more or fewer apples *at any given price*, and that has not happened. Review Chapter 3 for a list of changes that can shift the supply curve.

8. c. is correct. If you draw a graph with supply and demand shifts for each answer, it will help you see why. In choice c., the rise in income shifts the demand curve rightward and the cheaper transportation costs shift the supply curve rightward. Each of these shifts causes equilibrium quantity to increase, but they have opposite effects on price, so the ultimate effect on price is unknown. Choices a. and b. are incorrect because they shift the demand curve for gasoline rightward, and cause price to rise. Choice d. causes the demand curve to shift rightward and the supply curve to shift leftward, each contributing to a rise in price—once again, no ambiguity in price. Both of the events in choice e. cause the demand curve to shift leftward, decreasing price—once again, no ambiguity in price. Also, in choice e., quantity decreases, rather than increases as required by the problem.

9. c. is correct (see Ch. 17 in the comprehensive (Micro-Macro) textbook, or Chapter 4 in the Macroeconomics paperback).

10. e. is correct. (See Ch. 17 in the comprehensive text, or Ch. 4 in the Macro paperback.)

11. d. is correct. Choice a. would be included in consumption spending, and b. and c. would be included as investment spending.

12. a. is correct. Choice b. is a transfer payment, not included in government purchases nor in GDP. Choice c. is consumption spending. (A government worker is acting as a household when purchasing goods and services for private use.)

13. a. is correct. We count the following to get GDP: consumption spending of \$5 trillion, business spending on plant and equipment of \$1 trillion; housing construction of \$0.5 trillion (included in investment); change in inventories of minus 0.7 trillion (included in investment); government purchases of \$3 trillion; and net exports of \$3.2 trillion – \$4 trillion = minus 0.8 trillion. The total is \$5 + \$1 + \$0.5 – \$0.7 + \$3 – \$0.8 = \$8.0 trillion. Transfer payments and taxes are not part of production, so are not counted in GDP.

14. a. is correct. GDP measured by the expenditure approach or the factor payments approach (total income earned by resource owners) are the same. Note that choice e. is equal to total wages and salaries only, since that is the only source of income not subtracted from the \$5 trillion total income in that choice. But total income of resource owners includes more than just wages and salaries; it also includes rent, interest and profit.

15. d. is correct. All the other choices incorrectly combine the expenditure approach to GDP (\$600 for the purchase of a consumption good) with elements of the factor payments approach.

16. e. is correct. The standard of living is typically defined as real GDP per capita. Since real GDP and the population are both rising by 2 percent, real GDP per person remains unchanged. Nominal GDP is irrelevant in calculating living standards, since it is not corrected for inflation.

17. d. is correct. (See Ch. 5 in comprehensive text, Ch. 18 in macro text.)

18. a. is correct. The inflation rate (percentage change in the price level) is ($160 – $150) / $150 = 0.0625 or 6.25%.

19. c. is correct. U.S. currency is not backed by anything of value (so it is not commodity money), and has no intrinsic non-money use (so it is not commodity money).

20. a. is correct. The other goods are not purchased by households, so their prices are not part of the CPI.

21. d. is correct. If the price level is not changing, the inflation rate must be constant at zero, not rising. All of the other combinations are indeed possible, and therefore incorrect choices given the wording of the question. For example, if prices are rising at an ever-faster rate, both the price level and the inflation rate will be increasing, as in choice a.

22. d. is correct. The real wage begins at $10 / 2.0 = $5.0 and rises to $15 / 2.2 = $6.82. The percentage change in the real wage is ($6.82 – $5.0) / $5.0 = 0.36 or 36 percent.

23. c. is correct. To see why, start with any nominal wage (we'll call it "X"). Also, set the starting price level at 1.0, so that the initial real wage is also X. Then, after three years, the nominal wage will be (1.03 x 1.03 x 1.03) X = 1.093 X. Meanwhile, the price level will be 1.05 x 1.05 x 1.05 = 1.157. Computing the new real wage, we get 1.093 X / 1.157 = 0.9447 X. The percentage change in the real wage is (0.9447 X – X) / X = –.055 or a decrease of 5.5%.

24. c. is correct. The nominal interest rate is ($550 – $500) / $500 = 0.10 or 10 %. The real interest rate is approximately 10% – 2% = 8%.

25. a. is correct. Choice b. is a simplifying assumption. Choice c. is *not* an assumption of the classical model.

26. b. is correct. (See Ch. 20 in comprehensive text, Ch. 7 in macro text.)

27. b. is correct. With the wage greater than equilibrium, labor supply will rise above its equilibrium level, and labor demand will drop below its equilibrium level, creating an excess supply of labor. Choice c. is wrong because, with the wage above its equilibrium level, employment will be less than full employment. Choices d. and e. are wrong because, as employment changes, it will cause a movement *along* the production function, but not a shift of the production function itself.

28. d. is correct. In the classical model, output is determined by the level of employment (from the labor market) and the position of the production function. Choice d. shifts the production function up, increasing output even with the same level of employment. While the other choices would each increase a sector's spending, they would not affect the labor market or the production function; they would only crowd out some other sector's spending by the same amount, leaving total spending unchanged.

29. e. is correct. In the classical model, a rise in the interest rate will *increase* saving and *increase* business demand for loanable funds. It will not affect the government's demand for loanable funds.

30. a. is correct. The rightward shift in the labor supply curve would cause an increase in employment, and—via a movement *along* the production function—an increase in output. The interest rate would not rise. (Actually—because an increase in output and income would increase saving—the interest rate would fall, although the text does not carry the analysis of an increase in employment that far.)

31. b. is correct. The total demand for loanable funds curve will shift leftward, resulting in a lower interest rate, a *decrease* in saving along the saving or supply of funds curve, and no change in output. (If the tax increase changes incentives, it could actually decrease output, but would not increase it as in choice a.)

32. c. is correct. With a surplus, the supply of loanable funds becomes saving *and* the budget surplus. The demand for loanable funds will be just planned investment. Because the loanable funds market clears, we will have saving + budget surplus – planned investment. Subtracting saving from both sides gives us budget surplus = planned investment minus saving.

33. b. is correct. You can see this by drawing the labor market diagram, and shifting the labor supply curve rightward. Then—as employment increases—we move rightward along the production function, increasing output. e. *might* be correct if we were discussing the short run. But since the problem specifies the long run, we assume that the labor market clears, i.e., that the wage rate will adjust to eliminate any excess supply of labor.

34. a. is correct. The number of workers is 50 million x .8 x .5 = 20 million. Labor productivity is output / workers = $50 billion / 20 million = $2,500.

35. a. is correct. An increase in labor supply, with no other changes, will move us rightward along the economy's production function. Labor productivity can be drawn as the slope of a line from the origin to the point on the production where the economy is operating. As employment increases, the line becomes flatter and productivity decreases. Choice b. *increases* productivity, as does choice c. since it will shift the production function upward.

36. b. is correct. Since the question refers to the long run, we use the classical macro model. In that model, the increase in saving will lower the interest rate, increase investment, raise the capital stock higher than it would have been, and shift the production function upward at a faster rate. Choice a. is incorrect because while it would shift the demand for labor curve rightward, employment (and therefore output) will not change as long as the labor supply curve is vertical. Choice c. increases the deficit, harming growth (although the policy might be favored based on other, non-growth criteria). Choice d. (through crowding out) and choice e. (by discouraging new capital expenditures) both cause investment spending to decrease, slowing down the upward shift in the production function and slowing economic growth.

37. d. is correct. One of the major points of the chapter "Economic Fluctuations" in your text (Ch. 22 in the comprehensive text; Ch. 9 in Macro text) is that shifts in labor demand and labor supply cannot explain real-world recessions.

38. a. is correct. (See Ch. 22 in comprehensive text; Ch. 9 in Macro text.)

39. c. is correct. The deficit is equal to government purchases minus net taxes, or 1,000 – 300 = 700.

40. e. is correct. Net exports (NX) are equal to exports minus imports, or 400 – 500 = –100.

41. d. is correct. The formula is: Y = 400 + .9(Y – 300) + 4,000 + 1,000 + (–100). Solving for Y gives us .1Y = 5,030 so Y = 5,030 / .1 = 50,300. (See Appendix 1 to Ch. 23 in comprehensive text, or Ch. 10 in Macro text).

42. e. is correct. The multiplier is 1 / (1 – MPC) = 1 / .1 = 10, so a $1,000 billion rise in government purchases would cause a $1,000 billion x 10 = $10,000 billion rise in GDP. (See Ch. 23 in comprehensive text, or Ch. 10 in Macro text).

43. c. is correct. The multiplier for a change in taxes is equal to –MPC / (1 – MPC) = –.9 / (1 – .9) = –9. Using this multiplier, the change in GDP is $1,000 (–9) = –9,000, which is more than 1,000. Alternatively, you could resolve for equilibrium GDP with taxes equal to $1,300 billion (which is $1,000 billion higher than initially), and discover that GDP drops by $9,000 billion. (See Appendix 2 to Ch. 23 in comprehensive text, or Ch. 10 in Macro text).

44. d. is correct. Net exports are part of aggregate expenditure. Choice a. moves us *along* the economy's aggregate expenditure line. Choices b. and c. will shift the aggregate expenditure line *downward*.

45. b. is correct. Draw a graph of this situation to help you see why: the equilibrium GDP is where the AE line intersects the 45-degree line. If GDP is greater than this level, the AE line will lie *below* the 45-degree line, which tells us that total output is greater than spending, with the unsold output being added to inventories over the period. Choice a. is wrong because the statement tells us nothing about whether unemployment is high or low or "excess," nor does it tell us where we are relative to "full employment." Choice d. is also wrong: total investment could be negative only if inventories were *falling,* and the drop were greater than the value of *planned* investment (which is total investment excluding the change in inventories). But inventories are actually rising, as stated. Choice e. is wrong because planned investment is a given in the short-run macro model, and even if it did change, the problem gives us no information about how.

46. e. is correct. All of the other are part of the "M1" definition of the money supply, and also included in other definitions, such as "M2."

47. e. is correct. The members of the board of governors are appointed by the President to 14 year terms *with* the approval of the Senate.

48. e. is correct. The balance sheet will show an increase in *both* assets (the $10,000) *and* liabilities (the funds now owed to the bond dealer).

49. e. is correct. Required reserves are equal to the required reserve ratio times total demand deposits, or .25 x $500 million = $125 million. The information about bonds and property and buildings is irrelevant.

50. d. is correct. Total demand deposits will increase by the government bond purchase ($100 million) times the demand deposit multiplier (1/RRR = 1/.25 = 4), so that total demand deposits increase by $100 million x 4 = $400 million.

51. c. is correct. While some of the other choices may be correct as statements, they have little to do with preventing banking panics.

52. b. is correct. Remember that GDP and total income are the same in macroeconomics, and an increase in income will increase the amount of wealth people want to hold as money. Choice a. (a rise in the interest rate) moves us rightward *along* the money demand curve, but doesn't shift it. Choice c. (a drop in employment) would, if anything, shift the money demand curve leftward, because it would probably be associated with a drop in GDP.

53. d. is correct. When the Fed purchases government bonds, it is increasing the money supply. Choices a., b., and c. follow directly.

54. b. is correct. There is an excess *demand* for money, which is equivalent to an e excess *supply* of *bonds*.

55. a. is correct. The action by the Fed will *decrease* the money supply, *raising* the interest rate and *decreasing* real GDP.

56. a. is correct. An increase in taxes will decrease equilibrium real GDP at each price level, shifting the AD curve leftward. Choice b. will shift the AD curve rightward, and choice c. describes a movement *along* the AD curve.

57. c. is correct. Choices a. and b. shift the AS curve upward.

58. e. is correct. The AD curve will shift *leftward* and the price level will *fall*. (Note: As a consequence, over the long run, the self-correcting mechanism will kick in, and the AS curve will shift *rightward* and the price level will *fall*, the opposite of choice a.)

59. d. is correct. Changes in the money supply are not part of the self correcting mechanism; all of the other choices will occur as the economy self-corrects via a leftward shift of the AS curve.

60. d. is correct. The rise in oil prices will shift the AS curve upward. To prevent output from falling (a recession), the Fed will have to increase the money supply in order to shift the AD curve rightward. But this will make the price level rise by more than it would have without the active monetary policy.

61. a. is correct. The other choices result in either output rising or the price level rising, or both.

62. c. is correct. (See Ch. 28 in comprehensive text, Ch. 15 in Macro text.)

63. b. is correct. The increase in the money supply would increase U.S. income (depreciating the dollar) and also lower the U.S. interest rate (depreciating the dollar further). Choices b. and c. would appreciate the dollar. (See Ch. 28 in comprehensive text, Ch. 16 in Macro text.)

64. d. is correct. Poles will want to buy U.S. assets, increasing their supply of Zlotys. Simultaneously, Americans will want to buy fewer Polish assets, decreasing the demand for Zlotys. The result is an excess supply of Zlotys. With the exchange rate fixed, there can be no appreciation or depreciation of either currency.

65. e. is correct. Countries with relatively low inflation rates have *appreciating* currencies. Choices a., b., and c. have it backwards. The dollar will *appreciate* against the pound and the Euro, and the pound will *appreciate* against the Euro.